The New Kings
of
New York

The New Kings
of
New York

RENEGADES, MOGULS, GAMBLERS,
AND THE REMAKING OF
THE WORLD'S MOST FAMOUS SKYLINE

By Adam Piore
for *The Real Deal*

Edited by
Stuart Elliott and Hiten Samtani

THEREALDEAL

The Real Deal

The Real Deal
450 West 31st Street
New York, NY 10001
www.therealdeal.com

Printed in the United States of America
First Edition: April 2022
Library of Congress Cataloging-in-Publication Data
Name: Piore, Adam, author.
Title: The New Kings of New York / Adam Piore
Description: First edition. | New York: *The Real Deal*, 2022
Identifier: ISBN 978-1-7379434-0-2

Contents

Introduction

I t was the kind of triumphant moment the billionaire developer Steve Ross had been working towards his entire career.

The haunting voice of Grammy nominee Andra Day was soaring across the vast, sun-drenched plaza of Hudson Yards, while a troupe of Alvin Ailey dancers leapt and tumbled around her. Backstage, the 78-year-old Ross, trim, bespectacled, with a booming voice and prominent ears, was leading a procession of VIPs toward the threshold of "the Vessel," the $200 million public art installation at the center of his megadevelopment on New York City's Far West Side. As they stepped into the beehive-shaped structure and mounted the first of the Vessel's honeycomb of stairs, a line of blue-robed Gospel singers appeared on a landing above them and launched into an emotional call-and-response with Day.

"You're broken down and tired, of living life on a merry-go-round."

"Rise up!"

"And you can't find the fighter."

"Rise up!"

"But I see it in you, so we gonna walk it out."

"Rise up!"

No one appeared to notice the irony that lyrics meant as a rallying cry for the oppressed should serve as the soundtrack for Ross and his entourage of one-percenters — Martha Stewart, private equity titan Henry Kravis, Senator Chuck Schumer — as they took in the full scale of the $25 billion project with its Rolex and Fendi stores, $35 million penthouses, and gleaming office towers. Indeed, at the opening ceremony of Hudson Yards that beautiful early spring day in March 2019, speaker after speaker emphasized how much the new development, billed as the largest private mixed-use project in North American history, would help New York City soar to new heights.

"This will ensure we continue to attract the best and the brightest," Ross proclaimed.

It was the same message that former Mayor Mike Bloomberg and his deputy Dan Doctoroff had used to sell the public on the project back in 2005, along with the generous package of tax incentives that went with it. The redevelopment of New York City wouldn't just be good for builders like Steve Ross; they'd promised back then and Ross promised now. It would be good for all New Yorkers.

As Anderson Cooper took the stage with a man in a seven-foot-tall Big Bird costume and fired a cannon with confetti into the ebullient crowd, it was almost as if nothing had changed. As if this was still the same optimistic, pro-development world it had been back in the halcyon Bloomberg days, when local politicians and the media eagerly embraced that message, waxed poetic about the bucolic experience of walking the newly created High Line, and celebrated the city's status as the global financial mecca and burgeoning tech hub — a city where the likes of

Amazon and Facebook were swallowing up office space and Google had spent over $3 billion acquiring real estate over the past decade.

But on the other side of the velvet ropes, the pitchforks were out. Simmering class resentments were roiling New York City politics and feeding a populist backlash — one that was now impossible to ignore. The opening of the massive complex came just weeks after progressive New Yorkers had risen up against the very policies that made it possible and successfully upended a hard-won deal that would have offered Amazon $3 billion in tax incentives — similar to those enjoyed by Ross at Hudson Yards — to build a sprawling corporate campus on Long Island City.

Just how much things were changing was apparent not from the celebrities and politicians in attendance that day — but those who weren't. Absent from the festivities were two officials who would normally be among the most likely to bask in their glow: New York Governor Andrew Cuomo and Mayor Bill de Blasio.

The truth was that in the years since Bloomberg had left office, and Ross had won the coveted assignment to build the project, many New Yorkers had grown fed up with the specter of ugly, needle towers for the rich sprouting up on the edges of Central Park, the so-called "Billionaires' Row," casting shadows across the Great Meadow. They'd read tawdry tales of how Russian oligarchs, Malaysian embezzlers, and Latin American drug lords were using $70 million penthouses to launder their dirty money, creating ghost towers and driving up land prices which in turn deprived city dwellers of affordable housing. They'd looked upon the tech-bro arrivals Downtown and wondered what had happened to all the artists. And they'd watched with alarm as their own rents soared and cost of living spiked. Many had begun to feel that the gritty, artsy, egalitarian New York City they'd always identified with was slipping away. Certainly, some in the media seemed to feel that way.

In the days leading up to Hudson Yards' coming-out party,

commentators turned their attention to the glittering new development and contemplated the tall walls of its luxury shopping mall, looming over 10th Avenue, like fortress battlements shutting out the rest of the city. They declared it a potent symbol of everything that had gone wrong.

Hudson Yards, architecture critic Michael Kimmelman opined on the front page of the New York Times a few days before the opening, "is, at heart, a supersized suburban-style office park, with a shopping mall and a quasi-gated condo community targeted at the 0.1 percent."

"It gives physical form to a crisis of city leadership," he continued, "asleep at the wheel through two administrations, and to a pernicious theory of civic welfare that presumes private development is New York's primary goal, the truest measure of urban vitality and health, with money the city's only real currency."

New York magazine's Justin Davidson lamented the wholesale transformation that had overtaken the city. Every time he approached Hudson Yards, Davidson wrote in a cover story, he felt "a volatile mix of wonder and dejection in my chest."

"I can't help feeling like an alien here," he wrote. "I suppose this apotheosis of blank-slate affluence is someone's fantasy of the 21-century city, but it isn't mine. Again and again, I have wondered who wanted it to be like this, and when it became a foregone conclusion."

One could argue with the sentiments. Ross certainly did, calling his critics and politicians supporting them "irresponsible." The project, he argued, would draw the kind of talent the city needed. Yet in truth his gleaming new development was a legacy of a different time. The ceremony that day in March 2019, billed at the time as heralding a new beginning, would in fact become far more significant for the ending it would come to represent.

The first two decades of the 21st century were a giddy, hyperbolic era of both dizzying highs and deep, dark lows. The headlines throughout the city told the story: The largest residential and commercial development in North America, the largest condo conversion in the history of the world, the largest hard money loan ever recorded, the most expensive penthouse ever sold in New York, the most expensive office skyscraper sale in history, the tallest condo ever built.

But now a new winter was coming. Within months, 95 percent of Manhattan's office space would sit empty amid a pandemic, restaurants would go out of business, and retail stores would be boarded up in a scene reminiscent of the 1970s — only this time covering the entire city rather than just the South Bronx.

Neiman Marcus, Hudson Yards' anchor tenant, would declare bankruptcy and pull out of the project. And the city would stand at a crossroads.

This is a book about where we have come from as we consider where we want to go next. It's about why the city wanted to develop Hudson Yards in the first place, and how Steve Ross came to build it. It's about what happened to all those New York neighborhoods Manhattan used to be famous for, and the tens of thousands of affordable housing units that disappeared in the first decades of the millennium. It is about why all those skinny skyscrapers for the 1 percent now ring Central Park, and how they got there. It's also about why and how New Yorkers built the High Line, constructed miles of new bike paths, and transformed a place that once teetered on bankruptcy into an urban oasis that many New Yorkers joyfully embraced — until they realized they could no longer afford it. Most of all it's about the men and women who were at the center of this transformation, and the fortunes they won and lost in the process.

It's a truism that every New Yorker enjoys a good real estate yarn — whether it's about that friend who found a miraculous, rent-controlled one bedroom on the Upper West Side for $700 a month, or the Russian oligarch who shelled out $88 million for a penthouse with Central Park views to house his college-aged daughter and hide his assets from his ex-wife.

In New York, where even going to the deli can be an adventure, there's a story behind every apartment — how the broker had a bad toupee, how a stoned tenant failed to vacate the premises for the open house — or how, upon moving in, you and your girlfriend discovered a mouse and named him Boutros Boutros-Ghali, or found a nick in the marble counters of your new 57th Street penthouse. A successful real estate conquest constitutes the archetypal New York City hero's journey, requiring from its protagonist ingenuity, skill, pluck, and often a twist of fate.

Perhaps that's why in New York City, to become a successful real estate developer is to become a figure of public fascination and intense scrutiny. To become a "mogul" is to develop the wizardry to conjure up that most precious of big city resources, the big game we all hunt for: a nice apartment. Or a gleaming corner office with Hudson River views. In this book you will meet those wizards, and tour the incestuous, gilded realms they inhabit, and the ruthless, high-stakes battlefields upon which their fortunes, their influence (and in rare cases even their very own apartments) hang in the balance. The cast of characters is a colorful one. It includes wily titans like Ross, Gary Barnett, and Harry Macklowe, and dynastic scions such as Rob Speyer, Will Lie and Arthur Zeckendorf, Joe Rose, and Kent Swig. You'll meet renegades, gamblers, brilliant strategists, thoughtful policymakers, and reckless speculators, all of whom have changed the city — for better and for worse.

In other words, this is a book with a lot of real estate stories. Not the small kind, but the big ones that make possible the thousands of little adventures we all enjoy.

This book also tells a larger story. It charts the final leg in the transformation of America's greatest city from a near-bankrupt urban combat zone into the land of Billionaires' Row and Hudson Yards — a luxury playground for the global 1 percent that 1970s New Yorkers — Mayor Abe Beame, the regulars at Studio 54, Howard Cosell of "The Bronx is burning" fame — would scarcely recognize. It's a transformation echoed in other world capitals, and one that few would have predicted.

"When I came of age a half century ago, everybody believed New York was over — that because so many people were leaving, the city was dying," said Alex Garvin, a former member of the New York City Planning Commission, of the 1960s and '70s. "There were thousands of abandoned apartments all around. The crime rate was crazy, and all of the experts had a death sentence for the city."

During the '70s — the decade in which many of the moguls in this book were laying the groundwork for the empires they control today — the city hemorrhaged hundreds of thousands of manufacturing jobs and lost more than 800,000 residents, akin to shedding the population of modern-day San Francisco or Washington, D.C. The 1980s were marked by high crime and a battle to take the city back.

Often, it took a special kind of personality, or a pair of steel balls, to thrive in this environment. Ross, who arrived from Detroit in 1968 at the age of 28, is a good case study.

He moved to the Big Apple hoping to parlay his experience as a tax attorney specializing in public housing deals into a career in real estate investment banking. But within three years, his audacity had cost him two jobs. His short career on Wall Street had come to an end after a particularly fractious meeting of Bear Stearns's investment committee. The group approved one of Ross's investment ideas and an associate suggested letting the young attorney run the deal.

"I don't have any confidence in Steve," said one of the partners, who had repeatedly clashed with Ross.

"Fuck you," Ross shot back, violating the sacrosanct corporate pecking order. "I don't have any confidence in you."

The newly unemployed and unemployable Ross, determined to stay in the city, wrote out a business plan, borrowed $10,000 from his mother, and used what he learned as an attorney to begin bidding to build government-subsidized housing.

In the years that followed, crime skyrocketed. Public health clinics and hospitals shuttered. Some schools could no longer afford toilet paper. Hundreds of recovering drug addicts slept outside Gracie Mansion for nine days to protest the closure of programs that had helped them get clean.[1] Rather than pay property taxes, some landlords simply walked away from their buildings. Others set them on fire so they could collect the insurance money. And yes, the Bronx burned. Everyone had given up on New York.

But Ross had tapped an unceasing faucet for federal funds — and found a recession-proof training ground in which to learn his new trade. When the city emerged from the darkness, he had the skills and experience to make it big — and the connections to save him when he faltered.

And he was not the only developer whose colossal self-regard during this period would prove advantageous. In early 1975, Donald Trump, a young Queens native with a golden pompadour and a talent for self-promotion, struck his first big Manhattan deal to purchase the Commodore Hotel, a once grand but by then ramshackle money-losing enterprise on East 42nd Street. The situation in the city had become so bleak, the New York Times noted that "even the Chrysler Building across the street was in foreclosure." Trump's father, Fred, who had made his fortune building meat-and-potatoes middle-class housing in the boroughs, compared his son's efforts to buy the hotel to "fighting for a seat on the Titanic."

---

1 Phillips-Fein. "No, Not Again." *New York Daily News*. April 23, 2017.

But Trump would not listen, and, like Ross, was able to bend the situation to his advantage. Prior to signing the contract, Trump talked local politicians into granting him an unheard-of 40-year, $56-million tax abatement, and near carte blanche to reimagine the site as he saw fit. Many would gripe that the decisive factor was Trump's political clout. His father had known Mayor Abe Beame for 30 years, and young Donald had many of Beame's closest political associates on payroll: publicist Howard Rubenstein; lobbyist, lawyer, and fundraiser Abraham "Bunny" Lindenbaum, and his son, zoning wizard Sandy. Trump's lobbyist at the time was Louise Sunshine, who also served as chief fundraiser for New York Governor Hugh Carey's reelection campaign.[2] For advice on playing hardball, he relied on Roy Cohn, the infamous lawyer who had advised Senator Joseph McCarthy.

But coming as it did at the very bottom of the market, pushing the deal through also took an uncommon combination of chutzpah, sangfroid, and hubris. For a time, the cocktail would allow Trump to ride the city's recovery to the very heights of moguldom—until he overextended himself and came crashing back to earth in the great real estate bust of the late 1980s.

In New York City, and in this book, it's not an entirely unique narrative. And though it's true that Trump, with his carnival-barking "truthful hyperbole" and status as the nation's first developer-in-chief, is in a league of his own, it's also true that there's a little bit of Donald Trump in most of the developers you'll meet.

Just a little. The industry has no shortage of loud-mouthed moguls. But it also has plenty of quiet operators who prefer to stay in the shadows, letting their money call the shots. You won't see the number-crunching

---

2   Blum, H. "Trump: Development of a Manhattan Developer." *The New York Times.* August 26, 1980.

corporate sharks at Fortress or Blackstone, for instance, with their vast war chests of institutional money and Ivy League pedigrees, tweeting out insults or letting their passions get the best of them. They will, however, embrace the opportunity to make "the world's largest hard money loan" and later push their borrower to the brink of financial ruin to make him pay it back.

And then there are the scions. The Speyers, Swigs, Zeckendorfs, and Rudins, who grew up steeped in wealth and were tasked with tending to property dynasties built by their forefathers, often come across as more polished than the outer-borough brawlers who built their empires from scratch. Kent Swig, for instance, who embarked on an epic real estate spending spree Downtown, was known for his sunny demeanor and charm rather than for the ruthlessness that characterized his father-in-law and mentor Harry Macklowe, a first-generation striver who became infamous after his contractors knocked down a pair of homeless SROs in the middle of the night without a permit.

Yet if you look closely enough, you'll find that behind most of the skyline-shaping developments of recent years, as well as the operatic failures, there's usually at least one big-talking promoter who scoffed at doubters, defied conventional wisdom, and, with utter confidence, claimed they had the deal of the century. Along the way, they scored public funds, found partners from all over the globe to share the risk and headaches, cast a spell on bankers, and stubbornly followed a vision that only they could see — or even if they couldn't, pretended to see.

"If you listen to everybody, you're doomed for failure to start with," says Ross. "You've got to have your own mindset and you've got to understand what you're doing. You can't live with conventional thinking when you're doing these kinds of things."

The rewards for such an approach can be immense. The last time Ross was interviewed for this book, he strode into his capacious, Central

Park–facing corner office in the tower he built, reached for a phone on his desk, and bellowed into the receiver: "I told you we should have made that goddamned trade!" On the other end was the general manager of the Miami Dolphins, the NFL team Ross purchased in 2009 for a total of more than $1.1 billion. It was two days before the NFL draft.

Today, New York City is home to nearly 100 billionaires, according to Forbes, with those from the real estate pack only matched by those in finance. They include Ross, Richard LeFrak, Jerry Speyer, Charles Cohen, Jane Goldman, Steven Roth, Jeff Sutton, Ben Ashkenazy, Larry Silverstein, Mort Zuckerman, David Walentas, and, if you believe him — many in the industry don't — Donald J. Trump.

In demeanor, swagger, and ruthlessness, they can be reminiscent of the studio chiefs of Hollywood's Golden Age or the robber barons of early 20th century New York. But the boldness comes at a cost. While the good times can be intoxicating, they are invariably followed by epic hangovers. And when things get ugly, prison-yard rules apply.

The ever-present specter of sudden ruin might help account for the uncommon level of bravado, machismo, risk, and the litigation for sport often seen in the industry. The late Sheldon Solow, who was the third-richest New York real estate billionaire, had been involved in an estimated 200 lawsuits, going after everyone from business rivals to his neighbor's houseguests. Harry Macklowe spent months in court with Martha Stewart, who owned the property adjoining his East Hampton getaway, in a dispute over whether he was allowed to plant trees and hedges.

In his autobiography, a seminal read for today's moguls, the great postwar developer William Zeckendorf Sr. (whose grandchildren, Arthur and Will Lie, you'll meet in this book) shared a childhood insight that has become somewhat of an industry mantra.

After school, Zeckendorf was slated to fight a far larger kid and fully expected to get beat up. By the time class let out, he was so frightened he ran down the stairs to meet his tormentor, anxious to get his drubbing over with. When his opponent spotted the boy rushing towards him, he mistook his panic for gusto and flinched. That moment of weakness gave the future developer and master assembler newfound courage to attack. The other boy gave up after just one or two punches.

"It taught me a lesson that later applied in business every bit as much as it did in a high school playground," Zeckendorf wrote. "If you show hesitancy or fear, you may already be half-defeated. If you put on a bold front, and fight with everything you have, you can win. Moreover, once you have won a few battles, you are usually left alone: in the jungle, no animal thoughtlessly attacks the lion."

It would be a mistake, however, to attribute New York's transformation solely to force of personality. While many of the characters here deserve credit for their audacity and vision, their ability to create vast fortunes and the physical overhaul of the city that is so obvious today are as much a byproduct of the fundamental demographic transformation that has washed over New York as anything else.

"The evidence of the late '70s suggests that the New York of the '80s and '90s will no longer be a magnet for the poor and the homeless," the Times wrote in 1979, "but a city primarily for the ambitious and educated — an urban elite." The paper noted the phenomenon's curious name: gentrification.

It was a prescient comment. Over the years that followed, that second New York would continue to grow, merge with, and then wipe away the old. And if the defining image of the city in the 1970s was that of buildings set alight by their owners, by the late 1980s its iconic counterpart had become a photograph of three words scrawled everywhere: "Die Yuppie Scum!"

Between 1978 and 1986, the average price of a Manhattan co-op apartment increased 500 percent. By 1986, 21,500 luxury apartments were under construction, the vast majority of them on the Upper East and Upper West Side. It was just the beginning of the revival, which would also include the explosion of a relatively new type of housing: the condo.[3]

The great real estate recession of the late 1980s and early 1990s put a temporary stop to the party. But by the mid-1990s, the city had largely recovered, and the boom was poised to pick up right where it left off, guided by the heavy hand of Mayor Rudy Giuliani.

That is where this book begins. A time when crime plummeted, in the days just before the growing divide between the top 1 percent and the great unwashed would see its starkest expression in Manhattan, and housing would become the priciest and most desired luxury good of them all.

Indeed, over the next two decades, New York City became a magnet for the superrich, not only those who made their fortunes locally on Wall Street and in media, but also the global elite from Moscow to Abu Dhabi, who came to see Manhattan as the ultimate destination for a pied-à-terre — or a stash pad for their money, what the appraiser Jonathan Miller called the "modern-day Swiss bank." Developers who understood that shift, and actively encouraged it by giving the ultra-wealthy more and more ostentatious options to buy from, profited handsomely.

"Not many people understood people were making so much money in the 2000s," said Arthur Zeckendorf, the grandson of Big Bill and one of the developers of 15 Central Park West, the most successful condominium of the era. "We were aware of that."

This is not meant to be a comprehensive guide to all the real estate activity that has led to this state of affairs. Rather, it offers a behind-the-scenes picture of what it's like to operate at the highest levels of the

---

3   Scheurman, Matthew. "The Zeckendorf Family." *The New York Observer.* December 18, 2006.

industry, how some of the big deals get done, and what it takes to shape our built environment. It's also a chronicle of what happens when the market crashes and the vultures move in.

But most of all, this is a book about the dawn of New York real estate's second gilded age, the opportunists who sought to exploit it, and the adventures they had along the way.

PART ONE

I

Come East, Young Cricket

Harry Macklowe
and the Education of Kent Swig

When Kent Swig first ran the numbers, they were so shocking, he ran them again.

It was 1998. On one side, there was Midtown Manhattan, where most of the city's real estate titans had made their bets, where vacancies were low and where prices were steep. Then there was the area below City Hall in Lower Manhattan — an area that didn't even really have a name, but that as far as Swig could tell had the same city government, the same transportation system, and similar demographics. The hotels there had solid occupancy. The retail and office scene was robust. Zoning laws had even been modified to allow landlords to convert antiquated office stock to hotels or condos. Why, then, were prices there so much lower?

A few days earlier, a broker had approached Swig with a chance to take over a bid on the old Bank of New York Building at 48 Wall Street. Swig, who'd been looking to do his first big development deal, had toured the property and been blown away. He had always been a history buff, and the building had a compelling story. Built in 1929 in the Colonial Revival style on land owned by the Alexander Hamilton–founded Bank of New York, the imposing stone façade on the corner of William Street stood watch over the famous thoroughfare synonymous with finance. Standing on the street, gazing upwards, was like looking back in time.

From its base, 48 Wall rose more than 15 stories before retreating off the street, its majestic limestone towers telescoping in a series of setbacks that culminated in a slender spire topped with a huge sculpture of a federal eagle. Just above the lobby level, three tall-arched windows looked out on the narrow street, and from outside Swig could glimpse the building's grand interior. Inside, a cantilevered marble staircase led up to an old banking hall on the second floor, where three enormous brass chandeliers hung from vaulted ceilings above floors hewed of checked marble.

The deal came with generous terms. The bank was selling the building in preparation for a move to One Wall Street, which it had acquired after a merger. But it promised to stay in the building for a full year after the deal closed and continue to pay rent, which would give Swig time to cook up plans. After a year, it planned to vacate the entire building, with no pesky holdout tenants standing in the way of whatever vision Swig had for the site. There were plenty of options — it could be commercial, residential or a hotel.

More than 20 groups had bid. The auction was in its second phase, but one of the three finalists, Vornado Realty Trust, the giant real estate investment trust founded by the pugnacious Steve Roth, was dropping out. Was Swig, the broker asked, interested in stepping in?

Swig's calculations showed that land in the area was worth about $200 a square foot. But a bid of $37.5 million — considered high enough to win the day — would pencil out to only about $130 a foot. He'd be getting the site for $20 million less than it was worth — before factoring in the beautiful, cash-flowing office building sitting on it.

"It didn't make sense!" Swig would crow years later.

It didn't make sense if you were an optimist, like Swig. Despite a penchant for elegantly tailored business suits and cufflinks, the 37-year-old Californian always looked as if he'd be more comfortable in a T-shirt, board shorts, and flip-flops, thanks to his light eyebrows, perpetually sun-cooked lips and shaggy blond locks.

Swig was undisputed real estate royalty — the grandson of the legendary Benjamin Swig, who had built the famed Fairmont Hotel chain and left his descendants the 50-story W.R. Grace Building on 42nd Street — as well as the son-in-law and protégé of Harry Macklowe, the scrappy, self-made builder of "midnight demolition" fame.

Though there were some pioneers in the area — a Bronx-born former lawyer named Steve Witkoff had started out buying properties in Washington Heights and seen promise in Downtown — most looked at the area and saw a glut of antiquated, unwanted office space. They saw the dark days of the recession that had just passed and the long list of speculators ruined when the market had taken a dive. They saw risk.

But Swig saw opportunity. He was ready to make a big bet on New York, which had recovered from the financial despair of the 1970s and the crime of the 1980s and 1990s and was now being seen as a safe, profitable place to do business under Mayor Giuliani. If the "investment thesis" brewing in Swig's head checked out, it wouldn't just be the one building he would buy in the area. There was no telling how big a chunk of the Downtown apple he might bite off.

Swig had grown up 3,000 miles from New York, surrounded by horses, chickens, and dogs in a bucolic stretch of California's Marin County, just down the road from where George Lucas would build Skywalker

Ranch.[4] His family's roots were in the Midwest. After starting out buying small retail stores in Iowa in the 1930s, Benjamin Swig had formed a partnership with Jack Weiler and began building what would become a $1 billion empire. The Swigs retained a number of Manhattan holdings including 1411 Broadway, 437 Madison Avenue, 711 Third Avenue, and the Grace Building, names that Swig can still recite today with the same ease that others recall long-deceased childhood pets.

From the very first time Swig visited the city when he was 10 — staying at the Carlyle, visiting the Statue of Liberty, taking the Circle Line around Manhattan — he was enthralled. The city back then was gritty and in decline. But Swig could see his future. "The energy — the soul — I'd never felt anything like it," he said decades later.

It would take a little while, and Swig would go a rather circuitous route, but he would return.

After majoring in Chinese history at Brown, Swig moved to China, living for five months in a city south of Shanghai called Hangzhou. There, he took daily jogs with a People's Liberation Army minder, who followed his wide-eyed charge by bicycle and diverted him away from areas of the town that were off-limits. Swig returned to San Francisco for law school, intent on mastering international law and going back to China. But his fate as a real estate scion intervened.

Swig's father got cancer, forcing Swig to step in and run the family business. He was surprised to find he enjoyed the creativity of the work and that his affable nature made him a natural dealmaker. And when his father grew sick a second time, Swig put together the deal that would change his life. After a partner backed out of an acquisition in Los Angeles, Swig was charged with finding a replacement. Swig had been

4   Gupta, Pranay. "A True Believer in Building Relationships." *The New York Sun*. May 5, 2005.

reading about Macklowe's developments in New York City and decided to cold-call and pitch him the deal. Not only did Swig persuade Macklowe to fly to L.A. and invest, he set off a relationship that would have a profound impact on both men's personal and professional lives.

In 1986, when Swig moved to New York for a few months to manage some of his family's investments, Macklowe invited him over for dinner, ostensibly to "meet his family." In reality, Macklowe was playing matchmaker — introducing Swig to his daughter, Elizabeth. Macklowe, it seems, was looking for both an acolyte and a son-in-law. Liz found out, canceled dinner, and went out with a friend instead.

Some things are just meant to be. That night, Swig was to meet an old law school pal at Saloon in Yorkville when he was spotted in line by Liz. She recognized him from her father's office and approached him, and the two started talking. In 1987, Swig moved to New York permanently, married Liz, and began apprenticing under Macklowe.

It was a job that offered Swig a crash course in the skills one needed to excel in New York real estate: creative thinking, media management — and bare-knuckled grit and ruthlessness.

Macklowe tapped him to oversee the construction of a Midtown hotel just off Times Square on West 44th Street. The hotel was already mired in controversy. In an incident that would make Macklowe notorious, his contractors had cleared the way for construction by demolishing a pair of single-room-occupancy buildings that sat on the site. They chose to do so in the dead of night, just hours before a citywide moratorium on SRO demolitions — triggered by the homelessness crisis — was to take effect. Eager to beat the deadline, the contractors demolished the buildings with no permits and neglected to turn off the gas, which could have caused an explosion.

In a city where gentrification and development had already begun to roil local politics, what would become known as the "midnight demolition" set off a firestorm and gave Harry Macklowe a dirty name. And though the district attorney eventually exonerated Macklowe of his contractors' actions, he was still forced to pony up $2 million in fines. The incident would be mentioned by default in every piece of press he received for years to come.

The name Macklowe, the New York Daily News said at the time, is "a watchword for everything furtive and underhanded in the real estate business."

"He's willing to bet the house, and he is a scoundrel," longtime New York Times reporter Charles Bagli, who covered Macklowe for decades, would later recall. "So something is going to happen in the end. And of course, it always infuriated him that the midnight demolition, which happened in the '80s, haunted him for the rest of his life."

Swig assumed the role of spokesperson for the project, allowing Macklowe to deflect. It seemed a small price to pay, for the development offered Swig a direct role in one of the more remarkable transformations in recent New York City history, that of Times Square.

Macklowe's site was located just two blocks up and one block over from "the Deuce," a stretch of West 42nd Street between Seventh and Eighth avenues that Rolling Stone had deemed "the sleaziest block in America" and that later inspired David Simon's HBO series. Once a middle-class entertainment center, Times Square had ceded that role to Lincoln Center in the mid-1960s, according to Columbia professor Lynne Sagalyn, whose "Times Square Roulette" documented the revitalization efforts.

"During the 1970s and 1980s, West 42nd Street became synonymous in the minds of a worldwide public with violence and crime, flaunted deviance and pornography and urban decay," Sagalyn wrote. The waiting rooms and concourses of the nearby Port Authority Bus Terminal, meanwhile, were a favorite homeless hangout. They served as both a hunting ground for shysters looking to scam new arrivals to the city and an entry point for a seemingly endless supply of would-be criminals to step in and replace those who had been arrested.

"If you city planners set out to make a place for dope peddlers, you couldn't plan anything as good as Times Square," one young drug dealer told two sociologists tasked with studying the area the decade of Swig's arrival,[5] according to Sagalyn's book. "I get off the bus from Detroit without a penny in my pocket. I walk up to the blood bank on Forty-second street, where I sell a pint of my blood, take the money, and go just four doors away where I can buy me a knife. I use the money left over to go into one of them all-night movies, where I slit open the back pocket of the first sleeping drunk I see. I take his money down the street, buy myself an ounce of smoke, find myself a doorway, and begin selling. I've been in town less than an hour and I'm already in business."

Macklowe's development site was located just outside the bullseye of the sleaze, at 145 West 44th Street between Sixth and Seventh avenues. On the block was a "hot-sheet" hotel, where prostitutes and their johns came and went at 30-minute intervals at all hours of day and night. Yet there was reason for optimism.

Even in the years before Swig's arrival, across town in the Midtown East business district, the wrenching bankruptcies of the mid-1970s had become a distant memory. And by the early '80s, development on the East Side had hit such a frenzied pace that many were worried the area was becoming overbuilt. So in 1982, the city had designated a West Side "growth area" from Sixth to Eighth avenues between 40th and 60th streets, an area that hadn't seen construction since the early 1970s. To entice developers west, the planning commission offered a zoning carrot, allowing developers to build 20 percent higher. It also created urgency: Any project without

---

5   Sagalyn, Lynne B. Times Square Roulette. *The MIT Press*. August 29, 2003.

foundation walls up by May 13, 1988, would lose the bonus.

By the time Swig arrived in 1987, the zoning bonus had brought over many developers. And the looming deadline set off a frenzy of last-minute activity. Plywood barricades and scaffolding were everywhere on the streets around Times Square, and to the north a small army of hardhats was engaged in a frenzy of demolition and digging. Bruce Eichner and VMS Realty were building a 450,000-square-foot office tower on Broadway and 46th Street. Up on 52nd and Broadway, Rudin Management was at work on a 35-story office tower. Larry Silverstein was assembling a project on Seventh Avenue at 47th Street, where he planned to build the Palace Hotel.

Macklowe was not afraid to delegate, and he gave his charge wide powers. Swig was an eager pupil.

He'd be up and working at 6:30 a.m., break for dinner with Liz and get back to it until midnight. "Harry said, 'Here's the project, you know, go forth.'" Swig recalled. "I had not been a developer of any project before, so there were a lot of things to learn. I was probably working 18-hour days. It was one of the greatest graduate programs anybody could ever do."

Swig did everything from hiring the architects and engineers to purchasing all the furniture, fixtures, and equipment. He did the research, designed the hotel, laid it out, and later set up a management company to operate it. Macklowe sat in on weekly project meetings with the architects and the construction teams.

Swig also learned, and then refined, the art of New York City urban combat — an art that would come in handy when he was building his own development empire in the 2000s.

To deal with the hot-sheet hotel, and to keep riffraff off the block, Swig formed a block association with other owners and ran it with Larry Feldman, a developer who was putting up a 40-story office tower on 45th Street between Sixth and Seventh avenues. The members paid dues and had walkie-talkies, which they used to share problems and note suspicious goings-on. They even persuaded the local police to run a sting: The married owner of the problem hotel was promptly busted attempting to solicit an undercover cop. That gave the developers the leverage to make him clean the place up, and things on the block began to improve.

Swig identified a key competitive edge for the new hotel. At the time, all of the city's conference spaces required off-site lodging. He suggested to Macklowe that they offer conference space on the premises. The area allocated for conference space eventually grew to three floors and became an integral part of the hotel. The project, a glassy 52-story 638-room structure, would come to be known as the Hotel Macklowe (today, it is the Millennium). It hosted a number of marquee events, including the marathon World Chess Championship between Garry Kasparov and Anatoly Karpov in 1990.

By the early 1990s, Swig had moved on. The end of his apprenticeship was hastened by the same factors that would take out a number of prominent developers: the great crash of the late 1980s. Macklowe filed for Chapter 11 bankruptcy on one apartment building and would eventually turn the Hotel Macklowe over to Chemical Bank to avoid foreclosure. As new development ground to a standstill in the early 1990s, and Macklowe struggled to stay afloat, both he and his protégé agreed: It was time for Swig to put out his own shingle and show the world what he could do.

As Swig sat in his office analyzing the Bank of New York deal and contemplating Lower Manhattan all those years later, he was struck by the similarity to the situation he had encountered in Times Square. Some of the lessons he learned under Macklowe clearly applied here. The first was that New Yorkers were so jaded, they often missed changes that were obvious to everyone else.

"New Yorkers sometimes know so much about their own city that they don't look at it with fresh eyes," Swig said.

Many were still nursing a financial hangover from the go-go 1980s. Spurred by favorable tax laws promoting office development and the Wall Street boom times, Downtown developers back then had kicked into high gear. And by 1986, more than 10 million square feet of office space had been created in Lower Manhattan. Then came the calamitous "Black Monday" stock market crash in October 1987. Massive layoffs, company closings — most notably the collapse of financial giant Drexel Burnham Lambert — and the belt-tightening of the recession followed, and office vacancy rates in the area spiked to record highs. Those tenants that remained had their pick of the space, and many moved out of the old stock and into the newest buildings.

By 1994, an estimated 25 million square feet lay vacant, an amount equivalent to all the available office space in Pittsburgh. Most of the empty space was in huge pre–World War II buildings, cursed with asbestos, low ceilings, unsightly columns, aging equipment, and floor plates designed for an era in which typists and secretaries ringed the outer areas of every office.

In 1993, a 325,000-square-foot building at 5 Hanover Square, assessed at $14.3 million, sold for $9 million, or $28 a foot. The following year, the 300,000-square foot 30 Broad Street, assessed by the city at $18.9 million, sold for $6.4 million, or $21 a foot. But just as in Times Square, there was some hope.

Several years earlier, City Hall had convened a task force on Lower Manhattan, and the Real Estate Board of New York, the industry's biggest trade group, had lobbied for aggressive action. It was already clear from the experience of the Upper West Side and other areas that people were returning to Giuliani's New York en masse. They needed places to live. If Downtown could be turned into a 24-hour district, if transportation could be improved, perhaps that old office stock could be put to better use — perhaps it could be converted to residential.

The area, city planners noted, was already anchored by Battery Park City on the west shore and the South Street Seaport and South Bridge Towers on the east shore. Some predicted redevelopment would proceed along the shores, then move inland.

In Times Square, Swig believed the construction of the Hotel Macklowe and other big projects had fundamentally altered the character of the place. But nobody seemed to see it. And even if you didn't agree with that, it seemed to Swig, it was hard to deny the impact the long-delayed implementation of the Times Square Redevelopment Project had on the area. Yet it took years for people to realize that Times Square had changed.

"You ask New Yorkers, 'What's your opinion of Times Square?,'" Swig would explain decades later. "'It's seedy. It's prostitutes. Never go there.' Then all these new buildings came up, and now, 'What do you think of Times Square?' 'It's seedy. It's full of prostitutes and crime. Never go there.' Okay. "Then a unique thing happened. All the infrastructure, millions of square feet, brand-new hotel rooms, residential, all there. And you still ask New Yorkers, 'What do you think of Times Square?' 'It's seedy, crime-filled, prostitutes,'" Swig concluded, throwing up his arms in exasperation.

Only after "The Lion King" had opened in 1997, Swig recalled, did New Yorkers, at the theater with their children, begin to look around, open their eyes and say, "Where am I?!" "Their eyes were open because of 'The Lion King,' and then all of a sudden, everybody goes, 'Oh my God, Times Square!'" Swig said.

As he contemplated the deal, Swig thought about his grandfather, who had a plaque on his desk that read: "Nothing can be achieved if all possible objections must first be overcome." Swig liked that people thought his studying Chinese history was unusual. Now he liked that people didn't see what he saw Downtown. The key to success, Macklowe had taught Swig, was "vision." You needed to see what others didn't. And you needed to have enough faith in your vision to follow it.

It was something Swig felt so strongly about that he sought to cultivate a persona that emphasized his uniqueness, injecting some pizzazz into the staid conservatism of the real estate world. He donned sharp suits, in grays and navy blues, but matched them with purple shirts, soccer ball cufflinks, beaded bracelets, and a tequila string around his wrist. He built a closet in his Midtown office to store his surfboards, which he showed off to visitors. He decorated the walls with expensive art by edgy icons — a huge Warhol print of Mao Zedong with pink and blue lips, a Damien Hirst painting depicting a needle with blood on it.

"You can think out of the box, you can be as creative as you want," Swig would later say. "Just because it hasn't been done doesn't mean it's not a great idea. Everything has issues and problems, and if you get limited or intimidated by every obstacle that you confront, you're never going to get anywhere."

Swig decided to bid on the Bank of New York building. And he won.

To buy the property at 48 Wall, Swig and his partner David Burris, also a Macklowe alum, teamed up with the Corsair Group, a real estate investment bank. And by the time Swig won it, he was convinced he'd scored the deal of a lifetime. In the Times, Bagli dubbed Swig's winning bid "surprising" and warned that the price fed a "rising fear that the market is out of control."

Just three years earlier, a 525,000-square-foot office building down the street at 25 Broad had sold for $10 per foot, less than one-tenth the $123 a foot Swig and Burris had bid to win their prize. But Swig's timing, in this instance at least, would prove fortuitous. And the buy would be the first of many — a preamble to one of the most epic spending sprees of the early aughts, and a journey that many in the industry would later recall as the most emblematic of the times, leading to one of the great busts of the cycle.

II

You Are Not to Talk, Young Man

The Rise of Steve Ross

S teve Ross wasn't big on chitchat. When he rang his old friend Ken Himmel in his Boston office one quiet afternoon, he got right to the point.

"How quickly can you get to New York City?" Ross asked. "Can you come for dinner? I have something I want to talk to you about."

"Yeah, I could get there," Himmel replied, a faint Boston accent coating his words. "What are we doing?"

"Just come," Ross said.

It was 1996. Himmel, a snowy-haired, retail and mall whiz with wide-set blue eyes and an affable air, knew the 56-year-old Ross well enough to know that whatever he wanted would probably be worth his while. He finished up what he was doing — which wasn't much, it had been a slow few months — and headed to Logan Airport to catch the shuttle to LaGuardia.

That night, Ross took Himmel to the Post House, a steakhouse on East 63rd Street, a couple blocks over from Central Park. It was some spot to take Himmel, a lifetime Red Sox fan who'd come of age in the '40s and '50s. Plaques marked the places where the Yankee sluggers Joe DiMaggio and Mickey Mantle had regular tables back in their day.

"I'm planning on bidding on the old Coliseum site," Ross revealed.

Himmel's ears perked up. Ross was talking about possibly the biggest development opportunity in a generation.

The Coliseum was a hulking, windowless, two-block-long concrete rectangle on the western side of Columbus Circle, topped on its southern edge by a drab, 26-story office tower. But mostly it was a monument to misguided city planning. Knocking it down would signify the shift to a city built on, by, and for private wealth.

The city and the MTA had been talking for years about replacing it with a new development. But previous efforts to do so had been derailed by the financial meltdown in the 1980s and opposition from civic groups. Now, the development was in play again. Whoever won the rights would become an instant macher in New York City and, if they could handle the delicate politics, would make millions of dollars in the process. It would arguably be the most important city real estate project of the new millennium.

Ross had a simple question for Himmel: would he be willing to join him?

The men had known each other since they were in their early 30s, small fries with big dreams. They had joined a networking group made up of up-and-comers, dubbed "the real estate roundtable of young guys." The group was drawn from the ranks of developers all around the country and met twice a year at beachy resorts. Himmel and Ross had grown particularly close.

In some ways, they were opposites. Himmel, with his folksy demeanor, had thrived early in his career thanks in part to the very skill Ross lacked — the ability to be a loyal, nonthreatening soldier — and had endeared himself to older mentors. After graduating from Cornell University's hotel school, he'd convinced a Boston entrepreneur building Hilton franchises to take him on as his assistant. He later supervised construction of the Ritz-Carlton hotel at the Water Tower Place in Chicago, which opened in 1975 as one of the country's first true urban vertical mixed-use projects. Getting that job had been a key break in Himmel's career, giving him a seat at the table for planning meetings with Thomas Klutznick, a pioneering developer of vertical malls.

After Water Tower wrapped, Himmel headed back to Boston and found a site for Klutznick's next mixed-use project: the 3.5 million-square-foot Copley Place. Himmel had since gone on to build vertical malls across the country, an experience that would inform his big venture with Ross.

Ross had taken a different path. He was a former tax attorney from Detroit who, like a number of the city's leading developers, had helped others make millions in real estate before deciding he wanted his own piece of the action. In his late 20s, he had quit his job the day after Robert F. Kennedy was shot — life had suddenly seemed too short — and moved to New York, where he'd been hired — and fired — from no less than two white-shoe financial firms in his first 18 months. (That's what happens at Bear Stearns when you say "fuck you" to your boss in the middle of an executive meeting.) Ross had focused early on building his own company and honing his developer chops by taking advantage of government subsidies available for affordable-housing projects.

As his own boss, Ross was a no-nonsense tactician, willing to admit his own weaknesses. He'd taken stock of what he was good at: structuring and explaining deals, telling people what he could do for them, seeing through to the heart of the matter. He'd approach well-connected collaborators and offer them pieces of deals simply to help him win them, and made a concerted effort to seek out young, ambitious architects and builders willing to teach him what he did not know about the nuts and bolts of development.

Ross had started with $10,000 from his mother, an expertise in tax shelters and syndication and an ace in the hole — his uncle was Max Fisher, a businessman who had built one of the largest gas station chains in the Midwest before selling it to Marathon Oil, then dabbled in real estate.

By the end of the decade, Ross had created 5,000 units, built up a staff, and moved his offices to a prestigious address. He signed a long-term lease for a building at 10 East 52nd Street, which was connected to Olympic Tower, the city's first luxury condominium. A precursor to Trump Tower and a whole slew of high-end buildings catering to rich foreigners and celebrities, Olympic Tower had snagged worldwide headlines for its opulence and famous residents, including billionaire Saudi arms dealer Adnan Khashoggi.

By then, the city had begun to emerge from its tailspin. A writer for Forbes provided a snapshot of Ross's adopted city in transition: He noted that outside the Citicorp Center on Manhattan's "fashionable East Side" (just a few blocks from Ross's new offices), "sleek, well-groomed couples strolled...casually onto the nearly empty streets nearby, as if it were daytime." The Upper West was still "unfashionable" and full of half-boarded-up tenements and weed-filled vacant lots, but was perceived as safe enough that at 1 a.m., a cheap jazz club there saw a sizable clientele of mostly white Midtowners.

"So where are the fires and looting, the nightmare mugger, the chaos and poverty of Wasteland New York? They exist. The vast, empty South Bronx moonscape is still out there, where abandoned buildings burn in the silence and there is no one left to watch," the Forbes writer wrote. But "nowadays, something else clearly exists, too: a new mood of stability and optimism that hasn't been seen in years."

"There have always been two, coexisting, New York Cities," he continued. "One was the immigrant blue-collar city, the sweatshop city, the melting pot you came to with only two hands and hope; the other was the affluent New York, the mecca for people with an edge who wanted to Make It Big. It is the first that is dying, the second that is enjoying the new bloom of revival."

Ross made his first foray into market-rate housing in 1985, when he acquired a big site on Third Avenue between 93rd and 94th streets from a developer who couldn't finish the job. On it, Ross would construct Carnegie Park, a 31-story 325-unit doorman rental building.

Soon after, he was selected to build one project at Battery Park City and then managed to take over three sites that had been failing.

When the market turned in the late 1980s, Ross, like Harry Macklowe, hit a tough patch. In the race to develop, Ross overleveraged his company and signed some recourse loan deals that would have allowed lenders to go after the rest of the company if Related defaulted. Over the next couple years, Related was forced to restructure $100 million in unsecured debt and, in late 1992, raised $40 million by selling a 30-percent stake in the company to friends and family, including his uncle Max Fisher.

By the time of his dinner with Himmel, Ross was on firm financial footing and ready to take the next big step. He could see his prize out his office window.

The day after their dinner, Ross took Himmel to his ninth-floor office on 58th and Madison and showed him the patch of land directly to the west across the park that he'd coveted for years.[6]

---

6   Grant, P. "Developer Ross Savors Win of Coliseum." *New York Daily News*. August 3, 1998.

To any ordinary civilian passing through it, Columbus Circle would have seemed an unlikely object of desire. It was a windy, dirty, dead space in the city — a place you barely noticed unless you were stuck in traffic. The graffiti-smeared statue of the famous explorer that gave the circle its name was marooned in the middle of a junction where five different streets came together, causing chest-tightening, horn-blaring gridlock, often backing cars and trucks down Eighth Avenue, all the way back to 53rd Street. You could smell the diesel.

The property was also depressing. Columbus Circle had long been dominated by the New York Coliseum. Since 1956, the foreboding convention center on the southern edge of the circle had cast a pall over the area, though it had occasionally drawn crowds to special events like the International Flower Show. Out front in 1971, an assassin had gunned down the Cosa Nostra boss Joseph Colombo during an Italian-American civil rights rally (an incident later dramatized in Martin Scorsese's "The Irishman").

But not much happened there anymore. By the late 1980s, the Coliseum had become a zombie building with just a few tenants — unless you counted the homeless people living in the sprawling shantytown outside it, or the drug dealers and prostitutes who lurked in its shadows.

But bleakness was not what Ross pointed out to Himmel. This was a chance for them to propel Ross's adopted home — and both their careers — to new levels.

The Metropolitan Transportation Authority, which owned Columbus Circle, was seeking new bids to redevelop the area, "to participate in the renaissance of this most important area of this city," then-MTA chairman Virgil Conway said.

Ross recognized Columbus Circle as a place he could leave his boldest contribution to the skyline, not just a visual legacy, but a metropolis-defining one. (It was a move that would pay off so spectacularly that 20 years later Ross would be in a position to build the biggest project of them all, "the largest private development in U.S. history": Hudson Yards).

Redeveloping Columbus Circle, Ross told Himmel, "would be like building the Rockefeller Center of the 21st century."

The central location of Columbus Circle, at the bottom of the park, and the junction between several major subway lines, was ideal. It was a gateway between Midtown and the residential Upper West Side. Though the area was dead now, it was easy to imagine a bustling hub — that is, if a developer could somehow open the space up and find a way to draw people in.

Ross knew that Himmel, like him, reveled in the complexities of real estate development. It was part of the reason they got along so well. Himmel liked figuring out mixed-use spaces, how to put it all together, how to "activate" a space. Ross loved the challenge of assembling parcels through intricate land deals, absorbing the rhythms of construction schedules, watching his creations turn from ideas into buildings. Most of all he enjoyed taking on new challenges, pushing himself, and proving he could succeed where others had failed. In high school he'd grown to 6'2" and 215 pounds, big enough to play offensive lineman on his high school football team. He still liked to win.

Ross knew that every other real estate macher in the city was probably running the same mental calculations he was. If you tried hard enough, you could almost hear the murmur of lawyers, accountants, and developers across the city huddling around polished conference room tables with sweeping views high above the city, plotting. Who can we get to back us on this? Who can we snare as an anchor tenant to get an edge over the other bidders? What do we have to do to convince the city and the state? There were plenty of bigger fish, and Ross badly wanted to beat them on this. Being selected would immediately establish the winner as one of the city's most prominent builders — or burnish the reputation of one already in that pack.

And indeed, they had all been lying in wait. There was the ever-loquacious Donald Trump, who was already promoting a newly opened office, hotel, and condo tower on the northern edge of the circle, the Trump International Hotel & Tower New York, while trying to convince the world his well-chronicled financial problems were in the past. The first time the city and state had solicited bids to develop the Coliseum site, he had placed not one but two bids, including a proposal to build a 100-story tower, the world's tallest at the time. The Donald had lost then. But now that the initial project had been abandoned — after a tortuous series of failed negotiations between the city and billionaire real estate magnate Mort Zuckerman's Boston Properties, with opponents such as Jackie Onassis and Henry Kissinger — he would certainly be back. The fact that he had recently completed the Trump International across Columbus Circle gave him even more reason to try. Larry Silverstein, the Brylcreemed, ever-scrappy billionaire developer of 7 World Trade Center, would also throw in. Millennium Partners, a development firm run by impeccably well-connected former City officials that had just completed a mixed-use project across the street from nearby Lincoln Center, was said to be partnering with Goldman Sachs. Ross would probably even have to beat out the owners of Rockefeller Center, the billionaire Jerry Speyer's dynastic real estate development firm Tishman Speyer, which was backed by blue-chip global capital.

To run the selection process, the MTA had hired Ben Lambert, chairman of Eastdil Secured, a real estate investment banking company. Lambert was more than a decade older than Ross, had done business with Ross's uncle Max Fisher, and had watched Ross blossom from neophyte into industry player. But he considered him a longshot.

"Steve had been doing all sorts of deals," Lambert, who died in January 2021, recalled. "But he was not the obvious choice. He hadn't really been in my judgment or in my awareness an important developer."

Not that Lambert expected that to stop Ross. Indeed, Ross's mother was fond of reminding her son that as a kid growing up in Detroit, he had drawn the attention of the elementary school principal — who took his father aside and cautioned him that his kid had "spirit."

"Be very strict," he'd advised. "But make sure you don't break him."

Upon arriving in Manhattan to try his hand at real estate, his "spirit" had irritated not just his superiors in finance, but perhaps the city's most iconic developer, William "Big Bill" Zeckendorf, the man behind the United Nations complex. Ross had accompanied his new boss, the president of the investment-banking firm Laird & Company, to a meeting with Zeckendorf to discuss the sale of a Park Avenue property. Ross had felt compelled to add his two cents when he realized his boss was about to agree to a bad deal. His input didn't go down well.

"You are not to talk, young man," Zeckendorf barked from behind his elevated desk. "You're just here to listen."

In Ross's mind, the seeds of an audacious proposal had already begun to form. Cynics would scoff when they learned of the details. Some would warn him he was courting failure and financial ruin. His scheme, they would say, might work in suburbia, but never in their cosmopolitan city. Ross couldn't be serious. Could he?

For on the site of the zombie office tower and former homeless encampment, Ross envisioned a high-end shopping mall. It was a project that would come to symbolize a more siloed New York, in which the global wealthy lived and shopped in their ivory towers, cut off — and by virtue of shell companies, hidden — from the rest of the city.

But back then, there were plenty of reasons for that vision to be seen as absurd. For one thing, Ross's Related had never built anything like it before. The company had found success developing affordable housing projects around the nation, and owned a number of office buildings as well as a handful of higher-end residential properties. It had even begun to develop a small mixed-use project in Union Square. But it was certainly fair to ask: Other than your standard big-city developer hubris, what exactly qualified Ross to build a two-million-square-foot vertical retail mall with 50 shops?

Manhattan was its own beast, the kind of place where people turned their noses up at malls, a symbol of suburbia. Why go to a mall when you can go to Soho or walk across the park to Fifth Avenue? Or shop at the cute little boutique just down the block? Malls were great in the suburbs when there was nothing else to do. They were convenient. But the streets of Manhattan were far more interesting.

New York was littered with cautionary tales about malls. None other than Melvin Simon of Simon Property Group, the leading mall developer in the nation, had built an 11-story mall on the old site of Gimbels, near Herald Square, in partnership with Big Bill Zeckendorf's son, William Zeckendorf Jr. It had been, in the words of Big Bill's grandson William Lie Zeckendorf, "a fiasco."

By 1996, the mall's vacancy rate was hovering around 25 percent, its upper floors a ghost town. No one could be bothered to shop above street level, a strange phenomenon that seemed to infect all New Yorkers. A block away, the Herald Center, a 10-story mall backed by deposed Philippines President Ferdinand Marcos, offered an even bleaker lesson in the dangers of vertical retail. Within months, stores like Brookstone, Ann Taylor, and Saks were gone, replaced by Daffy's, Payless ShoeSource, and the Department of Motor Vehicles.

"Every retail broker in New York would have told you back then that New Yorkers will not go up two or three floors to shop," William Lie Zeckendorf recalled of Ross's proposal. "I certainly never thought it would work."

But in those months when the parameters for the site bids were set, Ross was not interested in what other New Yorkers thought would or wouldn't work. Much of what he knew about vertical malls, he had learned over the years through long conversations with Himmel. Ross suspected that if he could recruit his old buddy to the effort, success would be his.

Unlike the legions of skeptical New Yorkers, Himmel saw right away why vertical shopping would work in the area. Both the site where he built Copley Place and the former Coliseum space were large, centrally located patches of no-man's-land surrounded by human activity — Himmel called them "holes in the doughnut." Copley Place had been built on a formerly inactive site located between the Mass Turnpike and the twin skyscrapers of Hancock Tower and Prudential Center.

"You had enormous density all around you," Himmel recalled of the Boston project. "And there was this hole in the middle of the city. So if you filled it with uses, and you connected to all the streets, and you connected to the Prudential Center, common sense would tell you, you had a pretty good chance of developing a lot of retail traffic. Traffic generates sales. So there's a lot of demand."

Ross described the same phenomenon at work around Columbus Circle. To the north, Broadway and Upper Broadway had a significant amount of retail, restaurant, and residential density. You had Lincoln Center drawing people to the area for cultural events. ABC was headquartered at 66th Street. To the west, on 59th Street and 10th Avenue, you had the John Jay College of Criminal Justice. Fordham's law school was on 62nd Street. To the south, there was the northern edge of Midtown and the 57th Street corridor. In between it all, dead center, was the traffic-choked circle, and the largely empty former site of the Coliseum.

Even if you didn't draw the tourists over from the high-end shops of Madison and Fifth avenues, it looked pretty promising.

"The traffic stopped when it got to Columbus Circle, because there wasn't much to draw you to come here," Himmel recalled.

And yet, Ross told Himmel, "you were in the most strategic location visibility-wise in the whole city — here at the corner of Central Park South and West."

Ross and Himmel also had something else going for their plan. Ross believed in New York City. He was certain it was on the cusp of a fundamental shift.

Manhattan in those final years of the 20th century was not yet the playground for the rich it would later become. But something was happening — Ross and other developers could sense it, and see it in the numbers. By 1990, most of the city's high-income neighborhoods, including the area just north of Columbus Circle, had regained the population they had lost during the calamitous 1970s, and then grew further. The rest of the city would soon follow suit. It was easy to see that the supply of new housing was not keeping pace with the influx of new residents, which had only fed a building boom and speculative frenzy as the '80s drew to a close.

That frenzy had been temporarily halted by the aftershocks of the 1987 stock market crash — which by the early 1990s had proven catastrophic for many New York City developers and nearly bankrupted Ross. But by the mid-1990s, the city had bottomed out and began to recover. Crime began falling steeply. And the tough talk and zero-tolerance policing policies of Mayor Giuliani — though anathema to many liberal New Yorkers — was exactly what developers believed was needed to continue the rehabilitation of the city's battered image and speed up the flood of affluent families and young people moving in from the suburbs.

True, you couldn't yet see the housing revival in the rents: Between 1990 and 2000, rent would increase a modest 1.9 percent citywide — 3 percent in the most rapidly gentrifying areas — and actually would decline in many areas. But things were poised to explode.

In Manhattan, the new arrivals were for the most part more educated, with the overall share of those in the city with a college degree rising from just over 21 percent in 1990, to over 25 percent in 2000, to nearly 35 percent between 2010 and 2014. They were increasingly members of the new Starbucks-chugging knowledge economy, the kind that eschewed Sears and JCPenney in favor of the upscale brands Ross and Himmel envisioned for their mall. The ranks of hedge funders and finance bigwigs who opted to stay in the city rather than head to suburbia were also growing.

In the days following their dinner at the Post House, when Himmel and Ross convened in Related's office at 625 Madison Avenue and began to plot out their approach, Ross could take Himmel to his window and point to signs that the gradual upscaling of the area around Lincoln Center had reached the very edges of the circle.

Towering over the far side of Columbus Circle at 60th Street and Broadway stood Trump's newly opened project, a sleek black obelisk on the site of the old Gulf and Western Building, a project that was perhaps the most hyped luxury development of the year, thanks to the tireless machinations of the irrepressible developer.

After a very public fall from grace, Trump had come roaring back. Never mind that he had been forced to sell off his 280-foot yacht, his Trump Shuttle airline, and that he'd had a soap opera affair chronicled in the tabloids cavorting with a Southern belle named Marla Maples and had divorced his wife Ivana. Never mind that he had reportedly owed, at one point, $8.8 billion, $975 million of it personally guaranteed. In 1994, he unveiled his latest luxury project at the top of Columbus Circle. The site was occupied by a tower with structural problems that caused it to sway in strong winds, sometimes causing nausea. In collaboration with General Electric, Trump planned to fix the structural problems and transform the building into the Trump International Hotel & Tower, a 52-story luxury hotel and apartment complex built around the original steel frame. To do this he would rely on the prolific New York architect Costas Kondylis, who incorporated new elements including a massive steel brace to stiffen the structure, and prevent it from moving in the wind.

"We think this is the best project in New York by a factor of 10," Trump had told reporters at the groundbreaking, adding that his building across from Central Park has "the best views anywhere, anywhere in the world."

When it opened just a few months before the MTA solicited its bids, Trump proclaimed his new project "the most important address in the world," and noted that it included a restaurant run by Jean-Georges Vongerichten, whom Trump pronounced "the best chef in New York."

Trump's building was already commanding the highest nightly hotel rates on the West Side, and drawing a steady crowd to Jean-Georges' restaurant at its base, which buoyed Himmel's vertical mall high-end restaurant pitch.

The building's residential condos, meanwhile, exceeded all expectations.

"When Trump started getting over $1,000 a square foot in that building — I had to double-check the numbers, they seemed so high," Barbara Corcoran, founder of the real estate brokerage Corcoran Group, noted at the time. "That really set off prices in the upper-upper-end condo market."

But Himmel knew Ross's project would live and die by its retail.

He understood how to get people to cross into the dead space of the circle and how to get them to ascend. He had relied on this knowledge in many previous projects, and it would later prove key if they were to win the bid. The keys to creating the necessary retail traffic, Himmel was convinced, lay in recruiting high-quality restaurants, helmed by name-brand restaurateurs such as Gramercy Tavern's Danny Meyer or The French Laundry's Thomas Keller.

"It all comes down to food," Himmel said. "I've always believed that — from the very beginning."

In the suburbs, Himmel knew people would drive 45 minutes just to eat at a good restaurant. To get to and from these establishments, especially if you placed the restaurants on a high floor, customers would ascend and descend through the mall and often stop to check out the retail. Himmel saw no reason the same dynamic wouldn't apply to New York City.

But that would come later. Meeting at Related's office, Ross and Himmel and their financing partner William Mack agreed that they would need to lay more groundwork and establish more credibility for their project before going after their desired tenants. They also would, of course, need to win the deal.

Recruiting a premium hotelier would be a key first step, one that would help draw everyone else who would sign on.

"It was a no-brainer for residential and hotel, because if you could get up in the air here, you had unbelievable views of Central Park," Himmel said. "Trump had already established a luxury hotel market. He'd already done the breakthrough project across the street."

To set the tone, the three decided to pitch what Himmel considered the world's premier brand: The Mandarin Oriental hotel.

"Bringing the Mandarin Oriental hotel to Columbus Circle said something very important about the credibility of what we were doing," Himmel said. "Retailers and restaurants could sort of look at all this and say, 'Wow, I mean, the location's great. The density's fantastic around it, and they're demonstrating clearly this is going to be an incredibly high-quality project.'"

To design their vision for it, the partners turned to Skidmore, Owings & Merrill's David Childs, of Willis Tower fame, who offered two sleek towers, with a curving front that mirrored the circle. Through the doors of the new building would lie a vast and inviting indoor public space, separated from the foot traffic outside by a glass wall that rose several stories, designed to maintain the feel of continuity with the street outside and draw people in.

Ross was bullish as he submitted his bid in late 1996. Now all he could do was wait.

III

Unto the Sons

The Zeckendorfs and 515 Park

While Ross sought to reshape Columbus Circle and make the jump from striver to titan, two young men with serious developer pedigree were wistfully eyeing a drab brick office building on the southeast corner of Park Avenue and 60th Street on the Upper East Side. They dreamed of knocking it down and replacing it with a monument to luxury more appropriate for the new New York.

William Lie Zeckendorf, 36, and his younger brother, Arthur, 35, regarded the building with a proprietary air. The small stake they retained in the property was practically all that remained of what had once been among the city's largest development portfolios, birthed by their grandfather, the swashbuckling postwar developer William "Big Bill" Zeckendorf Sr.

Over the previous decade, their father, William Zeckendorf Jr., had constructed some 30 buildings, worth more than $30 billion, becoming a key driver of the residential resurgence of the Upper West Side and Union Square, and building the mammoth office and residential complex Worldwide Plaza in Midtown. Backed by Japanese conglomerate Mitsubishi, Zeckendorf Jr. had purchased the Park Avenue office property in 1989 for $38 million, intending to knock the building down and develop it himself.

Then in the early 1990s, the market turned, the creditors moved in, and Zeckendorf Jr. — just like his father before him — had lost it all.

Before entering semi-retirement in New Mexico, he had sold his two boys what remained of his stake. It wasn't much. Mitsubishi was by then carrying the majority of the mortgage and was eager to get out of the deal. By 1996, William Lie and Arthur were gunning to raise the funds needed to buy them out.

They certainly had plenty of pockets to tap into. The brothers had been raised on Park Avenue, attended exclusive private boarding academies (Will went to the Taft School in Watertown, Connecticut; Arthur, St. Paul's in Concord, New Hampshire) before graduating from Tufts University. Will had gone on to Harvard Business School and married a debutante, while Arthur had gone directly to work for his father, and wed a member of the Junior League. They summered in the Hamptons, lunched with other second- and third-generation developers, and were extremely well-connected.

Invariably described as "intensely private" and "low key" in the media, and "calmly rational"[7] by associates, the brothers' public image was in direct contrast to that of their late grandfather.

In his time, the bald, rotund developer had been a national icon,

---

7   Scheurman, Matthew. "The Zeckendorf Family." *The New York Observer*. December 18, 2006.

pictured most famously in the back seat of his limo, wearing a homburg, a three-piece suit, and tan leather gloves, clutching a telephone to his ear. "Big Bill," who told stories about his own pistol-toting ancestor, an Arizona pioneer, could be quite a cowboy himself: He was known to live on the edge, relying on short-term high-interest financing to grow his empire.

"I'd rather be alive at 18 percent than dead at the prime rate," he once declared,[8] showing his willingness to take big risks to stay in the game.

Big Bill sometimes had as many as five or six projects going at a time. He put together the transformative deal for the site that became the United Nations headquarters and was considered to be the most significant developer of his time. In 1965, however, his highly leveraged chickens finally came home to roost, and he was forced to declare bankruptcy.

Conversely, Will and Arthur, who share the same warm brown eyes, thick curving eyebrows, and small, tight smiles, favored conservative business suits and relied more on numbers and 40-page business plans than force of personality to sell their ideas. Their confidence was more of the understated, attended-the-right-schools type, though Arthur, the bald one, was considered shy, and Will, with a full head of hair, gregarious.

Where Ross hoped to draw the public into Columbus Circle with his master plan, the Zeckendorfs' vision for their site, while equally bold, was quite the opposite: the complex they envisioned would be an enclave of opulence and luxury catering to the richest of the rich, a gated haven in the sky intended to one-up even the great prewar co-ops of the first gilded age.

They would dress it in French marble, build a sumptuous lobby and entrance halls, and construct living rooms with 30-foot ceilings, fireplaces, and marble bathrooms. There would be wraparound terraces, servants' quarters, billiard rooms, and climate-controlled wine cellars. They would have a gym

---

8   Putzier, Konrad. "Developers Who Rise from the Dead." *The Real Deal*. November 1, 2015.

and state-of-the-art kitchens. And the apartments would be huge, as large as 6,000 square feet. This would be an urban palace with all the old-world class of a grand Fifth Avenue building, and all the new-money accoutrements of the modern age — though only a select few would ever see the inside of it.

Yet the Zeckendorfs' plan did have one egalitarian twist. Unlike the older, exclusive co-ops of the Upper East Side — which had famously rejected a long list of luminaries from Barbra Streisand to Richard Nixon to Diane Sawyer — buyers here would have no need to jump through hoops for the elitist co-op boards. Hailing from New York aristocracy themselves, the Zeckendorfs took aim at one of its most time-honored symbols.

The Zeckendorfs left the co-ops behind and decided to build a condominium. The only price of admission would be money — heaps of it.

It was a decision that helped set off the wave of ask-me-no-questions deals by superrich buyers that would come to dominate Manhattan, such as the Russian oligarch Dmitry Rybolovlev's $88 million purchase of a penthouse at the Zeckendorfs' 15 Central Park West years later. A flurry of builders would scramble to cater to this elite buyer pool, leading to a wave of condo development.

At the time, however, the plan for their Park Avenue condo was about as well received in the boardrooms of New York City financiers as Ross's improbable vision for an upscale vertical mall in Columbus Circle.

"You name it, we pitched them," Will recalled. "No one believed us."

"There was not a big appetite," Arthur added. "Not at all."

"Hell-o! Location, location, location!" one broker snidely remarked to a reporter at the time. "You won't see any real Park Avenue blue bloods moving in there. It's too far south."[9]

---

9   Lockwood, Charles. "Big Rich Digs." *Grid*. January 2000.

The brothers were keenly aware that their site was surrounded by offices, hotels, and apartments, well away from the more desirable all-residential blocks seen further north on Park. They knew that what they were proposing to build would be considered an outlier.

But, in some ways, that was exactly the point. Both had received their real estate schooling across the park in the far grittier realms of 1980s West Side Manhattan. And if they had learned anything from their father, it was the need to be able to look at a development site and visualize the future, not the past — to follow that vision, and "ignore the losers" you beat out to win the project, along with all the other doubters.

Such vision, they'd seen firsthand, had the power to transform neighborhoods.

Working for their father in the 1980s, Will and Arthur had closely tracked the influx of young, gentrifying families moving back to Manhattan, and built housing to accommodate them, often in marginal neighborhoods like Union Square and Upper Broadway, where crime and drug dealing had scared away other developers. Their no-nonsense projects had played a key role in the revitalization and gentrification of the West Side up and down the Broadway corridor.

"We would really pack them in so we could keep the price points down," Will recalled. "It was tight. It was not prewar-style co-ops. It was efficient, hardworking apartments at a price point meant to get up-and-coming families to buy."

Will's initiation into the business had been a series of terrifying trips down to Union Square, where drug addicts lurked in the doorways of abandoned buildings and you "felt like you were going to get mugged any second."

"I was scared to tears," he admitted.

Across the street from what was then a notorious needle park in Union Square, his father and brother would build Zeckendorf Towers, a million-square-foot mixed-use development. Costing $225 million, the complex would eventually house a 22,000-square-foot grocery store, 300,000 square feet of office space, and over 600 condos. When it opened in 1987, the traffic it helped draw to the area accelerated its evolution into the thriving public square it is today.

Up on 96th Street and Broadway, where the Zeckendorfs would eventually build the 400,000-square-foot 32-story Columbia condominium, some of the locals were so menacing that the Zeckendorfs had to meet potential partners and financiers around the corner on 97th Street and West End Avenue, where foot traffic was light and doormen swept the sidewalks and chased away undesirables.

"We would do most of the talking there," Will recalled. "Then you walk quickly by the properties, and you go back to West End Avenue because we could at least walk around the neighborhood without being harassed."

At the groundbreaking, protestors opposed to market-rate housing had sparked a "quasi riot," chanting "go back to the East Side," and the police had dispersed the crowd.

The Zeckendorfs' marquee project to date was Worldwide Plaza. The three-building mixed-use development, in partnership with developer (and national squash champion) Victor Elmaleh, rose in the middle of Hell's Kitchen, a neighborhood then defined by its pawn shops, bodegas, and freewheeling crime; the undesirables, driven out of Times Square by the city's revitalization efforts, had showed up right at their stoop. While the elder Zeckendorf focused on leasing the office space, Arthur had headed up efforts to sell the 660 condo units, many of them directly across the street from a local high school for troubled, often violent teenagers, who would gather on the sidewalks every afternoon and harass passersby.

The privileged young brothers from Park Avenue had thus spent time in the trenches. Their apprenticeships had taught them the dangers of hubris and the cruelties of the market. As conditions in the late 1980s began to turn, they had begged their father to slow down. He hadn't listened.

In 1993, after a couple of stressful years spent helping unwind their father's projects, Will and Arthur had finally gone out on their own. They were so relieved to be out from under the cloud of crisis that they considered a wide array of new ventures, ranging from partnering with the Florida Seminoles to opening casinos down south, to bidding on military housing.

But they settled on returning to what they knew best: the brothers offered up their project-management expertise to banks looking to finish repossessed development projects. Then, in March 1995, they lunched with another industry scion named Kent Swig.

The three had known each other, and followed each other from afar, for most of their lives. Their families had been doing business together as far back as the 1930s, when Benjamin Swig and Big Bill had partnered on projects. As they got to talking, they realized they were at similar career inflection points.

Over lunch, Kent Swig had talked about the challenges he and his partner David Burris faced as they looked for ways to break in as developers in their own rights.

"I'm looking for a platform on which to do business," Swig explained. "If I buy individual buildings and things, it takes time and effort for me to do it. I can't afford a lot of staff right now. Then if I go run it, I can't afford to go buy all the stuff. So what I'm looking for is to take over a company that has lots of issues. Buy it right, clean it up, use it as a platform, and leverage a career."

"That's exactly what we're looking to do," Swig recalls the brothers telling him.

Realizing acquiring a real estate brokerage would help toward this end, the three budding moguls decided to join forces, forming Terra Holdings.

They found precisely the vehicle they were looking for in Brown Harris Stevens, a venerable residential brokerage founded by Harry Helmsley which had name recognition, but no computers and an antiquated phone system. The company was hemorrhaging money, and had 136 lawsuits against it "because Helmsley Enterprises put everything not good into the company, and nobody would buy the company because it was filled with problems," Swig said. At the time, it had been caught up in an epic kickback scandal that roiled the industry and had resulted in scores of indictments in the property-services business, 17 at the firm alone.

The new buyers would later recall a short, emotional meeting with the seller, Leona Helmsley, wife to the master syndicator and property magnate Harry Helmsley. Though she had earned the moniker "Queen of Mean" for her notorious outbursts and tyrannical behavior, the Chanel-clad matriarch showed the third-generation princelings a different side that day.

"She could be very charming when she wanted to be," Arthur said of Leona, recalling her being very emotional. "She remembered how fond Harry was of my grandfather. She's a very thoughtful person."

It was in fact from this purchase — and the vantage point it offered them of the market — that the brothers became convinced the city was ready for the high-end development they wanted to build.

The brokerage firm gave the developers access to an unparalleled source of market intelligence: a team of agents out on the streets interacting with top-end buyers and sellers, along with pricing information coming in from sales at the 128 co-ops and condos they managed. (In 1999, Terra would acquire brokerage Halstead as well.)

Of the 10,000 apartments Brown Harris Stevens managed, a third were on Fifth and Park avenues, including many of the city's most exclusive and expensive addresses, among them 720, 730, and 740 Park, the Dakota, and 1 Sutton Place. The firm had been the exclusive agent on the sale of the late Jackie O's Fifth Avenue pad.

"What do you need in the market?" Will would ask the brokers. "What do you think is underbuilt? What are your clients looking for?"

One message began to emerge very clearly.

"We literally cannot find our customers an eight-room Park Avenue co-op, because they're not around," Will recalled the brokers telling him.

The city's blue bloods, Will and Arthur were hearing loud and clear from their brokers, were now more and more eager to stay put in New York even after starting families — or were moving back here. The inventory for what had suddenly become the hottest commodity on the market — large mansions in the sky — had not been added to for decades.

In the 1980s, there hadn't been a need for new construction of large apartments, because there was still a relative glut of the East Side prewar co-ops created by the legacy of white flight. You could still, Will recalled, "buy one for a song." But that was no longer the case, and, Will added, "there were no condominiums to compete."

It seemed an ideal way to re-enter the development market.

To pitch their new project, the brothers had worked up a slick presentation, complete with demographics, a detailed business plan, and renderings, which they had carried to conference rooms around town and lobbied to as many as 15 different potential investment partners.

"Park Avenue has long been the most coveted address in America, and for the first time in six decades discriminating buyers have the opportunity to purchase a new home in a landmark building," promotional materials declared.

This would be their first solo developer project, a 43-story limestone palace. And they were certain that if they could win the financing, the project was so ambitious it would immediately put them on the map.

But by 1997, time was running out to buy out Mitsubishi and take control of the site. The Japanese conglomerate was said to be in talks with

Trump and Steve Witkoff, the savvy, Bronx-born real estate attorney-turned-developer with a big Downtown portfolio.

"I had a flat-out handshake to buy the deal at $15 million, with paper going back and forth," Witkoff recalled, speaking about the debt for the Zeckendorfs' Park Avenue site.

But then the Zeckendorfs got a lucky break. Jules Demchick, a developer and principal at JD Carlisle, called "out of the blue," and offered to pay Mitsubishi substantially more — Witkoff recalled the number being more than twice what he had agreed to pay. The banker called Witkoff and informed him the deal was off — Mitsubushi wanted to see how much they might get on the open market.

Just as Mitsubishi was preparing to accept bids to sell the note, the Zeckendorfs, after three attempts, finally convinced Dan Neidich of Goldman Sachs' Whitehall Investment fund to bite, and help finance their vision for the property.

A few months later, Neidich's team informed the brothers that Goldman had arranged to purchase the note from Mitsubishi, paying roughly 33 cents on the dollar, or $20 million.[10] The Mitsubishi note had been officially ripped up.

The brothers' elation, however, was tempered by a little hardball from Whitehall. Arthur received a phone call from Neidich's right-hand man, Ralph Rosenberg. Rosenberg, today head of KKR's real estate division, informed them he was calling from first class on a flight en route to Paris, and that the phone would lose its connection once the plane got two miles over the U.S. border. The brothers, he said, needed to agree to the terms before he was out of range or the deal was off.

"It means more to you guys than it means to us," Arthur recalled

---

10   Garnarine, R. "Super-Luxury Condo Market Broadens." *The New York Times*. July 10, 1998.

Rosenberg telling them, as the brothers hunched over the speakerphone in their office on 770 Lexington Avenue. "We have plenty of deals. And if you guys don't agree we're just going to tell the bank we're out and this goes in the dead-deal pile."

"We'll take your deal," Arthur recalled replying.

It was a small hiccup. When the brothers had begun pitching the deal, they had suggested they could sell the condos for over $1,000 per square foot, a number many had dismissed out of hand. But by then, the market had recovered and Trump was already getting those prices across the park, which meant that even with the hard terms, they would still make out like bandits.

In the end, their estimates would prove conservative. The sumptuous, full-floor residences they would unveil just a couple years later would go on to break all pricing records, influence the course of development in the city, and help launch a new era of uber-luxury residential in the new millennium that would transfix, and transform, the industry.

The Zeckendorfs were just getting started.

IV

I, Columbus

The Time Warner Center Site

Ross's plans for the Coliseum site, with the glitzy Mandarin Oriental and a roster of fancy restaurants and retail tenants, were far more glamorous than those of his rivals. Bruce Ratner and Daniel Brodsky, for instance, were anchoring their project with a Sears and offering up mid-level residences.

In the spring of 1997, state officials announced their five finalists for the site. Ross's Related was one of them, with the MTA's representatives, Eastdil's Ben Lambert and real estate attorney Rob Sorin, taken by his vision of a luxury destination. The other finalists were Ratner and Brodsky, Tishman Speyer, Trump, and Millennium Partners.

Lambert and Sorin had been instructed by the MTA's chairman, Virgil Conway, to negotiate tentative contracts with each of the finalists to make sure the eventual winner could not use their victory as leverage to wring new concessions out of the city and MTA.

"Go out and get a feel for this and speak to these people and kind of try to get them to where you feel like you need to get them to, but not to like their best and final thing," Conway told them.

The pitches and the tenor of the negotiations varied widely. Trump brought all the bluster and showmanship you'd expect. One negotiation at Trump Tower was interrupted by a phone call from Today Show host Bryant Gumbel, according to Sorin. Trump had the call put through to his big desk in the middle of the meeting and, as Sorin and Lambert waited, he used hand gestures and mouthed words to convey to them that Gumbel was calling to get advice about his divorce.

Though Trump had credibility in the neighborhood thanks to his presence on its northern edge, he "probably had the biggest mountain to climb" to win, said Sorin, given the lack of "institutional structure and quality" in his organization.

Ross's firm was also a long shot, without the likes of a Rockefeller Center under his belt, like Tishman Speyer, or a Brooklyn MetroTech, like Ratner. But Ross's passion for his project, the creativity of his vision and his personal connection to the site worked in his favor.

"Look, I stare at this thing every day," he'd proclaim. "I want to do this deal!"

By July, Ross was hearing that it was Millennium Partners in pole position. The firm's leader, Christopher Jeffries, who had achieved a certain degree of fame by marrying Rita Hayworth's daughter, had several things going for him. One of his partners was Philip Aarons, a connected former development official in the Koch and Dinkins administrations. They were fresh off the hugely successful construction of Lincoln Square, a $250 million, 47-story mixed-use megacomplex just north of Lincoln

Center,[11] with a 12-screen Loews that would become the highest-grossing theater complex in the country, a seven-level Reebok health and fitness complex, and 600 rental apartments and condos. Millennium had since launched similar projects in Washington, Boston, and San Francisco and had become prominent figures of urban resurgence.

On the Columbus Circle site, Millennium proposed to build a 2.1 million-square-foot, 750-foot-tall tower on top of the existing Coliseum structure, with a luxury Westin hotel, entertainment center, and health club.

But what really set the Millennium bid apart was an audacious set of guarantees that Jeffries had offered, guarantees no other developer was willing to match.

The company had agreed to pay more than $300 million upon signing the contract. They also promised to pay for the site and proceed with the deal even in the event community groups sued and litigation delayed the project — an unlikely outcome, but one that had derailed previous iterations and many others like it across the city.

On Friday, July 25, Jeffries was in the Hamptons when he received the call.

He was to fly back to Manhattan by helicopter immediately to work through final issues in his contract so that the MTA could make an announcement. He arrived around 4 p.m. that day, according to Sorin, and went through the final details. Unofficially, the deal was Millennium's.

"We were satisfied with their financial representations," Lambert recalled. "The design to the extent that we knew what they were going to do with the site was acceptable to the MTA and they presented a very, very plausible picture of what they could do. They had already done quite a bit of development so we knew their experience level was good."

11   Rothstein, Mervyn. "Lincoln Square: Growth and Doubts." *The New York Times*. April 17, 1994.

The following day, an article leading the Metro section of the New York Times reported that state officials had "tentatively recommended" Millennium as the winner, and the MTA board hoped to ratify the deal the following Wednesday.

Millennium's willingness to pony up a $300 million deposit ensured "this thing won't drag on for years," the Times quoted an anonymous "senior state official" as saying. Years later, Ross recalled the wave of disappointment that washed over him when he picked up the paper that morning. He reminded himself the city still had to sign off and that "you can't believe everything you read in the news." When pressed for comment at the time, Ross and the other bidders were said to be "angered," claiming Millennium would never actually honor the promise to proceed should litigation erupt. They vowed to press their case with Mayor Giuliani, who had veto power over the plan.

In the end, they wouldn't need to. Because the news, it turned out, came as just as much of a shock to Giuliani as it did to everyone else. Informing the legendarily pugnacious mayor of its decision through the newspaper was not, events would prove, a particularly effective way for the MTA to win his blessing.

Giuliani had tasked the head of his Planning Department, Joe Rose, with overseeing the review effort and advising him on the project. Behind the scenes, Rose and his team had been working to slow down the pace of negotiations between the MTA and the bidders. Rose had thought he was succeeding, and regularly reminded the MTA that the city would look to weigh in. Rose also had a personal connection to the project.

Trim and perpetually tanned with a boyish, presidential smile, Rose was born into the third generation of a storied New York City real estate family and grew up on Park Avenue. In the 1920s, brothers Samuel and David Rose planted the seeds of an empire by building apartments in the Bronx, then passed the baton to a second generation of Roses —

brothers Frederick, Daniel, and Elihu, who "consolidated" the holdings in Manhattan and expanded into other cities.

Joe Rose had studied city planning and international relations at Yale, followed by graduate work in government at Harvard, and then worked as a special assistant for Urban Affairs to U.S. Senator Daniel Patrick Moynihan. He was a passionate student of New York City, contemplating its rise and fall, and considering what it would take to revive his hometown.

He understood that there were many ways to fight crime — beyond the controversial policing policies advocated by his boss, the mayor. In particular, Rose was influenced by William "Holly" Whyte, the great urban theorist who had observed that drug dealing and violence are often exacerbated by the absence of a critical mass of normal pedestrians in public spaces.

Rose had long felt Columbus Circle was a "lost opportunity," a site that took away from the city rather than added to it. He had been involved in the efforts to redevelop the Coliseum site from the beginning, and to him the unfolding events were like a recurring bad dream.

He saw Columbus Circle as a key link in a great chain of four sites so centrally located that they could be transformed into junctions of humanity and energy that would not only draw more people in, but send ripples of vibrancy outward, drive up land prices, and draw demand to the areas surrounding them. They were Bryant Park, Times Square, Madison Square Park, and Columbus Circle. It was at Bryant Park where Whyte had showcased his ideas; a few years earlier the City Planning Department had commissioned him to conduct research on precisely what it took to revitalize an area. Many of the suggestions he made were modest and easy to achieve — places to sit, access to sunlight, a setup that allowed people to gather and watch people. Whyte held out Bryant Park as a prime example of a badly designed public space, and suggested that by opening it up and making it more visible from the street, and creating cafés and other attractions to draw in the public, the dope dealers and homeless could be driven out.

In the mid-1980s when the city and state had selected Boston Properties to redevelop Columbus Circle, with a plan for office skyscrapers, Rose had pleaded with those in government to reconsider, warning not just that they were missing an opportunity to change the city for the better but that they were likely to face a potent public backlash should they approve the sterile project. City officials had ignored him then, and the proposal had indeed sparked a public backlash. Boston Properties eventually pulled out.

This time he was on the inside — but now it was the state that seemed unwilling to listen.

"This is a place that has the opportunity to create a great destination, to do something special!" Rose had argued to Giuliani and anyone else who would listen. "This is about the future of the city."

He had been very explicit with the MTA and the leading bidders that Giuliani wanted a "significant" public-use component to the project, a museum, a concert hall or something that would make it a destination rather than a utility.

"You have to activate space, bring people, bring positive uses in as a way of displacing negative uses. If you have abandoned spaces — neglected or underutilized, something is going to congregate there," Rose argued.

The Saturday the Times story broke, Rose was at his own Hamptons beach house slated to represent Giuliani in a meeting with Millennium's Jeffries and MTA's Conway at the East Hampton home of Millennium's land-use attorney, Sandy Lindenbaum. He expected that meeting to focus on the issue of public space at the site.

Instead, when Rose stopped on the way to the meeting to pick up coffee, donuts, and the paper, he discovered that the state seemed to have already anointed Millennium.

The message was clear. "The state and the developer weren't interested in hearing what the city had to say," Rose said. "Their attitude was that they were negotiating with the MTA and we should get out of their way."

When Rose arrived at Lindenbaum's house, he was livid, and fairly certain his boss would be, too.

"What do you guys think you're doing?" Rose recalled saying.

"Don't worry about it," he was told.

Within minutes, however, Rose's phone rang. It was Deputy Mayor Randy Levine, informing him that the mayor planned to veto the decision. In the city, meanwhile, Giuliani went on the warpath.

"The MTA has really no concern for the future of the city," Giuliani said at his presser that day. "All they are concerned about is how much they make...They are going to have to make a lot of changes in order for me to be satisfied."

Giuliani then announced publicly that he wanted the winning developer to build a theater to host jazz, opera, or Broadway performances on the site that would connect it to Lincoln Center, a few blocks to the northwest.

"The MTA mistakenly believed that this was all about money," Levine said to a reporter. "We told them that it was never about money, that this was about a series of things, price being only one. The most important thing is the way the project enhances the neighborhood, because New York City has to live with this for the next 50 or 100 years."

After hanging up and informing the MTA and Millennium of Giuliani's intent to veto, Rose recalled the rest of the meeting as being "not very pleasant — there were words exchanged."

"The message," from the MTA and Millennium, Rose said, "was basically 'you broke it, you fix it. We had a deal here that was all ready to go. You think you're so smart, now this is all on you.'"

Ross took this last-minute reprieve as a sign to spring into action. The first order of business was finding a blue-chip anchor tenant for the office space. And he knew who to aim for.

Rockefeller Center was synonymous with NBC. For the Coliseum site, Ross wanted another media behemoth: Time Warner, which was said to be looking for a new headquarters. If Ross could get Time Warner to place its imprint on the circle, and relocate its thousands of employees to the area, it would be a huge boost to the bid. The sex appeal of big media would sit well with the city, he thought.

Ross didn't know Time Warner chief Dick Parsons personally. But he did know one of Parsons' board members, and convinced that board member to get him and his deputy, Jeff Blau, a meeting. Concerned Parsons might not take the meeting if he knew what it was about, they asked the board member not to disclose what they wanted to discuss.

When they arrived, things didn't exactly start off smoothly. After introductions, Ross and Blau mentioned that they wanted to talk about the Columbus Circle project.

"There's nine bidders, and I understand you're the ninth," Parsons told them, according to Blau. "And I don't need any real estate."

Ross had been prepared for that. "This isn't about real estate," he replied. "This is about marketing and branding and about featuring Time Warner."

The "world's greatest media company," Ross continued, needed a headquarters befitting its stature. This was about CNN broadcasting around the world from Central Park, about people seeing "Time Warner Center" each and every day, and in the process, elevating the brand. Time Warner was in "crappy office space all around the city." Why not centralize and upgrade it?

Parsons was intrigued. The meeting, originally a five-minute meet-and-greet, ran an hour and a half. And by the end of it, Parsons promised to have an answer within a day, and, if the answer was a "yes," board approval within 10 days.

Ross and Blau got their yes. Their bid was now anchored by one of the world's most recognizable brands.

While the drama between Giuliani and the MTA strengthened Related's hand, it weakened those of others. By January 1998, Millennium lost two key tenants: Sony Entertainment, which had opened talks with rival bidders, and Westin Hotels, which had gone and teamed up with Ratner and Brodsky. Millennium soon modified its plan to include a 425-room Ritz-Carlton hotel and the city's largest ballroom, but the momentum was no longer with them.

In February, Giuliani announced he had struck a deal to incorporate a 100,000-square-foot concert hall and home for Jazz at Lincoln Center into the project, and instructed all five developers to resubmit their bids setting aside space for the new venue. It was an expensive ask — since that space would detract from rentable office, retail, or condo square footage.

But Ross and Himmel didn't want to take any chances with the bidding. They contacted Rose to find out precisely what the mayor had in mind.

"Related's position was very explicit," Rose said. "They said, 'Tell us what to do.'"

The developer decided to make Jazz at Lincoln Center one of its centerpieces, placing it on the fifth level, in prime space that might otherwise be used to bring in retail revenue. It seemed a costly decision, one that their competitors didn't have the stomach for. To meet the requirement, it seemed to Rose, several of the contenders tucked in the public-use component as an "afterthought," most cramming it into a corner in the basement.

In contrast, Ross and Himmel recognized that devoting prime space to the jazz venue had benefits beyond simply mayoral benediction. The trickiest challenge of the project — precisely the challenge Rose was so eager to confront and the one Himmel knew to be the key to success — remained the question of how to draw people into the new development, how to activate the space in the center of a circle that had been a corpse for so long, and how to do so in the "vertical mall," a kind of space that had never before worked in Manhattan.

New Yorkers only shop at street level, was the saying. But the presence of a performing-arts center higher up could change that. Malls might be perceived as lowbrow things more fit for suburbia, but what could be more sophisticated than jazz?

In July 1998, the selection was announced: Related had won. The deal called for the firm and Time Warner to pay $345 million for the land. The demolition was to start the following summer, and construction was slated to be completed by 2002. The project would be monumental: A 2.1 million-square-foot development that would house the Time Warner headquarters, a 425-room Mandarin Oriental hotel, 325 luxury residential condos, and a 1,000-seat concert hall.

It would be the most significant project in Manhattan since the World Trade Center.

Steve Ross was already a successful developer. He was already wealthy and powerful. But without Columbus Circle, he would have been a passing mention in the history books of New York City. If he pulled it off, however, he'd be a central character.

And that, for Ross, was what it was all about.

V

A Second Gilded Age

515 Park, 48 Wall, and the Promise of 15 CPW

After closing on 48 Wall, Swig took stock of his options. All three types of buildings — commercial, residential, or hotel — would bring in similar income, and at first Swig thought he'd do a hotel. He negotiated a nonbinding agreement with Intercontinental Hotels to lease them the entire property.

After the Bank of New York vacated, he gutted most of the building and hired architects and engineers to design layouts. Then the Intercontinental Hotel pulled out of the deal. Swig took that in his stride and placed ads offering short-term residential leases, which he figured would buy him more time.

Then something curious began to happen: Swig started getting calls from commercial office brokers who wanted to rent the space to their clients.

"My ads were for residential units," he'd tell them. "You sure you're calling the right ad?"

The more ads Swig placed for residential, the more the calls came in from commercial brokers. If Swig wasn't renting commercial, did he know anyone who had a property like his that was?

"After a while, you get a bump on your head," Swig would later explain. "You figure, oh, there's a bump here. You should go look at that bump. So I re-explored the commercial aspect."

Swig was skeptical at first. The building had small floor plates, and the conventional wisdom pointed to a glut of office space. If it took three years to lease the place, he would go broke. Still, he commissioned Cushman & Wakefield to do a study. When he got the numbers, they jumped out at him. Though it was the big tenants and the big deals that grabbed the headlines, the average commercial tenant in New York, it turned out, needed less than 6,000 square feet — perfect for his building's layout.

That would, however, require a lot of individual deals. So he then looked at leasing volume. There, too, he found surprises. Downtown, there were tons of small tenants, but their options were limited. Either they could pay top dollar for space in the most modern of buildings, in a place like the World Trade Center, where floors were measured in acres, not in square footage, and they'd be lost in a sea of huge tenants. Or they could choose a rundown Class C or D building, even though much of that space was being converted to residential.

Swig's new building would never qualify as Class-A office space — you needed a modern glass façade for that. But its exterior was beautiful, limestone with the kind of prewar craftsmanship that died out after the Great Depression. Swig realized that if he could offer top infrastructure, heating and cooling, and beautiful mahogany elevators while peddling smaller spaces for those smaller tenants, he'd be meeting an unmet need.

The numbers worked, too. In the face of all the incentives for residential conversions, most people overlooked another aspect of the city's

Downtown revitalization plan: It contained a wide range of tax benefits for office tenants and for landlords willing to invest in their properties.

"Zero people were offering it, and yet that's what the market demanded," Swig says. "So I threw out the plans. Threw them out. Threw out all the ideas. Kept it commercial, and went out and leased."

Within 16 months, the building was fully leased — so fast Swig was convinced he could do it again. Just to make sure, Swig continued researching the area. If anything, it convinced him the demand was only likely to grow. Everybody seemed to be converting Downtown office space into residential. Nobody was staying commercial.

"Now there are some 17 million square feet downtown converted into residential in 75 or 80 buildings," Swig would recall years later. "Every single building on Wall Street, the most famous street of all the financial world, every single building on the south end is residential or hotel. Not one or two, every single one. There's no commercial buildings left."

If he found more properties, he and his partners would have the market all to themselves.

Meanwhile, more than 70 blocks to the north, the Zeckendorfs were putting the finishing touches on their temple to the city's growing wealth.

Rising on the corner of Park and 60th, their new white-limestone-and-beige-brick building added a slender new silhouette to the skyline, one that, with its deep-set rectangular windows and ornately carved street-level stone façade, caused most of the critics to deem it perfectly in tune with the prewar buildings surrounding it on the Upper East Side.

Their $100 million new development at 515 Park Avenue was not only the first luxury residential building in Manhattan to open in the new millenium, but it was also the most expensive. Apartments were selling fast. And no one could question their vision now.

After inking the deal with Whitehall, the Zeckendorfs had bought 11,000 square feet of unused development rights from a neighboring nonprofit, allowing them to rise 43 stories. They then hired Frank Williams, who had designed the Park Belvedere back in the 1980s, and looked to the stately co-ops of the Upper East Side for inspiration, cladding the building in French limestone, and, inside, forgoing Trumpian gold and brass in deference to more tasteful shades of silver and brushed nickel.

Any concerns that the location was too far south to sell had long been put to rest. The sales office opened in the fall of 1998,[12] and by then, the buzz that 515 Park would offer a new level of luxury was already building. The New York Times set the tone with an article that led the Metro section, headlined: "A Haven for the Super-Rich With Room for the Servants."

"In a city of gargantuan ambition, where the Wall Street boom and soaring corporate profits have bestowed fabulous riches on a few, it was perhaps only a matter of time until someone came up with 515 Park Avenue," the article began. It noted the building's fireplaces and 1,500-square-foot wraparound terraces; it described what seemed at the time an absurdly large five-bedroom duplex, for $12 million, and a four-bedroom penthouse with 360-degree views on the 42nd floor. After remarking on the tower's 15 climate-controlled private wine cellars, private gymnasium, and chandeliered lobbies, the article pointed out that 38 storage rooms could be rented "for those extra French Empire chairs and gilt mirrors."

"All this — the grand scale and the lavish opulence designed to push the upper limits of the real estate market — is meant to fulfill the fantasies and affectations of the underserved super-rich," it said.

The New York Observer, in a front-page article on 515 Park, evoked Bud Fox from the movie "Wall Street," blowing the windfall he receives after snagging Gordon Gekko as a client on an enormous penthouse.

---

12   Lockwood, Charles. "Big Rich Digs." *Grid*. January 2000.

Twelve years after the release of Oliver Stone's paean to corporate greed, the paper noted that a "luxurious apartment is once again the ultimate object of desire for the moneyed class."

In February 1999, eight months before construction was even finished, the Zeckendorfs announced sales of over $260 million, with just six of 38 apartments left to sell. Prices had broken all benchmarks, with condos selling at $3,000[13] a square foot — blowing away a record set by Trump at his Columbus Circle project.

The idea that so many had once doubted the Zeckendorfs could get $1,000 a square foot for their vision now looked quaint.

A deluge of other ultra-luxury housing was not far behind. By the end of 1998, the city had issued permits for 146 new construction projects, the most in a decade. About 80 percent were for apartments and condos, and some 12,000 new apartments, many of them luxury, were slated to come to market by 2001.

And for the first time, the glitz wasn't confined to the Upper East Side or Central Park West. By the late 1990s, the Soho loft market had exploded and was competing for the Wall Street moneyed elite. By 1998, a 6,000-square-foot space on Wooster Street, boasting a 3,000-square-foot roof terrace and a basketball court,[14] had fetched $4.5 million. The typical 2,500-square-foot loft in Tribeca was by then going for an average of $1.13 million.

"It was the first thrust into downtown as an upscale market," said Jonathan Miller, the appraiser and author of a prominent market report for brokerage Douglas Elliman. "It started in '97, '98, and then sort of peaked in

---

13   Tharp, Paul. "Zeckendrof Is Tops in High-Priced Digs." *The New York Post*. February 25, 1999.

14   Hevesi, Dennis. "Prices Send Loft Pioneers in Search of New Frontiers." *The New York Times*. February 21, 1999.

2000. The loft market downtown underwent gentrification and it became significant competition for these staid, prewar Park Avenue sort of things."

Among those jumping onto the ultra-luxury bandwagon was the titan-in-waiting Steve Ross, whose Related had shelled out more than $40 million in May 1998 to purchase 23 condo residences at 279 Central Park West, at 88th Street, out of bankruptcy. The palatial 24-story apartment building, designed by Costas Kondylis, had an illustrious past. Director Stanley Kubrick lived there and had used it as a setting in his Tom Cruise–Nicole Kidman flick "Eyes Wide Shut." Related planned to upgrade the façade and lobby, overhaul common areas, and refurbish two-to-five-bedroom apartments that would ask between $900,000 and $4.5 million.

"As superlative sites became available at very high prices, we determined that condominium development was the most appropriate type of building to build and finance a more attractive investment," David Wine, Related's president of residential development, told the Times of his company's decision to expand beyond mixed-income and affordable housing. Since 1995, the sales price for super-luxury condos went from "nonexistent" to between $900 to $1,100 a square foot, the article noted. And with the prospect of such large sums, developers were bidding up prices for prime development spots — pushing up their profits but also squeezing out those with plans to build more modest developments.

That October, Related also began building the Chatham, a 32-story, 100-unit tower at 65th Street and Third Avenue, designed by Robert A.M. Stern, and announced plans to build ultra-luxury apartments on an assemblage it had acquired in collaboration with Mack and AREA just south of the circle on 56th Street and Broadway, a complex they would call the Park Imperial. According to architect Ismael Leyva, who designed the layouts and interiors for the Chatham, a new sort of arms race was already underway by then.

"The market started changing," Leyva recalled. "Even the rentals started becoming more luxurious, in terms of material, the finishes and the bathrooms, with marble and nice fixtures. You have to be better than the other guy. People tend to go to a new building. So in order not to lose them, they have to do better."

Amid all of these developments, the Zeckendorfs contemplated their next project and arrived at what might be considered a rather surprising conclusion.

Their 515 Park, which some had worried would be too opulent, had, in fact, not been opulent enough. Since it was their first project, they had been on a relatively tight leash with their partners at Whitehall.

"We took the idea two-thirds of the way there, not 100 percent of the way there," Will would later reflect. "We broke up the lower floors into large apartments but not huge, two-bedroom, three-bedroom. Nice, but nothing tremendous."

Since the building had sold out — and sold out fast — it had proven their investment thesis. For their next project, the brothers hoped to build something even more lavish. They now had Whitehall's full trust. And they already had a perfect site in mind, one that Will had been eyeing for years.

In the 1980s, Will often spent his weekends walking up and down the Broadway corridor with a zoning map and a highlighter. When he found a potential development site, he marked it in blue or orange, highlighting parking lots, abandoned structures, and two-story commercial buildings far smaller than zoning rules permitted.

For years afterwards, he kept that map on his office wall, even as the Upper West Side transformed. Over the years all those highlighted sites, one by one, had been snapped up and built on. But as much as things had changed, through all those years, the biggest patch of color on the wall — the most tantalizing, promising, and elusive — had stayed largely as it was, its potential value unrealized.

The site spanned an entire city block between 61st and 62nd streets bounded by Broadway and Central Park West, directly across from the park, promising potentially stunning views of the precious urban oasis. On it was a parking lot, and the Mayflower Hotel. An unpretentious 18-story, 365-room[15] building, originally opened in 1926, the Mayflower was described in one guidebook as a structure that "hasn't been cutting edge in over 70 years."

With the rise of Trump International around the corner and the expected arrival of a new luxury development on the old Coliseum site to the south, Will and Arthur knew that this last, large undeveloped piece of property on the Upper West Side, just up the block from a subway station once notorious for knifings, suddenly looked as if it might soon become among the most desirable development sites in the city. But it would not be easy to snag.

The owners of this block-long assemblage were by no means blind to its potential. The pieces had been painstakingly acquired over the course of more than a decade by John J. Avlon, a businessman working on behalf of the Goulandris family, a Greek shipping clan. Avlon had bought the first piece of the assemblage back in 1973 as a long-term investment, suspecting the Coliseum would one day be replaced with something better. He had been turning away developers who wanted to buy his assemblage for so long, he no longer bothered to return phone calls. He was content to keep it as it was, wait for the city to revive and watch the values rise. Until the time was right.

Avlon was, however, anything but a passive investor. In the early 1990s, he had reportedly hired a number of lobbyists and consultants to convince the city to bestow special zoning status onto his block. And he succeeded

---

15   Dunlap, David W. "An Old and Comfortable Face Is Leaving the Park's Side." *The New York Times*. November 4, 2004.

in convincing the City Planning Commission to nix a requirement that mandated any new building to include multiple setbacks. Instead, he won support for a new scheme that would allow a 125-foot street wall on Central Park West to better blend in with the surroundings and enhance the site's development possibilities.[16]

One evening in 2000, Will was dining with Basil Goulandris, one of six trustees on the controlling entity, who confided that the family was finally getting ready to sell the whole prize.

"I've been trying to call John for years," Will told him.

"Don't worry," Goulandris replied. "I'll set it up for you."

"I was on it like you wouldn't believe," Will recalled. "I was all over that property. I knew it intimately."

One afternoon, the Zeckendorfs departed their East Side offices and headed across the park. At Avlon's penthouse office at the Mayflower, they were directed to take assigned seats around a coffee table and offered refreshments, while Avlon and an assistant looked on. That first meeting, and the ones that followed, had a similar script, according to Michael Gross's 2014 book "House of Outrageous Fortune," a chronicle of the building that would eventually rise on the site.

"Avlon would tell them the block wasn't for sale, but the corporation that owned it might be," Gross wrote. "That meant any buyer would face significant exposure to taxes and various corporate liabilities, even unfunded pension liabilities for hotel workers. Avlon also said that the remaining rent-regulated tenants in the building would be 'your problem, not our problem' — and quoted a 'very high price.' The property was, in fact, not yet for sale, and as they continued cultivating the block-teasing Avlon while he, in turn, studied them, the Zeckendorfs learned that they

---

16   Gross, Michael. *House of Outrageous Fortune*. Atria Books. March 11, 2014.

were only one of a number of parties circling it."

The other parties, it would later emerge, constituted a who's who of development, including Related, Vornado, Trump, Edward Minskoff, Elad Holdings, Tishman Speyer, and Millennium.

But the Zeckendorfs suspected that if Avlon ever did decide to sell, they might have an edge. In one of those first meetings around the time of 515 Park's opening, Avlon walked them out to his terrace and pointed to their new creation.[17]

"You guys got the highest price ever in the history of New York City," Arthur Zeckendorf would recall Avlon declaring. "You guys are the best."

"Look at the view from here," Avlon added. "You guys can get that type of pricing here. This site is worth a ton of money."

It was a prescient remark. The building that would eventually rise there, 15 Central Park West, would indeed be the full expression of the Zeckendorfs' vision, and for close to a decade the ultimate New York symbol of money and power. It became home to banking titans such as Sandy Weill and Lloyd Blankfein and luminaries such as Denzel Washington, and the most successful residential project in the history of the city.

17   Gross, Michael. *House of Outrageous Fortune*. Atria Books. March 11, 2014.

VI

The Rubble

9/11 and Its Aftermath

O n the morning of Sept. 11, 2001, Kent Swig was rushing to an appointment at 2 World Trade Center with his bankers at Lehman Brothers. Swig had a busy day ahead. It was his son's eighth birthday, and the family was heading to a magic show that evening. The New York City mayoral primaries were also happening, and Swig meant to vote before work but had gone to the wrong polling place.

Now, as he scrambled down the stairs to the subway on that cloudless day, he feared he might be late for his meeting. It was only when he entered the station and headed toward the 4 train platform that someone informed him that a plane had hit one of the World Trade Center towers and "all hell had broken loose Downtown."

There would, of course, be no meeting between Swig and his lenders that day.

Thousands were dead in the rubble of the World Trade Center. The U.S. was at war. And nothing Downtown would ever be the same.

In the weeks that followed, some developers would be thrown into the spotlight in ways they never imagined.

Larry "Energizer Bunny" Silverstein had gotten his start as a broker in the Garment District in the 1950s and built a portfolio with his father and his then-brother-in-law, Bernie Mendik. He had taken over control of the WTC site just six weeks earlier, after an extended bidding war with Vornado, Brookfield, and Boston Properties. Silverstein's $3.2 billion deal to secure the ground lease to the 11 million-square-foot complex was the biggest transaction in New York history. It had catapulted him to the top of the developer pecking order.

"I'm thrilled to pieces," he told the New York Times after the deal was announced. "I've been looking at the Trade Center for years, thinking, 'What a great piece of real estate, what a thrill it would be to own it.' There's nothing like it in the world."

Now he had become one of the key faces of the disaster. His precious new buildings had been reduced to rubble. The land he had fought so hard to gain control over had become a graveyard. Silverstein, like everyone else, was in a state of shock. But he was also a pragmatist.

"I ran into him — he was about to go into a place to have dinner, and I ran into him on the street on the Upper East Side," Mary Ann Tighe, the city's top office leasing broker and a key player in the post-9/11 rehabilitation of Downtown, recalled to *The Real Deal* about Silverstein. "We were standing in front of each other and I began to cry. And he put his arms around me and said, 'Sweetheart, gonna rebuild.' This is six o'clock on the night of 9/11."

Silverstein said the attacks gave him a sense of single-mindedness.

"It's funny, but I don't recall the focus [of my thoughts at that time], other than the disaster, and the magnitude of the problems we were facing as a result of it," he said in an interview with *The Real Deal* in 2011.

For many of the other Downtown landlords who would eventually come to be associated with the city's recovery, the sheer magnitude of the disaster that day blotted out any thoughts of business. It seemed almost as if the world were ending.

Steve Witkoff was in his office at the old Daily News building up on 42nd Street, and could see the smoke coming from the towers through his windows. At 9:59 a.m., he watched in horror as the South Tower came crashing down, followed 29 minutes later by its twin next door.

Witkoff rushed up to the Bronx to collect his children from the Riverdale School. Soon after returning home, he got a call from Bo Dietl and Mike Ciravolo, two old friends who were retired NYPD detectives. They suggested heading Downtown to help, which is how Witkoff ended up standing on a piece of mangled steel, on a rope line until five o'clock the next morning, holding the end of a long cord tied around the belly of a firefighter with a flesh-sniffing dog digging through the rubble of the massive pile of debris, searching for survivors.

Witkoff had seen New Yorkers go through hardship before. But what he would see in the days following 9/11 was well beyond anything he had experienced.

Born in the Bronx and raised on Long Island, Witkoff had started out in the late 1970s as an attorney at Dreyer & Traub straight out of Hofstra law school. As a young associate, he pulled 90-hour weeks working on real estate deals. But, like Steve Ross, he had longed to get in the game himself.

"Every day you were representing these swashbuckling guys who were entrepreneurial in their spirits," Witkoff said of his clients, such as Peter Kalikow, Arthur Cohen, and Howard Lorber. "They felt like rock stars to me."

Witkoff made his first property buy in 1986 at 29, borrowing $15,000 from his father and partnering with his Dreyer colleague Larry Gluck on a $240,000 building in Washington Heights. They financed it just like some of the deals they had worked on for clients, getting a loan backed by the government-sponsored Federal Home Loan Mortgage Corporation, Freddie Mac. Witkoff and Gluck soon left the law firm behind and set up shop as Stellar Management — the name being a combination of Steve and Larry — in a 150-square-foot office on Park Place.

By the time the market began to turn down in 1989, Witkoff and Gluck owned 10 properties Uptown. Unable to unload them — they had originally intended to be "deal guys" — they realized they would have to learn the ins and outs of real estate, including how to deal with frozen pipes and work with Albanian supers to save money on repairs.

Washington Heights at the time was still plagued by drug dealing, gangs, and violence, and Witkoff, chatty by nature, grew close to many of his tenants, hearing firsthand about tragic deaths and the scramble to make ends meet. He recalled one young mother he was friendly with inviting him up to her apartment for sex because she needed money to buy food for her children (he gave her the money and declined the sex). He discovered another family living illegally in the basement because they couldn't afford rent. (Witkoff moved them into an apartment.)

He learned to use a gun, and began carrying one Uptown in his gym bag. He spent New Year's Eve in 1991 in the basement of a building on 124th Street and Madison Avenue, helping his plumber with a sewage backup. For years, he kept a copy of the book "Tough Jews," a romanticized account of Jewish gangsters, on his desk.

Witkoff and Gluck made their Downtown debut in 1994. They realized they could buy a foreclosed office building around the corner from their headquarters for $4 million, less than $20 a square foot, and by relocating there save money on rent. Witkoff split from Gluck in 1997, and by 2001 he was a major player in the area. He had as many as 10 buildings there, including the magnificent Woolworth Building, a 60-story, terracotta-clad tower that was once the world's tallest skyscraper.

Several of his properties were now smack in the middle of what looked like a war zone.

After that exhausting night on the pile, Witkoff walked into the ornate lobby of his $146 million trophy, with its cathedral-like ceilings, bronze fixtures, and elaborate glass mosaics, and was surprised to find exhausted firefighters, police officers, and other first responders stretched out on virtually every inch of available floor space. Their clothes were covered in ash, and their hands were raw from digging through the rubble, he recalled, which made for a shocking tableau set against the marble floors and rich red carpeting of the tower.

Witkoff was so moved, he walked an American flag up to the top of the skyscraper — the elevators were out — and raised it. He moved a generator in, vowing to keep the building open no matter what. For the next 30 days, the building served as a staging area, and slept much of the 10th Precinct and first responders from other areas.

As the scope of the tragedy became clear — Osama bin Laden's al-Qaeda terrorists had killed nearly 3,000 people, traumatized the city, and pushed the U.S. to go to war — Witkoff began attending funerals and doing all he could to help out. He made a conscious effort to block out thoughts of what the tragedy might do to his empire.

He had purchased almost all of his buildings at an extremely low-cost basis, and most of his tenants were on long-term leases. When President George W. Bush visited the site on September 14, slung his arm around a firefighter and addressed first responders through a bullhorn, the Woolworth Building looming in the background, Witkoff was standing a few feet away, a guest of Police Commissioner Bernie Kerik.

"I decided it was beneath me to worry about my business," Witkoff said. "I remember thinking this can't be about business. And I was deeply inspired. It was, 'What can I do?' Guys who had uniforms on are walking up these staircases to rescue people, and they all died. They didn't go home to their families. That's when I remember thinking: 'I cannot do enough.'"

When the city did begin to take stock of the damage, however, the devastating destruction of property loomed among the most obvious, and expensive, consequences. Downtown had lost 15 million square feet of space, with nearly 13 million square feet destroyed and over two million square feet declared structurally unsound as a result of fires, falling debris, and building collapses.

An additional 11 million square feet were damaged, and roughly half would be taken off the market for at least a year. The World Trade Center/World Financial Center submarket totaled 40 million square feet, according to JLL — and half of that had been taken out by the attacks.

Downtown's future was unclear. A toxic cloud would hang in the air for months. Tenants in search of new space looked elsewhere. The overall area office vacancy rate, 6.2 percent in August 2001, would spike to 15.6 percent in the weeks that followed.[18]

The psychic shock of those two huge towers coming down also caused people to rethink what was possible. Around the city — around the world — some even began to question whether there was a future for skyscrapers at all.

Gene Kohn, founder of architecture firm Kohn Pedersen Fox, predicted to Scientific American that there could be a hiatus in skyscraper construction "lasting as long as a decade."

Related had launched sales at Time Warner Center just a month before 9/11. William Mack, Related's equity partner on the project, received an early indication of what the attacks might do to their marketing efforts.

---

18   Napoli, Michael. "Wall Street's Other Revival." *Institutional Investor*. March 2004.

One of his tenants threatened to pull out of another building Mack owned — in Pittsburgh.

At 64 stories, the USX Tower was the tallest skyscraper in the city. Prior to the attack, Heinz had been on the verge of signing a 15-year lease to occupy the top three floors. Now, the food-processing giant balked. What, they asked Mack, if terrorists took down their building next?

"That's when I said, 'Who's going to Pittsburgh?'" Mack recalled.

Mack's reassurances were not enough. Heinz went elsewhere.

"It's hard to put yourself in the position of people then. There was a great fear that anything that was a high-rise they'd be banging planes into, and the security couldn't be accommodated," he recalled.

Looking back years later, Related's Ross would downplay his own fears, claiming that by then he knew it would pass.

"Of course it was stressful," Ross said. "You're reading articles in the paper, and you're thinking, 'Would there ever be another high-rise in New York?' You know, you're wondering what's going on in the world. You react to it. But you don't crumble."

Ross and Mack still had 163 condos left to sell at Time Warner. And company executives admitted that a number of buyers had asked for time to reconsider. One friend of Mack's, who had intended to buy, informed him his wife refused to live above the 15th floor. He was not the only buyer they lost.

Slowly, however, the city's housing market began showing its resilience.

In November, Related announced that more than $45 million in condo contracts had been signed since the attacks, bringing the total to $105 million. A crawl compared to what had been expected before the attacks, but a positive sign nonetheless.

The condo market's brashest cheerleader was also back at it. In late November, a group led by Donald Trump beat out three other bidders with a contract to pony up $115 million for the 169-room Hotel Delmonico, a storied Upper East Side property on 59th Street and Park Avenue. Built in 1928, the property was converted into apartments by William Zeckendorf Jr. in 1975, then converted back into a hotel by different owners in 1991 (Zeckendorf still used the penthouse as a pied-à-terre).

Trump's deal, the Times' Charles Bagli wrote, was a sign that "the real estate market has not collapsed." Trump, Bagli noted, was planning on transforming the Delmonico into a condo-hotel, "not unlike" the Trump International Hotel and Tower across town at Columbus Circle. Trump would eventually name the development, perhaps predictably, Trump Park Avenue.

PART TWO

VII

Swig Goes Big

A Downtown Buying Spree for the Ages

Weeks after 9/11, Michael Bloomberg, founder of financial-services firm Bloomberg LP, was elected the 108th mayor of New York City. The ascension of a multibillionaire technocrat to the top job was to have a profound impact on the direction the real estate market would take.

Short, slight, with thin lips, a receding hairline and always fastidious in his dress, the new mayor could come off as robotic or wooden. Yet in the months following the greatest tragedy in New York history, there was something profoundly comforting about Bloomberg's unflappability.

A long-shot candidate prior to the attacks, Bloomberg pumped $73 million of his own money into his campaign, outspending his opponent five to one. He argued that New York needed a seasoned business executive to rebuild, and voters bought into that argument. One of his first tasks would be coming up with a plan for devastated Lower Manhattan.

Bloomberg's predecessor, Rudy Giuliani, and New York Gov. George Pataki had announced plans to create the Lower Manhattan Development Corporation to oversee the reconstruction of the World Trade Center site.

Two months later, in February, the City Council approved a zoning permit for the first new project in Lower Manhattan since the attacks. The permit went to the residential developer Glenwood Management and its grizzled chairman, Leonard Litwin. Glenwood planned to construct a 45-story residential tower, with 288 apartments, office space, and ground-floor retail on Liberty, William, and Cedar streets. The industry had planted a flag in Downtown.

In December 2002,[19] Bloomberg strode into the ballroom in Wall Street's Regent Hotel, a stately Greek Revival landmark that once housed the New York Stock Exchange.

Taking his place at the front of a rotunda,[20] he addressed the city's business leaders, unveiling his vision for the future of Downtown in a breakfast speech before the Association for a Better New York.

The "ailing" financial center that largely shut down at night would be transformed into a collection of neighborhoods — a vibrant 24/7 "urban hamlet" with housing, schools, libraries, and movie theaters, he said. West Street would morph from a six-lane highway into "a promenade lined with 700 trees, a Champs-Élysées...for Lower Manhattan."

Bloomberg told the business elite he would create a larger Battery Park, and entirely new parks over the mouth of the Brooklyn Battery Tunnel, stretching from the Battery Maritime Building to South Street Seaport. There could be baseball fields, an outdoor skating rink, and floating gardens.

19 Steinhauer, Jennifer. "Mayor's Proposal Envisions Lower Manhattan as an Urban Hamlet." *The New York Times*. December 13, 2002.

20 Mahler, Jonathan. "The Bloomberg Vista." *The New York Times Magazine*. September 10, 2006.

He envisioned 10,000 new apartments south of Chambers Street in two new neighborhoods: one near Fulton Street and a second south of Liberty built around a new park. He also called for tax breaks to attract foreign companies and direct transportation links to the nearby airports.

"We have underinvested in Lower Manhattan for decades," Bloomberg said. "The time has come to put an end to that, to restore Lower Manhattan to its rightful place as a global center of innovation and make it a Downtown for the 21st century."

The plan had a $10.6 billion price tag. But with $21 billion on the way from the federal government, 9/11-related insurance money, and newly authorized "Liberty Bonds" for new housing Downtown, it was not fanciful.

"Moving forward," Bloomberg declared, "Lower Manhattan must become an even more vibrant global hub of culture and commerce, a live-and-work-and-visit community for the world. It is our future. It is the world's second home."

Covering the speech, the Times noted that Bloomberg had devoted only 20 seconds of its 31 minutes to the WTC site.

He didn't need to. That came on December 18 in a widely covered event in the Winter Garden, the glass, tree-lined, indoor atrium on the edge of Ground Zero, when some of the world's top architects presented their visions for the site. Daniel Libeskind's proposal to build five skyscrapers, including a modern crystalline centerpiece with a towering spire that would be called Freedom Tower, would be selected as the winner in February 2003. The footprints for the original towers would be transformed into a memorial.

When the planes hit, Kent Swig had just completed the renovation of his Bank of New York Building and had been preparing to go on a major buying spree. After the attacks, he decided to wait and see how things unfolded.

He had made one significant real estate play, however. In 2002, Swig and his wife, Liz, had demonstrated they possessed the requisite $100 million in liquid assets and moved, with their two young sons, into a 16-room, five-and-a-half-bath duplex at 740 Park Avenue, the city's most prestigious co-op.

Every morning on the way out to work, Swig would nod hello to moguls such as Ronald Lauder, Steve Schwarzman, and David Koch. Liz decorated the Upper East Side apartment with "funky art and color-coordinated candy," according to a press report. She was featured in a 2003 New York Magazine article exploring how to have a successful dinner party, right alongside Diane von Furstenberg, Tina Brown, and Joan Rivers.

To celebrate her brother Billy Macklowe's birthday, Liz had several hundred pounds of slate, wildflowers, and climbing accessories shipped in, and served trout wrapped in foil. The menu was superimposed over a photograph of a shirtless Billy, a noted outdoorsman, dangling from a cliff. Swig and Liz spent their weekends at a four-acre waterfront estate in Southampton and took surfing trips to Australia.

By the summer of 2003, Swig was done waiting. He had concluded he might just be looking at a transformational opportunity.

He announced that 48 Wall was 96 percent leased and that he had refinanced the $55 million loan on the property.

Swig commissioned a study that found that in 2000, more than 34 buildings in Lower Manhattan, representing almost 13 million square feet, had been converted to residential, creating an even more profound shortage of high-quality office space in smaller buildings. If he could replicate what he had done at 48 Wall, there was plenty of demand.

Swig was still perplexed by the price differential between Midtown and Downtown — a gulf that, after 9/11, had grown even more vast.

"I looked at a massive tragedy and said, 'I'm down in this area, what the hell is going on?' I looked at my business plan and said, 'Does it make sense?

Yes.' Perception has gone even further down, and nothing has changed."

That summer, Swig bet on his gut, paying $52 million for 5 Hanover Square, a 25-story office tower built in 1962. He announced plans to convert it into a "luxury boutique-style office complex," with better bathrooms, new elevators, floors of Italian travertine marble, and an all-glass façade. Within a few weeks, the building had picked up several new tenants and was 98-percent leased.

In November, Swig and partner David Burris teamed up with Iranian émigré and diamond mogul Asher Zamir to buy 44 Wall Street, a gem built in 1927, for less than $200 a square foot.

He kept going, buying the 36-story 80 Broad Street and another 25-story building next door. He snapped up 110 and 130 William Street. These were the go-go, subprime, pre-bubble days, with low interest rates and readily available credit. Swig, readily backed by Lehman Brothers, had his fill, and then some. By the time he was all done — by the time Swig instructed his assistants to throw out any incoming offering sheets because he didn't want the temptation — he had a portfolio that exceeded $3 billion.

"I went and bought everything I could," he recalled. "I started in 2003, and bought until January 2006. I bought every single property I could possibly buy. I was buying buildings all under $198 a foot. Never paid more than $198. Land was trading at that time probably for $250 a foot. So either I bought the land cheap and got a free building, or I bought a building and got free land, but nobody was doing it. Everybody was looking at me like I'm a fool."

"The market was mine," he added. "Nobody was doing this. Everything that moved, I bought. Literally bought every building. If it came up, in three days, I bought the building. When brokers came to me, and said, 'Here are eight buildings, three million feet. Pick wherever you want,' I'd say, 'I'll have all of it.'"

VIII

The Time Warner Effect

The Malling of Manhattan

Seen from the bottom of Central Park as one walks west towards Columbus Circle today, Time Warner Center's two angular, glass-and-steel towers rise 750 feet above a sleek, two-story atrium that hugs the rounded contours of a circle.

Often, it's not Ross's towers themselves that draw the eye, though, but the gap between them.

Perfectly aligned with Central Park South, the street running along the southern boundary of the park, the broad notch of empty space at the far western end of the traffic circle pulls the gaze upwards to the ribbon of blue visible between a sparkling glass-and-steel edifice seemingly cut into two halves — as if the broad thoroughfare continues on once it reaches the circle, leaping the atrium, flying through the notch, and carrying the eyes of cynical New Yorkers away from the crowds and up to the heavens above.

Throughout the 1990s, Ross had visualized a building that would somehow draw people into the empty space. The architect David Childs gave shape to that vision. He started by diagnosing the problem, recognizing that the Coliseum's windowless, hulking profile had cut Central Park South off from the West Side as effectively as if somebody had built a giant concrete city wall on the far west side of the circle. Meanwhile the sheer bulk of the building combined with the frequently gridlocked north-south traffic in the circle to create an equally potent blockage between Midtown and the residential Upper West Side. It was a chokepoint, stuck like a bone in the throat of Manhattan.

To open up the circle, Childs looked to design a building that would somehow knit together the disparate parts of the city that fed into it from four directions, rather than break them apart. He also needed to unclog the circle and allow it to flow.

The city was already working on improvements to better regulate traffic flow, so that cars approaching from the disparate parts of the city could feed into the circle from all four directions and pass through it with relative ease. Still, Childs knew there was no way to physically extend the main east-west thoroughfare at the bottom of Central Park through Columbus Circle to Manhattan's West Side. The grid pattern wouldn't allow it, and his two-towered building would stand in the way. But he could create the illusion of continuity.

The notch of blue sky, and the alignment of the towers, was a subtle yet effective touch. When viewed from the center of the park, the towers appear to be arrayed at an odd angle in relation to one another. In fact, they are set at the same diagonal orientation as Broadway, which slices through New York's otherwise regular street grid and feeds into the circle from the north, then continues downtown at the same angle from the circle's southern end.

Beneath the towers at street level, Childs hoped to create a glittering public space, one that somehow incorporated the natural movement of the surrounding areas and beckoned pedestrians in. It was separated from the foot traffic outside by a multi-story glass wall to maintain the feel of continuity with the street and park outside. The upper floors telescoped back, mirroring the contours of the street outside, as if the entrances to the shops were located on indoor sidewalks rising in tiers from the ground level.

It was left to Himmel and Ross to populate the inside with attractions that would act as a magnet.

Related had settled on one big draw: high above the atrium on the other side, through a wall of interior windows, the auditorium of Jazz at Lincoln Center was visible from below. Visitors who timed it right would sometimes catch the melodic tones of trumpets, pianos, and saxophones drifting down from the venue during an evening performance.

To draw non-concertgoers into the seven-level mall, Ross and Himmel had approached the famous restaurateur Danny Meyer, whose Union Square Cafe many credit with helping revive that neighborhood. But Meyer wasn't feeling the vertical-mall concept — he told Himmel he just couldn't imagine people taking an escalator.

The developers got a more welcoming reception from Thomas Keller, owner of the world-renowned Napa Valley restaurant The French Laundry. To sell him, Himmel and Ross flew out west and drove up the coast to have dinner one night at the restaurant, and laid out their vision for an upscale collection of eateries. In the 1980s, Keller had owned a well-regarded French bistro in Lower Manhattan that catered to the Wall Street crowd. He knew the city well and had been eyeing a return.

Unlike Meyer and other doubters, Keller wasn't bothered by the idea of a vertical mall. In fact, he saw it as a potential advantage. As a restaurateur in an urban environment, he noted, you could control everything that happened once your guests walked in the door — but very little outside, beyond, perhaps, the awning. On cold, windy days, when it snowed or rained, guests would try to get through the door as quickly as possible, run to the bathroom to fix their makeup or hair, and check their coats. It could create a frantic energy.

A mall, it seemed to Keller, might actually allow guests to acclimate.

"It doesn't really matter where you are," Keller said. "Because your experience as a guest in my restaurant begins once you walk through my front door. It's a much better environment walking through my front door after you've come through the mall which is a conditioned space."

Not only did Keller agree to sign on and open the restaurant that would come to be known as Per Se — named the city's top restaurant several years later by the New York Times — he agreed to "curate" the overall dining collection at Time Warner Center, recruiting other top chefs.

To help woo retail tenants, Himmel hired Marvin Traub, the 70-something former chairman of Bloomingdale's, as a consultant. The venerable department store was the master of corralling tony brands in its space, just as Related would need to do here.

"I was bringing him [Traub] to every meeting with me, because I was sure I could get the meetings," Himmel recalled. "I had to be sure I got into all the right people and Marvin got me into all the right people."

Related quickly discovered that their location was both a blessing and a curse. Because of their proximity to Fifth Avenue, it turned out, few of the highest-end luxury stores were willing to take space in Time Warner — it was too close to their flagships. But Related hoped to find the sweet spot in what Himmel calls "bridge brands" — brands like Coach, Stuart Weitzman, Hugo Boss, Williams-Sonoma, and Michael Kors — which would draw healthy foot traffic.[21]

---

21   Newman, Andy. "Traffic on Columbus Circle Finally Comes, Well, Full Circle." *The New York Times*. August 11, 1998.

The basement level had provided a quandary, and for a time the team had considered using it for storage. In the end they hit upon an innovative idea: Why not place a high-end grocery store in the space? It took a while to win Ross over, but eventually, the team inked a deal with Whole Foods, and, at Himmel's request, they sent a team on a tour of Harrods in London and other high-end European-style eateries to examine a more continental way of providing services for lunch.

It hadn't all been a smooth ride. After 9/11 came the recession, the Iraq War, and the SARS epidemic. There was even a fire, when debris left inside the walls behind the stove in the kitchen of Per Se burst into flames. Damage from the conflagration set back the opening of that restaurant for another three months — William Mack likes to joke it was beset by a series of Biblical plagues.

Still, by 2004 Time Warner Center was finally ready to open, and things were looking up: The 201 luxury condominiums were in high demand — including a duplex on the 76th floor, already purchased by David Martinez, a Mexican financier, for $42.5 million, setting a new record for priciest New York City residence.

The developers marked the opening with a massive celebration that was lapped up by the media. It was a coronation of sorts, the beginning of a new era, not just for Ross and Related, but for the area as well.

Standing on the third floor of the brand-new mall that night in February 2004, CNN's Larry King, his silver-haired bouffant brushed back and sprayed into "television-ready perfection,"[22] leaned over a railing and gazed through oversized glasses at Governor Pataki.

"How much if we both go over the rail?" he cracked to a nearby reporter.

Around them, some 8,000 guests in tuxedos and evening gowns,

---

22   Kuczynski, Alex. "At Towers' Opulent Debut, Even Guards Are Dolled Up." *The New York Times*. February 5, 2004.

drawn from the top ranks of the city's rich, famous, and powerful, sipped champagne and nibbled on risotto and mushroom tarts. They were entertained by actors dressed as Time Warner's Scooby Doo, Sylvester the Cat, and Tweety Bird, and by a Cirque du Soleil troupe.

Outside, limos choked the traffic at Columbus Circle in front of the entrance to the gleaming 2.8 million-square-foot retail atrium of glass, steel, and stone, a behemoth that was the biggest new building since the Twin Towers. Klieg lights illuminated the sky, dancing across the exterior facades of the center's twin 750-foot-tall, 80-story towers. And, on the red carpet were Sean "Diddy" Combs, in immaculate tux and diamond studs, supermodel Cindy Crawford, and the night's entertainment, the singer Jewel, who appeared on the arm of a professional bull rider in a white cowboy hat. The schmoozing was reminiscent of the annual scene at the Real Estate Board of New York gala, known in the industry as the "The Liar's Ball."

Guests could sample treats from celebrity chefs recruited by Keller — they included Gray Kunz, Charlie Trotter, and Jean-Georges Vongerichten. Sushi artist Masa Takayama offered tasting menus for $350. The mall's 50 shops included a J.W. Cooper store peddling $4,000 alligator boots and $20,000 gold belt buckles inlaid with diamonds. They were told they were there to celebrate the opening of New York City's "most important new building in a generation."

Looking back later, some would reflect on that night, and conclude that the opening of Time Warner Center marked a clear inflection point for the city.

"It's not that Time Warner was seen as the premier luxury development of all time, but it was the first successful mall in Manhattan in my view, and it catered to all the luxury brands," Miller, the appraiser, would remark years later — long after the condos had broken all records for resale value, and luxury shops were bringing in $1,500 a square foot, three times as much as comparable retail elsewhere in the country. Demand for Whole Foods and its upscale food hall was so great that the number of customers had exceeded the fire limit, and Related had to hire a guard to stand at the top of the escalator to make sure it stayed under capacity.

"It was one of the first steps towards a new urbanism for the wealthy — which is ultimately where the city is ending up," Miller added. "The opening of Time Warner was the foreshadowing of the overemphasis on luxury products — with housing being one of them — that would help define the next decade." That ethos would later reach a culmination in Related's Hudson Yards.

"That building changed everything," JDS Development Group's Michael Stern, the luxury developer behind the ultra-skinny Steinway Tower at 111 West 57th Street on Billionaires' Row, would later declare.

And indeed, after substantial champagne had been consumed, after a little bit of music and dancing, the comic Jon Stewart and CNN anchor Paula Zahn escorted Bloomberg onto a makeshift stage.

"Let me tell you, if Janet Jackson comes up here, I'm outta here," the mayor quipped, referring to the pop singer, whose Super Bowl "Nipplegate" scandal had erupted just three days prior.

Then Bloomberg made a promise. Time Warner Center was a mere beginning in "a stronger and healthier New York."

"There would be more openings like this!" He promised. "The best is yet to come."[23]

23 Furman, Phyllis, et. al. "The Best Is Yet to Come." *New York Daily News*. February 5, 2004.

IX

The Full Monty

15 CPW, the First Super-Condo

T he impact of Time Warner Center on the area around it was immediate, driving prices for sites around the park into the stratosphere.

On Central Park South, the Plaza hotel, which Trump had owned and then lost in his debt spiral, would sell in August of that year for $675 million.[24] The deal came to more than $800,000 per room, a city record at the time, and the buyer, a subsidiary of Israeli conglomerate Elad Group, planned to convert the 18-story hotel into condos. Brokers at the time suggested that six-room apartments there might sell for up to $20 million apiece — or about $4,000 per square foot, among the priciest asks in the entire city.

---

24   Weiss, Lois, et. al. "Plaza Sweet." *The New York Post*. August 14, 2004.

But what was coming at Central Park West would make even those numbers look small.

That spring, John J. Avlon finally began accepting bids on his block-long assemblage on Central Park West. He had been waiting for the completion of Time Warner Center, while continuing to meet with suitors.

When bidding kicked off, the Zeckendorfs and their partners had one crucial advantage. Avlon had hired an architect to design a conceptual model of a development site that would meet existing zoning regulations. But the Zeckendorfs had secretly hired their own architects and consultants, who had come up with a key innovation. Avlon's architect had designed a single building with a block-long base, limited in height by the more restrictive zoning requirements on Central Park West. But Peter Claman, the Zeckendorfs' architect, realized that if you divided the lot — and built two buildings instead of one — you could put up a second, far taller tower on the western portion of the lot, which fronted the far more generously zoned Broadway.

The bottom floors of the Broadway tower could be used to house amenities. The space above it would be extremely valuable real estate with park views. The addition of significantly more high-demand amenity space dramatically boosted the amount of money the Zeckendorfs could expect to make.

In the months leading up to the bidding, the brothers came up with preliminary apartment layouts to help calculate how much they could reasonably expect to sell units for. By maximizing views, and designing huge, floor-through apartments, they could be certain it would be a lot. Virtually every apartment would be large — the full realization of the idea they had first visualized before they started on 515 Park.

Once again, the brothers recruited Goldman Sachs' Whitehall to serve as a capital partner, as well as Eyal Ofer, a billionaire Israeli investor who they were planning on teaming up with on a different deal across town.

The Zeckendorfs also took a deep dive into the city's buyer pool, harnessing all the research firepower they had as owners of brokerage Brown Harris Stevens. Years later, in an interview in the sales office for their latest luxury condo, Arthur would pull out a graph tracking the wealth of the top 10 percent of New Yorkers and trace a finger over a line with a steep upward slope. From the 1990s and continuing into 2008, wealth for the top increased fivefold, he noted.

"Most developers don't intellectualize these things," Arthur said. "But this is a very interesting graph. Not many people understood people were making so much money in the 2000s. We were aware of that."

Many of the competitors went for counsel to Louise Sunshine, who had marketed both Trump International and Time Warner Center. But, thanks to their brokerage, the Zeckendorfs also had access to proprietary real-time information of their own.

By the time they received word that Avlon was ready to accept bids, the Zeckendorfs "had that deal completely designed, every apartment laid out," Will recalled. "We had checked the numbers backwards, forwards, and sideways."

They had also sold Whitehall on their vision to move the luxury needle as far as it could go.

Whitehall had advised them to bid their maximum on day one, and not assume there would be a second round of bidding.[25] They held little back, submitting an offer of $401 million for the land — a record price, and at $690 a square foot more than twice the going rate for land in Manhattan. The actual price was expected to be even higher, since the developers would have to buy out existing tenants at the Mayflower and pay taxes on the deal.

---

25 Bagli, Charles V. "Mayflower and Its Vacant Lot to Be Sold." *The New York Times*. May 27, 2004.

"We went in with our absolute best number day one," Will would later say. "We crushed the other numbers. I was never more confident in my life."

Soon after, the Zeckendorfs received a phone call summoning them to Avlon's attorney's office at 399 Park Avenue. When they arrived, Avlon informed them he would accept their bid, pending approval by the board overseeing the Goulandris family's holdings, then sent them into a conference room to sweat it out, while he called the board and they voted. When they got the nod, the Zeckendorfs were ecstatic.

But other suitors had a different reaction. Arthur heard that Steve Ross, upon learning Related hadn't been chosen, "broke his desk."

Others responded with disbelief at how much the Zeckendorfs had paid.

Most agreed by then that the Central Park West–Broadway parcel was among the choicest residential development sites left in the city. But the sales price was far higher than anything offered by Related, Steve Roth's Vornado, Edward Minskoff, or any of the other half dozen rival bidders. It was so exorbitant, in fact, that none other than Trump had called the pricing for the site "crazy" — and he had done so way back in 2001, when rumors of a pending sale had led some to quote a number that would turn out to be just half of what the Zeckendorfs would eventually propose to pay.

"If it's your money, this is a level of risk no one would take," one real estate executive told the Times after the sale became public in May 2004.

After the article appeared, Will came home to a message on his phone from his then mother-in-law. "Don't feel bad that you paid too much," she said. "Some of my favorite things I've brought in life, I've paid too much for."

Even Joe Rose, the man who had pushed so hard for a transformative project in Columbus Circle, wondered what they were thinking.

Rose and Will had lunch at the Regency on Park Avenue soon after the sale was announced, and Rose listened politely to his rationale. In order to make back the money, to handle the construction costs, the zoning challenges, the tax issues, and make the numbers "work," Rose realized, they needed to sell whatever they built there at $2,000 a square foot. Rose was extremely skeptical.

"Okay, if you think so..." Rose recalled telling Will. "They were betting that people would pay these unheard-of sums to be in that building at that location. Nobody was paying that."

The Zeckendorfs were making an audacious bet: in order to make their plans work, they would have to entice buyers to pay the kinds of prices one could get on the big avenues of the Upper East Side — even top them.

But this time, they intended to build a product that would command such prices. If 515 Park had been "two-thirds of the way" to their vision for a new kind of luxury, this new venture would go all the way.

"Our investment thesis on 15 Central Park West was that if you build the finest apartment house on three of the great avenues, which is Central Park West, Fifth Avenue, or Park Avenue, that you will be able to achieve extremely high prices," Arthur would later say. Everything had to be a "10," he added — location, views, size, quality, amenities, layouts.

"Now the proof was there, so 15 [Central Park West] could become a full realization of the idea," Will recalled. "So all-limestone, tremendous number of amenities, every single apartment large."

To make sure they got the design right after winning the bidding, the Zeckendorfs hired five architects, paying tens of thousands of dollars in fees to pit them against each other. They included Libeskind, the World Trade Center architect, who arrived clad in all black and wore a black glove. In the end, it came down to a competition between Cesar Pelli and Robert A.M. Stern, both of whom they paid to work up more detailed designs. Pelli, who had designed the famed Petronas Towers in Kuala Lumpur, submitted a more modern approach with glass curtain walls.

But Stern, with his ode to history and conservatism, won out.

In some ways, he was the perfect choice to deliver on the Zeckendorfs' mandate of a building meant to blend the grandeur of the past with the amenities of the present. As a student at the Yale School of Architecture — where he later became dean — in the 1960s, Stern had found himself far more inspired by the magnificent gothic structures he could see across campus through the windows of the school's drafting rooms than the mainstream ideas espoused by his professors, who argued for modernism, a school of architecture in vogue at the time that embraced a cold minimalism, and the generous use of glass and steel.

In the years that had followed, Stern increasingly incorporated design elements from the past into his commissions. Eventually, as the dean of his alma mater, and as a well-compensated designer for single-family luxury homes and institutional structures around the nation, Stern would emerge as one of the most prominent purveyors of what he calls "modern traditional architecture."

By then in his 60s, Stern cultivated a professorial air that stood in stark contrast to some of his flashier competitors. But if you looked long enough, you noticed whimsical flourishes, such as his tortoiseshell glasses or a pair of bright yellow socks decorated with blue anchors.

"The traditional languages of architecture can be reinterpreted in a modern way for modern times," Stern said. "Languages evolve but don't necessarily get abandoned."

Despite its traditionalist design, 15 Central Park West, however, was to be more luxurious than any new building in a generation.

"Having spent that kind of money," recalled Paul Whalen, one of Stern's principal architects on the project, "the Zeckendorfs decided that they had to shoot for the moon. That they had to put even more money into it to make it worthwhile. They had to do the best building ever to get their money out of it."

For inspiration, the Zeckendorfs joined Stern, Whalen, and Michael Jones, the other partner in Stern's firm charged with directly overseeing the project, for another walking tour of the great prewar buildings along the avenues fronting the park. On a beautiful sunny day in September, the small group met at the Central Park West site, and walked up to the Beresford on 86th Street, then took in the nearby San Remo. They hopped in a car to head across the park to inspect 740 Park Avenue and 1040 Fifth Avenue.

The Zeckendorfs had also arranged for access to a number of grand lobbies and examined the detailing on the bases of the building, the custom light fixtures, and the narrow gardens out front. They took note of the huge doors, with intimate yet grand lobbies, bright and welcoming.

Stern, who lived on Central Park West and had written a book about its architecture, had a clear vision from the very first meeting, according to Will. He was very particular about the materials — the building, he argued, needed to be light in color, and "should really be stone."

They had renderings made of stone, precast concrete, and brick. They also brought different kinds of stones to the half of the site that remained an empty lot, laid them out in thick slabs, and looked at the different rocks in the light. Eventually they narrowed it down to different types of limestone.

For a design, Stern's team resolved to blend some of the iconic qualities of Upper West Side buildings with the asymmetry and picturesque elements characteristic of the Upper East Side. Jones shared his vision for what he wanted the building to feel like: He pictured Fred Astaire and Ginger Rogers dancing under the stars, overlooking Central Park. He wanted to create something that captured the romance of New York City. Whalen visualized a "king of the world apartment — somebody flying in on their private jet, pointing out the building from the air, with its iconic top, and saying 'that's my terrace.'"

"You can't do that with most buildings," Whalen said. "It's not expressed on the outside. You just don't have the resources. We really wanted to express all that specialness on the outside."

And inside, they envisioned 16-foot-wide windows in the living room going down to the floor. Secondary bedrooms would have smaller windows, to give it variety, and make it feel intimate.

Most apartments built in the post–World War II era, Stern said, failed to address the "residential character and needs that people would like in a house," such as family rooms, generous closet space, high ceilings, and a gracious entrance. Now Stern and his team had the chance to shoot the moon — indeed, they had clients who could only succeed if they did "shoot the moon."

And so they set out to do it.

X

The Push for a
"New" New York
Doctoroff's Olympic Dreams

A procession of horse-drawn carriages pulled up outside the historic Plaza hotel on Central Park South. Just across the street, the long, stone walls marked the boundaries of Central Park, where sheets of orange cloth hung from towering, three-sided vinyl frames and billowed in the wind seven feet above the snow-covered ground. The artist Christo had erected 7,503 "Gates" on the 23 miles of walkways spanning the park.

It was February 2005, and city officials had been planning this spectacle for months. This was the night, they hoped, that New York City would help them win the right to host the 2012 Summer Olympics.

"Every one of the meetings and events we planned had just the right dusting of pizzazz," Dan Doctoroff, the city's Deputy Mayor for Economic

Development at the time, would recall in a memoir detailing his City Hall years.

After sunset, 13 delegates representing the 2012 International Olympic Committee site-selection team emerged from the Plaza Hotel and stepped into the carriages, manned by top-hatted liverymen, who conveyed them the few short blocks down Central Park South to Time Warner Center. Inside, a welcoming committee that included Meryl Streep, Matt Damon, Barbara Walters, and the "Perfect 10" Olympic gymnast Nadia Comaneci stood ready to take the stage at Jazz at Lincoln Center.

"What's great about my city is that it's a microcosm of the Olympics," Whoopi Goldberg said, as she loosened up the crowd. "We have Asian people making pizza. And Italian people making soul food. You don't see that anywhere else."[26]

Jazz great Wynton Marsalis took the stage, and the audience later proceeded to Mayor Bloomberg's Upper East Side townhouse to mingle with more luminaries and sing along with Paul Simon.

Doctoroff, a hitherto low-profile financier whose Olympic dreams a decade prior had propelled him into the ranks of Manhattan's power elite, was now tantalizingly close to realizing his vision, with New York, one of the five finalists, starting to make its pitch to host the 2012 games.

Though the selection was a few months off, it was clear that Doctoroff's yearslong efforts were to have a lasting impact[27] on the city.[28] Just a couple weeks earlier, the New York City Council and Bloomberg had finalized

26 Doctoroff, Daniel. *Greater Than Ever*. PublicAffairs. September 12, 2017.

27 Moss, Mitchell. "How New York City Won the Olympics." NYU Rudin Center. November 1, 2011.

28 *TRD* Staff. "10 Projects Born Out of NYC's Failed Olympic Ambitions." *The Real Deal*. February 3, 2018.

an agreement clearing the way for one of the most dramatic physical transformations the city had seen in a generation — the rezoning of a 59-block neighborhood adjacent to a proposed Olympic stadium, running from West 30th to West 43rd streets between Seventh and 12th avenues.

The rezoning allowed for a new residential and business district on the Far West Side, previously reserved for industrial use and long dominated by railyards, dilapidated brick warehouses, factories, and parking lots. Now, new office towers and apartment houses would rise next to the proposed Olympic stadium, and vibrant green parks and boulevards would abound.[29] And, thanks to the approval of a multibillion-dollar bond issue, a new spur of the No. 7 subway line would transport tens of thousands of Olympic spectators — and later simply New Yorkers — into the new space, along railroad tracks that would run a mile farther west from Times Square to 34th Street and 11th Avenue. In lieu of turning over the property and collecting annual taxes on the new buildings, the city would take ownership of new buildings and lease them back to developers for 30 years, with their payments going to pay off the bonds. That new city-within-a-city would come to be known as Hudson Yards.

It was the kind of transformative project that planners, architects, and politicians had been suggesting for decades. (Olympic planners would unearth proposals for developing the railyards in city archives dating back to the 1920s.) But only with the looming deadlines imposed by the city's Olympic bid, along with an innovative financing scheme dreamed up by Doctoroff to pay for the subway extension, were city leaders able to marshal the focus and political will to push it through.

The remaking of the Far West Side was just one part of a much larger land-use blueprint. From the beginning, the Bloomberg administration had

---

29   Bagli, Charles V., et. al. "Mayor and Council Reach Deal on West Side Development." *The New York Times*. January 11, 2005.

recognized the city's Olympic bid as the perfect catalyst to fundamentally reshape how the city used its space. Eventually Bloomberg would rezone 40 percent of the city, focusing on unused waterfront areas left over from previous eras when the city was a shipping and manufacturing mecca.

Among the areas also up for rezoning at the time were over 14 blocks along "the High Line," a rusting, unused elevated rail line that snaked along the edges of Chelsea, where an elevated pathway that all New Yorkers could enjoy was envisioned. The changes would affect an area just south of Hudson Yards, running from West 16th to West 30th streets bounded by Tenth and Eleventh avenues, and would allow the sale and transfer of "air rights" between different nonadjacent lots of land under and around the railbed, to placate landowners in the area who wanted the old tracks torn down.

That proposal, too, had been helped along by the Olympic push. Bloomberg officials needed City Council Speaker Gifford Miller to at least acquiesce to their plan to build a controversial Olympic stadium on the Far West Side (a pledge Miller would later renege on). To win it, Bloomberg had cut a deal to help pay for the new walkway. (Miller's former roommate at Princeton headed the main nonprofit pushing for the High Line, and his mother was a horticulturalist and prominent supporter of the plan.)

Across the East River in Long Island City, Doctoroff had settled on a largely vacant industrial area as the proposed site of the Olympic Village, and wanted to build a complex of 4,400 new apartments to house and feed 16,000 athletes, coaches, trainers, and other team officials. Once the games were finished, the area could be converted into middle-class housing. This would help accelerate the redevelopment of the Queens neighborhood into a new business enclave.

Indeed, economic development was the point. In the days after his January 2002 swearing-in, Bloomberg had highlighted the importance of the area, not just for the Olympics, but for the future of the city. Traveling to Long Island City with his new police commissioner Raymond Kelly, Bloomberg had summoned the media to a press conference just below the rumbling tracks of the Queens Plaza elevated train station. He promised to take on issues targeted by his predecessor Giuliani and called on the public to assist in the crackdown by reporting "quality-of-life" offenders: panhandlers, prostitutes, public drunkards, illegal street merchants, and disorderly homeless people.

"We have said repeatedly that we are not going back," Bloomberg declared, pointing to the dramatic crime reduction the city experienced under Giuliani. "We are going to take the better city that was bequeathed this administration and make it even safer."

In some ways, Long Island City made for the perfect tableau for a declaration of Bloomberg's overall ambitions, Doctoroff's dreams, and the challenges that needed to be overcome.

Dominated by low-slung industrial buildings and warehouses, city planners under Giuliani had honed in on the site as a promising alternative for companies considering moving back offices out of Manhattan. Many companies had chosen Jersey City, which had undergone a massive building boom and, which, long before 9/11, much to the chagrin of city planners, had begun to lure tenants away from pricier downtown digs.

To compete, the City Council had voted the previous July to rezone a 37-square-block area in Long Island City for new office towers and residential development. In the months that followed, the air was thick with the smell of diesel from heavy industrial equipment, and the sound of jackhammers, as crews set to work on new offices for MetLife, a separate 4 million-square-foot office complex, as well as a number of new residential projects. Even before 9/11, a task force formed by Sen. Chuck Schumer to address New York City's growing shortage of commercial space had recommended a major push to develop office properties in Long Island City, which was blessed with a number of mass transit options and close proximity to Manhattan.

The idea that the area could lure large corporate clients from other cities still seemed a long way off. But local boosters were optimistic the area's redevelopment could at least help stanch the corporate exodus from the city.

"For the first time in history, there is an opportunity for companies to stay in New York City and not pay anything more," Michael Bailkin, a Manhattan lawyer who has been a key player in the rezoning and redevelopment of Long Island City, told a reporter at the time.

Bloomberg and Doctoroff were chewing over similarly grand ambitions, which they would soon unveil.

In Brooklyn, the city was poised to rezone a 175-block area in Greenpoint and Williamsburg to allow for residential high-rises, low-rise commercial, and mixed-use buildings, and a two-mile-long public esplanade with a series of waterfront parks[30] not slated for Olympic activity.

In the Bronx, Bloomberg and Doctoroff were working to break the legal logjam that had tied up the redevelopment of the Terminal Market, a decaying facility near the Harlem River where Doctoroff hoped to construct a velodrome for Olympic track cycling and an arena for badminton. After the Olympics, it was hoped, a new market would rise.

New York's big developers were paying close attention.

Related's Steve Ross had been intimately involved from the very beginning with the Olympic bid, and planned to take a leave of absence to oversee the construction of the housing at Hunters Point in Long Island City should New York win. He had forged a close personal relationship with Doctoroff. Ross and many of his counterparts were also hungrily eyeing the rezoned Hudson Yards, realizing its scale would dwarf even the

---

30 Moss, Mitchell. "How New York City Won the Olympics." NYU Rudin Center. November 1, 2011.

Time Warner Center project.

For Doctoroff, it had all started, improbably enough, at a soccer game in New Jersey.

In June 1994, both the Knicks and the Rangers had been in the playoffs, and Doctoroff and a fellow financier named Andy Nathanson had attended nearly every home game together. It was Nathanson who suggested they extend the streak the following month with a World Cup soccer match across the river at the Meadowlands.

Doctoroff, 6'2", trim, with a curly mane of black-gray hair spilling over his broad forehead, had proven himself an energetic and enthusiastic date at local sporting events. But he would later admit to being unusually grouchy when they arrived at the stadium. It was a sweltering July day, Doctoroff's bus was stuck in traffic for an hour, and to top it off, he didn't even like soccer, he wrote in his 2017 memoir, "Greater Than Ever." But once he was inside the stadium, he found the experience electrifying.

Bulgaria was taking on Italy, and the 80,000-strong crowd was a feast of national colors, screaming, dancing, and cheering with every play. The energy, Doctoroff wrote, was like nothing he had experienced before.

"The stands were teeming with roaring Italian-Americans, and Bulgarian-Americans (and Italians and Bulgarians) standing, chanting, and singing, brandishing flags and painted bodies that screamed their national colors of white, red, and green."

On his feet the entire game, Doctoroff reflected on the ethnic diversity of his adopted home, and realized that you could replicate the dramatic emotions with other countries, too.

He then came up with the "vague notion" that would change his life. There should be more of this magic. There could be more of this magic. New York City, the global melting pot, ought to host the Olympics, he decided. It was a far-fetched idea. Certainly Doctoroff had nothing on his résumé to suggest he was the man to bring the Olympics to the city.

Still, he started paying close attention to news articles detailing preparations for the upcoming 1996 Olympic Games in Atlanta. His father was a judge, with access to the news intelligence database LexisNexis at a time before internet search engines were routine. After his kids went to bed, Doctoroff read about past games including those in Barcelona, Tokyo, and Los Angeles, scrutinizing the economic and social impacts on host communities. It was at first a passing interest, then became a hobby, and eventually, an obsession. Friends and associates thought it was an interesting idea, though no one expected him to be the one to make it happen.

Doctoroff approached the idea the way he approached most investments. He gathered string, sketched out the pros and cons, and slowly built a case. And he zeroed in on what would become the core of his pitch.

"The biggest benefit from hosting the Olympics wasn't really about the actual games at all," he would later write. "It came from the deadlines and international attention that forced cities to propose bold projects and then be accountable in the most public way possible."

Tokyo's 1964 games had helped it build its subway system. Barcelona had reimagined its waterfront. Atlanta built affordable housing and developed a downtown core. For Doctoroff, the idea of an Olympic bid was no longer simply about creating a spectacle that would bind and enthrall his fellow New Yorkers. As Doctoroff contemplated his adopted city, it was clear to him the games could recast it. He had long felt the city needed changing — he just hadn't considered that he might be the one to do it.

When Ross had first visited New York he felt he was "coming home to a place I'd never been." Swig had been intoxicated by its tempo and energy. Doctoroff, however, upon first visiting the city in 1968 at the age of 10, felt "hate at first sight." To him, the city was grimy, dilapidated, and depressing. Shortly after spying the "Entering New York City" sign for the first time from the back seat of the family station wagon, Doctoroff's eyes fell upon the imposing apartment houses of Co-op City in the Bronx.

There were "dozens of seemingly identical brown buildings," he said. "They seemed to be replicating, with more anonymous clones under construction, a vast bleak spreading mass. In the foreground was a dump."

"I am never going to live in this city," he recalled shouting out to his family. Not that anyone in his family would ever suggest such a thing.

Fate, however, intervened decades later. Doctoroff's wife, Alisa, was offered a job at HBO, headquartered in Manhattan, so he followed reluctantly. Soon after, the Harvard and University of Chicago law graduate landed an investment banking job at Lehman Brothers.

Doctoroff worked in the merchant banking group, and was assigned to structure a partnership between Lehman and Robert Bass, a billionaire Texan and private equity pioneer. After setting up the partnership that came to be known as Oak Hill Capital, Doctoroff jumped ship to it.

Doctoroff and his wife were textbook gentrifiers. They had purchased an abandoned townhouse on West 91st Street just a few months before that 1994 World Cup match. There were homeless people sleeping on the stoop and crack vials in the tree pit in front of his house.

Reading up on the history of the city, Doctoroff realized New York was still "saddled with land-use policies better suited to a bygone industrial and shipping era than to the final years of the 20th century." Huge swaths of land on the waterfront were left undeveloped, not because no one wanted to develop them but because they weren't allowed to. These areas, much of the 520 miles of the city's waterfront, were still zoned for industrial use.

Now, Doctoroff wanted to clear out the rusting wreckage of New York's blue-collar manufacturing past, and pave the way for a New York that would serve as a magnet for the global elite.

It was a tune some developers had been singing for decades—they had seen the city's "nostalgia" for its working-class roots derail many ambitious, potentially transformative projects. Though, of course, there had been more to it than that. There had been the legacy of Robert Moses, whose power grabs dressed up as development plays had soured many New Yorkers on major projects, the city's powerful core of entrenched interest groups and activists, and a thousand other crises to deal with. Beame had focused on the economic crisis of the 1970s, Koch and Dinkins on rebuilding the abandoned areas in the 1980s, and Guiliani was focused on cracking down on crime in the 1990s. But by the time Bloomberg came along, he could set in play the city's metamorphosis into a mecca for the superrich, making him the darling of developers.

The first person outside his family Doctoroff chose to approach with his Olympic idea was John Monsky, Oak Hill's general counsel. He referred Doctoroff to Alex Garvin, a member of the New York City Planning Commission who taught urban planning at Yale and had recently published a book on American cities. Garvin was connected — one of his protégés from Yale was Joe Rose, then Mayor Giuliani's planning czar — and Garvin had been pushing for the very kind of changes Doctoroff wanted to bring about. He immediately saw the potential of both to create the urgency needed to rezone the city and generate revenues that might be used to pay for infrastructure improvements.

"My mother used to say, 'I was born saying no first and asking questions next,'" Garvin said. "But I went to Dan's office, and he turned to me and said, 'What do you think about having the Olympics in New York?,' I said, 'I think it's a great idea!' He told me everybody else thought he was crazy."

Garvin knew that much of the city's zoning was obsolete. But he also understood that changing it would mean going against a powerful block of opponents led by a group known as the New York Industrial Retention Network, which had argued effectively that zoning should remain as it was to depress the value of the land, and keep it zoned for manufacturing to help the city retain the few blue-collar jobs that existed and keep open the possibility of attracting more. To Garvin, the best counter to that argument lay in the numbers: since the 1960s, New York City had lost 1 million manufacturing jobs. And they weren't coming back.

But he knew there were other obstacles to developing the waterfront, not the least of which was the lack of any transportation to connect it to the rest of the city, and the lack of a viable financing scheme to build it. An Olympic bid could help overcome both obstacles.

At first, Doctoroff bankrolled the efforts himself. Garvin set up shop in a conference room in Doctoroff's office on 56th Street and Madison Avenue, and soon he and his team had it plastered with lithographed maps depicting virtually the entire city at a scale of 50 feet to one inch. The "Sanborn" maps, originally created for use by fire insurance underwriters, included outlines of buildings, street names — even the location of fire hydrants, the widths of sidewalks and streets, details on the composition of building materials, and notation on prevailing wind directions.

Garvin's team compiled a list of all the facilities New York City would need to host the summer games, along with the space requirements. How much space would you need to accommodate volleyball courts and seating? What was required for wrestling, swimming, and diving?

Then, they pored over the maps. Having served in a number of housing-related posts in the Lindsay, Beame, and Koch administrations, Garvin was determined that the Olympic plans not require any relocations. But he was also quite sure there would be no shortage of vacant space to choose from.

Next, the team headed downtown to a police helipad on the East River, and started doing flyovers. Over the course of a dozen trips, Garvin took hundreds of aerial photographs and invariably discovered things that weren't on the maps. The final step was actual on-site inspections, mostly on Sundays so Doctoroff could accompany them.

On one flight over the Williamsburg waterfront, Garvin was struck by the vast empty spaces along the potentially picturesque patch of land, and realized it would be the perfect setting for a volleyball court. Later, he took the subway to the neighborhood to check out the area in person. Under Beame, Garvin had made loans to a number of relatively poor Puerto Ricans and Hasidic Jews in the area. But he was surprised to emerge from the subway and see an art store and Thai restaurant.

"This isn't the neighborhood I remember," he said. The Williamsburg gentrification was already beginning. Still, the site was perfect. And eventually it would be rezoned and become a waterfront park.

After about four months, Garvin and his team locked themselves in the office, and vowed not to come out or answer the telephone until they had a plan. Garvin placed yellow tracing paper over the map, and followed the train routes. One arm ran from the Meadowlands into Flushing Meadows-Corona Park and all the way out to Long Island, while the other ran from the East River to connect sites in Long Island City all the way to the west side of Manhattan. It formed a perfect X. The tracks could be used to move athletes and coaches between the competition sites and practice sites easily, avoiding traffic.

When Doctoroff saw the tracings, he dubbed it the "Olympic X," and from then on it would be the organizing principle of the plans. He began gearing up to sell the plan to the city's business and political elite.

In the winter of 1996, he got introduced to Bob Kiley, the president of what would later come to be known as the Partnership for New York City, a nonprofit founded by David Rockefeller that was composed of the city's top business leaders from real estate, finance, and law.

Over breakfast at the Drake Hotel, Doctoroff laid out the case for the Olympics and all the development it might spur. Kiley immediately saw the potential. He suggested Doctoroff prepare a presentation and deliver it to the group's board several months later. It was to be a pivotal moment.

Doctoroff and his team worked for three months on the presentation, hiring a design and production crew. The 28-minute presentation began with the opening scene from "West Side Story." The camera zoomed in to the slums of 1950s West Side New York, and then dissolved into images of Lincoln Center — the project erected after those slums were bulldozed that became the catalyst for the resurgence of the Upper West Side. He then made his case for "the catalytic impact" hosting the Olympics had on cities around the world, and revealed his plans to build a stadium on the Far West Side. He closed with the image of a little girl looking up at the Statue of Liberty, waving an American flag.

When he was done, the members of the Partnership — which included the CEOs of Time Warner, Chase Manhattan Bank, and a number of developers — gave him a standing ovation.

Things moved quickly from there. Word reached Giuliani, and a week later Doctoroff was with Hizzoner discussing his ideas. The managing editor of the New York Daily News called and asked Doctoroff to make his pitch to the news and editorial teams. That June, the paper ran a spread headlined "Going for the Gold: Let's Light the Flame and Host the Games."

"The proposal that New York host the Olympics in 2008 ignites the imagination," the editorial read. "The Daily News is proud to take a leading role in this effort. And to sound the rallying cry for others to join the push. For every New Yorker, nay, every American, has a stake in making the dream a reality."

Ross was an early convert. He had actually thought about starting an Olympic bid himself, recognizing it could "get things done that you couldn't otherwise get done." He had even traveled down to the 1996 summer games in Atlanta to learn how to go about it.

When Ross learned Doctoroff was already running with the idea, he immediately offered to help.

The two had a lot in common. Both were self-made men from the Detroit area. Both, by coincidence and connection, had come to own a stake in the Islanders hockey team. Both had been offered and seized the opportunity to buy into the team with big ambitions, and both would come to resent the way they were treated as "5 percenters," owning a minority share. The ownership group was dominated by its majority owner Howard Milstein, another real estate titan, who "didn't care to listen to anybody and he was just going to do the whole thing himself," according to Ross.

"We saw this as a meeting place of the world, we saw it as the world's second home," Doctoroff said. "We believed through crisis that New York would always rebound, and would manage thoughtfully. Steve was an optimist about the city, and I'm an optimist about the city, and I think to some extent that just bound us together."

Early on, Doctoroff had gone to see Lew Rudin, a legendary developer who along with his brother Jack headed one of the city's oldest real estate clans and was a leading advocate for New York. In 1975, in the depths of the city's fiscal crisis, it was Rudin who helped persuade major landlords to pre-pay $600 million in real estate taxes to help keep the city solvent.[31]

Doctoroff was supposed to have 30 minutes with Rudin at his office in a building he owned at 345 Park. But instead, he received a 90-minute master class in the factors that had led to the city's near-demise in the 1970s.

It was, Rudin explained, a "vicious cycle," of falling population and a plummeting tax base, which led to an inability to fund city services for such basic needs as crime prevention and sanitation, leading to more population and business losses, and more financial problems. Rudin, it turned out, had led efforts to bring the 1984 Olympics to the city — a contest eventually won by L.A. And he articulated for Doctoroff more reasons to do it.

"He essentially kind of laid out for me, sort of the history of the financial crisis and what happens when you don't invest," Doctoroff said. "And he

---

31 Bagli, Charles V., et. al. "Mayor and Council Reach Deal on West Side Development." *The New York Times.* January 11, 2005.

became a huge believer and one of the first funders of the Olympic bid because he understood instinctively the benefits of the Olympics which is a catalyst in getting things done, catalyst for the kind of investment that a city would actually need."

For Doctoroff, the meeting helped crystalize a concept that would become central to his time in the Bloomberg administration — that just as the city could be brought down by a "vicious cycle," it could also be elevated through a "virtuous" one.

The idea of what Rudin and Doctoroff called a virtuous cycle would later be expanded upon and popularized most famously by urban studies theorist Richard Florida, whose influential 2002 book "The Rise of the Creative Class" summed up an emerging consensus that gave the idea a more contemporary spin. In his book, Florida outlined how cities could inject new vibrancy into their downtowns by making the city desirable to members of what he called the "creative class," a mix of artists, intellectuals, and college-educated millennials, whose arrival would attract better employers, lead to the inevitable creation of new jobs, and boost tax revenues. City leaders could do so with quality-of-life amenities, like parks, vibrant nightlife, and restaurants, but also by offering generous tax breaks to help lure real estate developers and convince high-tech companies to set up shop.

It was a belief that was confirmed when Garvin strode into Doctoroff's office one day for their weekly chat, looking concerned.

"The plan doesn't work," he declared.

"What do you mean?"

"I can't get anybody by subway to the convention center where we have eight events going on, to the Olympic square to the broadcast center, to the press center — or to the stadium!"

"What do we do?" Doctoroff asked.

"Extend the number-7 subway line."

Garvin promised to return the following week with some financing options for the subway.

At the next meeting, Garvin laid out three photographs. One, circa 1903, depicted the East Side of Manhattan looking down Park Avenue from 46th Street. The picture was dominated by the old Grand Central Terminal and the East Side's sprawling railyards. The next picture depicted the same area but was from 1913, with the new Grand Central. In this picture, bridges had been built on top of and across the railyards representing 44th, 45th, and 46th streets on Park Avenue, which opened up the possibility of development.

The final photograph showed the area around the new infrastructure in 1930. Penciled over the drawing were all the new buildings that had been erected over the railyards during the course of the preceding 17 years, including the Yale Club, Waldorf Astoria, Commodore Hotel, and a whole host of others. Where before had sat only railyards, now sat an army of tall new buildings.

Garvin's message was clear. Every one of those new buildings represented millions of dollars in new real estate tax revenue for the city. The same transformation could be expected on top of the West Side railyards.

"I didn't have to explain to Dan that we were going to pay for the subway extension — he understood instantly that real estate taxes from all these buildings would pay for the capital improvements," Garvin said.

If Doctoroff could find a way to tap that anticipated new tax revenue in advance, the plan would pay for itself.

XI

Right Side of the Tracks

The High Line Effect

Doctoroff wasn't the only private citizen in the 1990s with a lofty vision that would manifest in the Bloomberg years.

In late 1999, a pair of young New Yorkers, Joshua David and Robert Hammond, would wind up sitting next to each other at a community board meeting. Their chance encounter would catalyze an improbable private campaign that would win over the city's political establishment and further extend Manhattan's millionaire playground through an unlikely vehicle, transforming an abandoned rail line into an elevated vertical park: the "High Line."

In 1999, David was a freelance travel writer with unrealized ambitions to be an architect, living in a basement apartment on 21st Street. While researching an article on changes in Chelsea, he noticed the hulking railbed about a block from his apartment, walked over and really looked at it for the first time.

"You couldn't see what was on top of it, but the rusting Art Deco railings gave it a sense of lost beauty, and the spaces underneath were very dramatic; they had a dark, gritty, industrial quality, and a lofty, church-like quality as well," he would later write. "It was shadowy and cool underneath. I didn't know what the thing was called."

David began to ask around. When he learned that the structure ran unbroken for 22 blocks, his imagination kicked in: "Wouldn't it be cool to walk around up there, twenty-two city blocks, on this old, elevated thing, on this relic of another time, in this hidden place, up in the air?"

Soon after, David read a Times report on how, for nearly two decades, City Hall and private developers had been trying to get the platform's owner, Conrail, to tear down the rusting, weed-covered elevated train platform, which ran 1.6 miles down Manhattan's West Side, from 34th Street to Greenwich Village. It had been used to transport cargo to factories and warehouses in the area, but was out of action by the 1980s.

Now it had a new owner, the CSX Corporation, which had commissioned a study to look at alternatives. The rusting tracks, 14 feet above the ground at their lowest and 50 feet wide at their narrowest, could support a wide range of public amenities if it were spared, the report noted, ranging from a bike trail to a rail service to restaurants and art galleries.

In the Times article, City Planning Commissioner Joe Rose, who had played such a prominent role in the Columbus Circle redevelopment, dismissed such proposals as "idle fantasy," and quipped that the city's efforts to get it torn down had dragged on so long that "this has become the Vietnam of old railroad trestles."

But David didn't see it that way. He called one of the CSX officials quoted in the article to find out if there was a group working to save it, and learned of an upcoming community board meeting at which they planned to present their study.

Robert Hammond, a 20-something Princeton grad who lived in the

West Village in an apartment at Tenth Street and Washington, also read the same Times article. Hammond had first spotted the High Line across the street from a neighborhood bar — on the wall outside, someone had posted an old black-and-white photo of a train running through a factory building. When Hammond looked across the street he saw the tracks. He had always liked the idea that a train used to run through his neighborhood.

At the meeting, David and Hammond exchanged cards. Though neither one had ever done anything like it before, they soon agreed that if they wanted the tracks preserved, they would have to be the ones to do it.

At the time, the area around the High Line was already in the midst of a renaissance, which made the debate about its future highly controversial. There was a lot of money at stake. And many developers who owned property underneath the tracks or in the area were eager to tear them down.

Priced out of Soho, a series of art galleries had opened up along 10th and 11th avenues around 22nd Street, lending an aura of shabby-chic to an area long dominated by taxis, auto-repair garages, and parking lots.

Meanwhile, the city's efforts to redevelop the rotting waterfront piers had resulted in the creation of the Chelsea Piers sports complex. Plans to create the Hudson River Park were proceeding. And with the buzz over Doctoroff's stadium proposal hitting the papers, the area seemed poised for transformation.

To the south, development in the Meatpacking District and Far West Side of Greenwich Village had already exploded.

In 1991, Rockrose Development, helmed by the Iranian-born Elghanayan brothers, purchased a five-block stretch of the High Line running from Bank to Gansevoort streets, demolished it, and built 265 apartments on Jane Street and a public plaza with a grove of Japanese pagoda trees, a majestic full-bodied species that exploded into thick walls of feathery, light green leaves every spring.

By 1999, at least eight other apartment buildings and two hotels were completed, under construction or being planned from Hudson Street to the Hudson River.[32]

Like Doctoroff, David and Hammond quickly recruited some powerful allies to help them in their efforts.

Hammond was good friends with Gifford Miller, the New York City Council member who would become Speaker during the Bloomberg administration. Hammond's best friend from college, Mario Palumbo, meanwhile, was working for a developer who had cut his teeth in government during the Koch administration and had a history of supporting art causes and quirky nonprofits. His name was Phil Aarons and he was one of the founding partners of Millennium, the development firm that had created Lincoln Square and almost beat out Steve Ross and Related for the Coliseum site.

To the High Line fight, Aarons brought a deep understanding of how to pull the levers of power, and went along with Hammond and David for their first meeting with a high-ranking CSX official at the World Trade Center. CSX, they were told, would remain neutral.

The trio proceeded to the Windows of the World restaurant, ordered champagne, and, as they gazed down upon the sparkling Hudson River, the city's skyscape, and the streets far below, clinked glasses and chose the name of their group: "The Friends of the High Line."

Meanwhile, ten days after Michael Bloomberg's improbable election victory in October 2001, Doctoroff received a call from Nat Leventhal, a former Deputy Mayor under Ed Koch. Leventhal had been tapped to head Bloomberg's transition committee, and said he had identified the ideal candidate to serve as the new Deputy Mayor for Economic Development and Reconstruction: Daniel L. Doctoroff.

---

32   Dunlap, David W. "In West Village, a Developers' Gold Rush." *The New York Times.* August 29, 1999.

During his run for office, Bloomberg had put an extension of the No. 7 line in his economic development strategy to revitalize the West Side, and he had contributed to the Olympic efforts.

Though Doctoroff professed reluctance at first, Bloomberg quickly shot down his concerns about how taking the job might prevent him from fulfilling his Olympic dreams.

"Where better to get things done in your plan than from City Hall?" Bloomberg said.

Doctoroff accepted.[33] Over the next six years, he would set out not just to implement the ambitious rethinking of space, but to revitalize the city. But first, he would need to disentangle himself.

Five days before becoming deputy mayor, in an arrangement cleared by the city's conflicts-of-interest board, Doctoroff received $3.2 million back from NYC2012, of the $4 million he had loaned. A day later, Steve Ross stepped in to guarantee a separate bank loan worth $3.2 million for the group.

From the beginning, Doctoroff embraced rezoning, and met early on with Amanda Burden, the glamorous new chair of the City Planning Department whose father was an heir to the Standard Oil fortune and whose mother was famous socialite Barbara "Babe" Paley. Over the course of Bloomberg's two terms, the administration would propose 140 separate rezoning actions — only two of which were defeated — and rezone 40 percent of the city.

The election of Bloomberg also offered a second chance to those pushing to preserve the High Line.

In their early Olympic plans, Doctoroff and Garvin had considered building the Olympic Village in Battery Park City North, and partly using

---

33   Doctoroff, Daniel. *Greater Than Ever*. PublicAffairs. September 12, 2017.

the High Line as a connector to bring athletes from the housing to a stadium on the Far West Side. But Doctoroff had not thought about the rusting tracks since abandoning that plan in favor of a village in Queens.

A few days after assuming his new post, however, Doctoroff received a call from Randy Mastro, a former deputy mayor under Giuliani who was now representing 38 landowners in Chelsea who wanted to knock down the old tracks. Mastro arrived for a meeting several weeks later with some of his clients, towing a wagon containing a huge chunk of concrete. The block, they claimed, had fallen from the rusting tracks onto a car below it, almost killing a passerby. The structure, they argued, needed to be torn down right away.

Burden, however, was a big supporter of keeping the tracks. "When I saw it the first time," she recalled in a 2014 TED Talk, "honestly, when I went up on that old viaduct, I fell in love the way you fall in love with a person."

And though Doctoroff acknowledges, "I didn't quite get it right away," Burden's support was enough to prevent the city from immediately making a move.

Eventually, Doctoroff began to see how the High Line might fit in with his overall plan for Hudson Yards. It was, it turned out, exactly the same elevation as the platform he and his team envisioned above the railyards. Doctoroff and Garvin[34] planned a broad boulevard running down the middle of the yards between 10th and 11th avenues which could feed directly into the new elevated park, one that Burden was aggressively pushing as Manhattan's answer to Paris's Promenade Plantée.

Doctoroff pledged his support for the High Line, he claims, in exchange for a commitment from Council Speaker Miller that the group would

---

34   Doctoroff, Daniel. *Greater Than Ever.* PublicAffairs. September 12, 2017.

not openly oppose the mayor's plan for a stadium on the railyards (a commitment, Doctoroff said, that Miller failed to keep).

In January 2005, all that prep work finally paid off: The City Council and Bloomberg hammered out an agreement on Hudson Yards that allowed the rezoning to pass, clearing the way for the construction of a new business district and the extension of the No. 7 line. The city also mandated that a quarter of the 13,600 new apartments planned for the 59-block district would be set aside for moderate-and-low-income residents. The moves followed state legislation that had authorized the $1.4 billion expansion of the Jacob K. Javits Convention Center a few blocks away.

But not everything worked out.

That June, Sheldon Silver, the powerful state assembly speaker, announced his opposition to the West Side stadium plan, which had become mired in controversy because of opposition to public funding and fears over traffic.

An Orthodox Jew who hailed from the Lower East Side and was known to adversaries and friends alike as "Shelly," Silver was a canny dealmaker who had ascended to the speakership in 1994.

In order to build the stadium, Doctoroff and Bloomberg needed state funding and the MTA's transfer of the land, both of which were subject to the unanimous approval of the state's Public Authorities Control Board, a three-person committee whose members were appointed by state Senate Majority Leader Joseph Bruno, Governor George Pataki, and Silver. Pataki's representative voted in favor, but when Silver joined Bruno in directing his representatives to abstain on the vote, the defeat was ensured.

Though Silver couched his opposition in pragmatic terms — he claimed he opposed the deal because it would distract attention from efforts to rebuild Lower Manhattan — Doctoroff suspected there were other reasons for his dissent.

Years later, Doctoroff would look back and concede he had been outmaneuvered in Albany by those with an economic incentive to thwart the West Side stadium plan, led by James Dolan and his father, Charles "Chuck" Dolan, a cable pioneer who had used his fortune to purchase Madison Square Garden and the New York Knicks. Fearing the competition to their sports stadium, the Dolans had hired a team of lobbyists to fight the stadium proposal in the state capitol. They included former New York Republican Senator Al D'Amato and Patricia Lynch, Silver's former press secretary, with whom he was known to be close.

Doctoroff would later work with Lynch on other issues, and she was not shy about letting him know where his earlier political efforts had come up short.

"In reflecting on the stadium battle," Doctoroff would write of Lynch in his book, "she said our biggest mistake was not understanding that Albany would be involved and not putting all our focus on Silver and Joe Bruno."

It was, as any real estate industry figure could have told Doctoroff, a rookie mistake.

The industry had long been devoted to gaming Albany. It was the largest single donor to statewide races and had mastered the art of lobbying to chip away at state-regulated rent control protections.

Doctoroff and Garvin came up with an alternate plan in Queens' Flushing Meadows, but the point eventually became moot.

In Singapore that July, with Doctoroff and Ross in attendance, the International Olympic Committee cast its final votes for the 2012 summer games. The winner was New York's perennial rival in the battle for global supremacy, London. Dan Doctoroff's efforts — including his courtship of the visiting olympic committee — had gone up in smoke.

On a Frankfurt layover back to New York, Ross and Doctoroff sat in the Singapore Airlines first-class lounge with Henry Kissinger, the former Secretary of State who was serving as a consultant to the committee.

"I could have told you you were never going to get it," Kissinger told them, according to Ross. "The rest of the world just doesn't like [George W.] Bush. It was a vote against the United States."

Doctoroff was devastated. But what he hoped the games would bring to New York City was already happening.

The Hudson Yards district had been rezoned. A new train station was en route. In mid-June, the City Council approved the High Line, adding fuel to a development frenzy that would further transform the Far West Side of the city. Surrounding land prices skyrocketed. An article in the New York Observer documented the impact: A local landowner named Benigno Serrano had purchased 12,350 square feet of land adjacent to the High Line at 23rd Street for $900,000 in 1986. He had sold it for $12.5 million to developer Alf Naman in 2005. Next door, another developer named David Kislin was already marketing condos in a 12-story glass tower, called High Line 519. Prices for the 11 units ranged from $860,000 to $3.4 million, and he had already sold five.

Down at 14th Street, meanwhile, André Balazs, the impresario behind the Hotel Mercer, was creating the 15-story Standard Hotel, in which he planned "to have this fascinating track running through" his building.

Initially, Ross would later acknowledge, he was no fan of the High Line. "When I first saw it, I thought it was stupid," he said.

The tracks would form an unnatural barrier, he argued, and people wouldn't want to cross under. It would have been preferable to tear it down and build a park at grade, he thought.

But once he realized it was inevitable, Ross quickly bought in, and was planning a project on the east side of 10th Avenue near the bottom of the High Line.

Nor was the halo effect of the Chelsea boom confined to the area overlooking the rusting railbed. Joe Rose, now a private citizen and a partner in the developer Georgetown Company, was building an office tower that promised to set a new standard for the area. The 10-story $100 million structure resembling a futuristic sail would be starchitect Frank Gehry's first New York City project, and would serve as the headquarters of IAC/InterActiveCorp, media mogul Barry Diller's company through which he controlled TripAdviser, Ticketmaster, and other online ventures.

"It's always been an area that has had a great deal of potential, and it's one we have lots of confidence in," Rose told the Observer.

By December 2005, 5,500 units of new housing were planned in the neighborhood. Height limitations and setbacks were put in place to preserve views, light, and open space. The High Line corridor, with its 6.7-acre park, was "like catnip to developers," the Times wrote, noting that of all the units in the pipeline, all but 1,100 were "for the fabulously well-heeled."

XII

Mogul Mania

Cashing In on the Resi Boom

Will Zeckendorf stood in the foundation pit of his Central Park West development site and smiled. It was an unseasonably warm fall day, and across the street in the park, parents pushed strollers down leafy pathways and office workers sat on benches munching sandwiches, while others lay on the grass, playing hooky, aware that the last remnants of summer would soon slip away.

The mood at the construction site was ebullient as workmen hoisted a 75-foot model of a building with a broad base and two majestic limestone towers up onto a specially erected scaffolding. The details in that rendering had been leaked to Times reporter David Dunlap a few weeks earlier, and he had billed his scoop as the answer to "perhaps the biggest mystery in Manhattan real estate."[35]

Two uber-luxurious towers would rise, a 19-story, 231-foot-high apartment house on the park side and a 35-story 550-foot-high midblock tower, separated by a private courtyard. Clad in 87,000 pieces of white limestone from the same Indiana quarry that had supplied the Empire State Building and the Metropolitan Museum of Art, the complex was to feature a 70-by-200-foot private cobblestone courtyard and driveway with an oval pavilion at its center and a glass-bottomed reflecting pool to the north. Beneath the glass, with light streaming downward from the sky, lay an Olympic lap pool and a 14,000-square-foot resident health club. There were to be 30 private climate-controlled wine rooms in a wine cellar, and a central octagonal tasting area; a private screening room large enough to hold 20, and an outdoor terrace with a meticulously manicured garden. And there was a residents-only private restaurant, where multimillionaires could fraternize just with their own kind.

The condos would start at $2 million. The grand prize, asking $45 million, would be a 10,700-square-foot, king-of-the-world penthouse with 14-foot-high ceilings, eight bedrooms, 10 full bathrooms, a screening room, library, and 800 square feet of terraces overlooking the verdant expanse of the park.

If you believed the Zeckendorfs could actually get those kinds of prices, the $400 million they had paid for the land and the estimated $900 million they planned to spend on construction no longer looked so crazy.

And indeed, although the world didn't yet know it, the brothers weren't just celebrating the start of construction that day. Standing in the foundation pit mingling with Arthur and Will's mother, Guri Lie, the architect Robert A.M. Stern, and a smattering of local politicians, were

---

35   Dunlap, D.W. "Redefining Public Space at the G.M. Building." *The New York Times.* March 2, 2005.

three members of the elite who had already committed to buy units. Among them was Jeff Gordon, the NASCAR racing champion, the first in a long list of celebrities that would come to include Denzel Washington, Robert De Niro, Bob Costas, and Sting.

Also present was the hedge-fund mogul Daniel Loeb, the notorious "activist" investor who had beat out another of his kind, corporate raider Carl Icahn, to snare the crown jewel of the building: the $45 million penthouse. The sight-unseen buy at its full asking price, a staggering $4,200 a foot, would be the talk of the town when it was leaked to the New York Post a few weeks later. The price set a new record for New York's most expensive residence, beating even the co-op record set earlier that year when Rupert Murdoch paid $44 million for Laurance Rockefeller's Fifth Avenue triplex.

After the groundbreaking ceremony, the Zeckendorfs led their small party to the sales office on the 44th floor of Carnegie Tower on West 57th Street, where they mingled in mock-ups of the condos' rooms and peered at a scale model of the building.

"It was a lavish affair with politicians and champagne — quite an extravagant, polite sort of thing — a big to-do," Will Zeckendorf would later recall. He reflected back on a different groundbreaking on another fall day — the start of construction for the Columbia a few blocks farther north all those years ago in 1981 with the shouting protestors, the signs, the people banging on the fence, the police. The sheer early-80s New York City craziness was utterly absent from the 15 CPW ceremony.

"Two bookends," he would conclude, "on the transformation of market-rate housing."

Indeed, that transformation seemed to many only to be accelerating. It was a function of how fast things were changing north of Columbus Circle that many of the bidders who had lost out to the Zeckendorfs a little more than a year earlier were already regretting not upping what had seemed an insanely optimistic price for the land.

"I called up one of our board members who is in his 80s and told him the price of the land and he asked what the cash flow of the building was," Vornado president Michael Fascitelli said at an industry panel of the block-long assemblage where 15 CPW was rising. "I kept telling him that there was no building, it was just land, but he kept saying, 'you don't understand, what is the cash flow of the building, the building!' It goes to show how much things have changed. Yet now, $700 per square foot looks great — I wish we had that deal." (In 2006, Vornado would make its own big play in the area, buying a site at 220 Central Park South and later building a new condo project there that would prove enormously successful in its own right.)

At the time, Fascitelli[36] lamented how difficult it was getting to make money in real estate in the midst of what many had already started calling a housing bubble. Land prices had risen so high, so fast, that it was impossible to build anything but condos and make a profit, he complained. The office market was also overheated. And even nontraditional methods of making money were getting harder.

In 2003, Vornado had bid on the GM Building and lost out to Harry Macklowe. But after losing the bid, Vornado had stepped up to provide Macklowe with $275 million in short-term high-yield mezzanine debt, with an adjustable interest rate that could top 15 percent. Now, however, long-term loans were so easy to come by, interest rates had fallen so low, and some institutions were so eager to lend that Macklowe had refinanced and paid the debt off early. Even after the $4.5 million prepayment penalty, Macklowe had still denied Vornado millions of dollars in interest.

"One of my colleagues came to me and pointed out that on one mezzanine

36 Geiger, Daniel. "Tight Market Is No Joke, Fascitelli Tells ULI Panel." *Real Estate Weekly*. September 21, 2005.

loan that was repaid early, we made a 44 percent gain," Fascitelli recalled. "I said, 'Great, so we made seven dollars.'"

Some were already issuing warnings that the good times couldn't last.

Among them was Jonathan Miller, the appraiser. In June, he'd gone on national radio lamenting the situation, warning that appraisals, which provide an estimate of a property's value that is then used to determine financing, were inflated and totally out of whack, and that the very structure of his industry was fatally "flawed."[37] In the residential world, brokers who arranged mortgages were the same people who decided which appraisers to use — meaning that in a climate where people no longer seemed to care about long-term risk, they were motivated to hire only the appraisers who would "meet their numbers" in deciding what a property was worth, and wouldn't get in the way of a deal.

"The systems of checks and balances no longer exist," Miller said.

Interest rates had dropped so low that everybody with good credit had already refinanced, bought, or sold, he believed. So many people had done so, he posited, that the pool of customers who met lending standards had begun to run dry.

In any normal world, lenders would have simply accepted the situation, or looked a little harder. Lending to individuals with questionable ability to pay the money back or on overvalued properties that were insufficient loan collateral was simply bad for business. But by 2005, it seemed, the normal concerns about risk no longer applied. A parallel universe was created by instruments of financial alchemy known as collateralized debt obligations, or CDOs.

Developed by Wall Street in the 1990s, CDOs consisted of loans chopped up into individual pieces and sold off to investors like bonds.

37 Miller, Jonathan. "'Appraising the Appraisers' on National Public Radio." *Miller Samuel Inc.* "Matrix Blog." August 1, 2005.

The riskiest pieces, which earned the highest rates of return, were the loans made to borrowers with troubled credit histories, borrowers whose only option was to seek "subprime," high-interest loans. Most lenders had traditionally approached subprime lending with caution, carefully calculating the risk-benefit profile and limiting the amount of loans they offered to dodgy borrowers. But the invention of CDOs changed things.

Thanks to residential CDOs, lenders no longer had to worry about what happened to the loans they issued in the long-term. Because they would no longer own them. As soon as these lenders originated a new loan and collected their fees, they could get it off their balance sheets, sell the risk to someone else, and never think about it again. As their popularity increased, CDOs became increasingly complicated and opaque — troubled loans were bundled with other loans in large packages, and it became more labor-intensive to understand all the constituent parts, what proportion of them was risky, and how likely they were to default. Swept up in the froth of the market, nobody really seemed to care. After all, homeownership was on the rise, investors were making money, and Wall Street was booming. Why slow down?

"Standards no longer mattered," Miller said. To get a loan, "you just had to have a pulse or fog a mirror, and I'm not exaggerating. We [appraisers] became the enemy to lenders. You're either a deal enabler or you don't get work."

Miller was so convinced there was a bubble, so frustrated, and so worried about his own business prospects, that he started blogging several hours a day to vent. Soon he became a go-to Cassandra, telling CNBC that 75 percent of the appraisals being written for banks "are not worth the paper they're written on." Many people dismissed his warnings as sour grapes and ignored him. Mostly people were too busy making money to care. But no one argued with the contention that the market was red hot. And it was red hot across the board.

The low cost of borrowing thanks to Fed chairman Alan Greenspan's historically low interest rates had not only turbocharged investment in residential and commercial properties, it also lowered the rate of return for pension funds, endowments, and others who relied on yield-paying treasury bonds to generate safe, steady income.[38] Many of those institutional investors had begun to look to real estate private equity funds and others to help goose their returns. Some did so by lending, partnering with investors, or pouring money into private equity "opportunity funds." Others looked for high-yield fixed income products that would pay more than bonds: CDOs. Greed — as much as naivete and mania — was inevitably a factor in the fall that was to come.

By 2005, CDOs pegged to large commercial properties, known as CMBS (Commercial Mortgage-Backed Securities) were in such high demand, they had become some of the most lucrative products produced by leading Wall Street banks such as Credit Suisse, Goldman Sachs, and Lehman Brothers. This increased the incentive for the banks to make large loans on commercial properties so they could create more products to sell to clients. Since the risk was passed on and demand was so high, lending standards plummeted there as well. The amount of cash required for collateral dropped considerably, and risk became almost an afterthought.

The hard-charging attitude of the bankers was perhaps best personified by Lehman's head of real estate, Mark Walsh, the man tasked with deciding what deals the megabank would back. Described as "a socially timid workaholic" from Yonkers in Andrew Ross Sorkin's 2009 chronicle of the financial crisis, "Too Big to Fail," Walsh was a favorite of Lehman CEO Dick Fuld and his deputy Joe Gregory.

"Walsh seemed immune to risk, which impressed Fuld and Gregory to

---

38   Bagli, Charles V. "Harry Macklowe Gambles Again." *The New York Times*. October 6, 2013.

no end," Sorkin wrote. "Each success bred hunger for more... Walsh had virtually unlimited use of Lehman's balance sheet and used it to turn the firm into an all-in, unhedged play on the U.S. real estate market."

Over at Wachovia, the in-house rainmaker Rob Verrone was so busy doing CMBS deals he had picked up the nickname "Large Loan Verrone." (Verrone once sent funeral roses to his longtime developer client Joseph Chetrit when Chetrit went to another lender on a deal.)

In Manhattan, where many of the Wall Streeters resided, the ballooning deal flow and the expanding profits meant huge bonuses. At the beginning of 2005, Wall Street paid out a record $18.6 billion in bonuses, ample gasoline for the fire that was the high-end New York City residential real estate market.

The year 2005 would see 90 residential sales of individual apartments at $10 million or above and 25 deals over $20 million — five times the number from 2004.[39] The most expensive properties were still co-ops and townhouses on the Upper East Side, but Central Park West and Central Park South were making their mark. And condos, an asset class that historically wasn't much of a force in the market, accounted for seven of the top 20 deals. Record-breaking contracts being inked regularly at 15 Central Park West, where deals would close in 2006 and 2007, promised to continue the trend.

Then there was the money pouring in from abroad.

Foreign buyers had always been a small but significant segment of the city's real estate market.[40] In the 1970s and 1980s, they had been key clients for the first luxury condos — the Aristotle Onassis–financed Olympic Tower, for one, had been home to the Saudi arms dealer Adnan Khashoggi,

39 Gregor, Alison. "A Family Tradition Yields a $5.4 Billion Coup." *The New York Times.* November 5, 2006.

40 "State of the Nation's Housing." Joint Center for Housing Studies, Harvard University. 2007.

who had hired a crane to hoist a grand piano into his penthouse through a window. And many of Trump's pioneering condo developments became known as "ghost towers," places where international buyers could park their capital even if they didn't spend much time living there.

After 9/11, there had been a dip in foreign buyers. But now they were back.

Because U.S. interest rates were so low, the dollar had become cheap relative to other currencies. From a low of around .85 to the dollar in January 2002, the euro began a steady rise, hitting 1.35 to the dollar by November 2003. Brokers reported that foreign buyers, particularly those from Germany and Russia, were taking advantage of the situation.

By the fall of 2004, some had begun to talk about a "foreign invasion." The new arrivals included the French and the Brazilians, but also the Malaysians, the Chinese, the Japanese, and plenty of buyers from the Middle East.

One of the most vocal moguls to embrace the trend was, of course, Trump.

"I happen to love a weak dollar," he told a reporter that year. "There's nothing better for New York real estate."

That year, Related's Time Warner Center had as many overseas buyers as domestic ones, according to Susan de França, then-president of residential sales for the developer. Joining the likes of Mexican-born David Martinez was Russian It girl Anna Anisimova, the daughter of metal magnate Vasily Anisimov, who paid $9.9 million for a penthouse soon after enrolling at NYU.

The publicity surrounding the Anisimova and Martinez deals were the exceptions. For many of the new arrivals, anonymity was a key amenity, as were the lenient rules for those who planned to use the apartment as a pied-à-terre. Unlike co-ops, which required potential buyers to provide reams of documentation and references to all-powerful co-op boards, who acted as gatekeepers and didn't need to justify why a potential buyer was rejected, condo buyers needed only to submit the highest bid and then cough up the money. Many sought to shield their identities by forming limited-liability companies (LLCs), shell entities that could be registered in places like Delaware where, some transparency advocates complained, less personal information was required to set up a new corporation than to register for a library card. Though many buyers did so for privacy reasons, others used LLCs to invest their ill-gotten gains secretly, turning the luxury New York condo into the next-generation Swiss bank.

XIII

Mr. Downtown Goes Uptown

Swig and the Sheffield

The moment Kent Swig stepped into the gloomy lobby of the Sheffield for the first time, he knew it was meant to be. To the untrained eye, the place was depressing. But Swig immediately saw the possibilities.

"It just popped," he recalled of that early 2005 visit. "It was like magic. It was extraordinary."

The 50-story red-brick rental tower just south of Columbus Circle offered park views from its upper floors and easy access to the newly minted Time Warner Center, with its Whole Foods, fancy eateries, and shopping mall just a block away.

Rose Associates had developed the property in the 1970s, and the 845-unit tower was the crown jewel of the family's sizable portfolio, one they had no intention of selling. But when superbroker Darcy Stacom said that developers eager to convert the property into condos would pay north of $400 million for it, the Roses had to listen.[41]

"She [Darcy] made us an offer we couldn't refuse," the company's president, Adam R. Rose, said.

Swig was one of those bidders with condo dreams. He would knock down the drive-through underpass that fronted the property and extend the first floor outwards.

"If you moved it out, enclosed this dark place and put glass on it," Swig would later explain, "this dingy exterior space became a magical interior space, full of light."

His vision for the building was more of a complete overhaul than the limited renovations his potential partners had in mind. But that was not a bad thing.

As Swig completed his tour, he grew more and more excited. It was serendipity at work again. Just as with that first Bank of New York deal, this one had fallen into his lap.

A few days earlier, Swig received a phone call from an Israeli émigré named Yair Levy, a new business associate he'd been talking to about a different deal. Levy and a partner, Serge Hoyda, had already prepared one bid for the Sheffield, but when bidding formally opened it proved so fierce that many of the 15 bidders were teaming up or finding new partners for a second round, and raising their offers.[42] Levy and Hoyda, who planned to convert the building into a condo, make some minor renovations, and then sell off the units, needed a third partner to put them over the top. Did

---

41 Gregor, Alison. "A Family Tradition Yields a $5.4 Billion Coup." *The New York Times.* November 5, 2006.

42 Geiger, Daniel. "Levy Runs Straight to Top with 'Lucky' Sheffield Bid." *Real Estate Weekly.* February 16, 2005.

Swig, they asked, want to take a look?

Levy and Swig made for an odd couple. Swig was 44, tall, blonde, and exuded an air of real estate royalty and California cool. Levy, 56, was short and swarthy, with bushy black eyebrows and shoes shined to perfection. He spoke with a thick Israeli accent, wore his hair slicked back, and left a miasma of cologne in his wake.

Levy had been working full-time since he was 13, starting by selling goods at Tel Aviv street fairs. He immigrated to the U.S. at 22, started a women's clothing line, and then plunged into New York City real estate in the late 1990s when the Garment District went into decline, following in the footsteps of many from that industry. To raise capital, Levy had borrowed against his home and snapped up a distressed property in Lower Manhattan at 133-135 Greenwich Street. As the market had rebounded and then soared, Levy's deals had grown bigger and his fortunes had risen. He sold a Third Avenue development site for $85 million, having paid just $33 million for it a few years earlier.

Levy and Swig had been recently introduced by Charles Dayan, another Israeli immigrant who had started out in the garment trade before moving into development.

"We didn't really know him that well," Levy said of Swig. "But we thought he was really very experienced."

At the Sheffield, Levy suggested they add on an additional $18 million to their initial $400 million offer, noting to his partners that Jews considered the number 18 lucky. The bid did indeed put them over the line, and at nearly $500,000 per unit, made national headlines.

Levy and Hoyda agreed to let Swig take the lead in renovating the property and dealing with tenants, thereby also becoming the public face of the project. But even helming such a meaty project did not satisfy Swig's appetite. He was immediately back Downtown, partnering with Colonnade Properties to pay $260 million for a 345-unit property at 25 Broad Street.

At over $750,000 per unit, it was a new record for a large building.

Again, Swig cheerfully laid out his case. He was well aware of talk of a "bubble," he said, but had again run the numbers carefully, and was sure he had a unique perspective. His command center was at 770 Lexington, which also happened to be the headquarters of Brown Harris Stevens and Halstead, by then two of the largest residential brokerage firms in the city. The boom was hard to miss there. The hallways were filled with jubilant brokers. Swig's partners on the brokerage, the Zeckendorfs, were in high spirits thanks to their 15 Central Park West.

"People talk about a housing bubble and it's true, prices are very very high, but there's no product out there," Swig said, citing a study produced by the wonks at his brokerages. There were about 53 percent fewer apartments available for purchase at that time than there had been just 24 months ago, he noted, and 13 percent fewer than there were 12 months ago.

The key to success would be the ability to physically transform the new properties and, in so doing, unlock value and meet that unmet need. Uptown, the plan was to unlock value by building taller. But at the Sheffield and at 25 Broad, value would come in converting the buildings into condos.

Unlike with ground-up condo projects such as Related's Time Warner Center or the Zeckendorfs' 15 CPW, Swig would have to convince existing rental tenants to either buy into his projects, or move out.

At 500,000 square feet, 25 Broad had been the largest office building in New York City when it was built in 1900. It had been gutted and transformed into a luxury rental property in 1994, and had zero rent-controlled or rent-stabilized tenants. Everyone there was on a market-rate lease.

Conversely, at the Sheffield, about 95 of the 845 units were stabilized. In New York, that meant those tenants were entitled to lifetime occupancy. But Swig felt that number was small enough that a conversion could move ahead.

For their part, the tenants at the Sheffield admitted to being intrigued by the prospects of new ownership, and were eager to hear what the partners might offer. They had followed the news of the auction closely, and many assumed they had hit the jackpot. They traded gossip and talked about next steps in the lobby, and elevators.

"We were all excited," Nancy Rovelli, president of the tenants' association, recalled.

Most tenants had been around in the 1980s, when many rentals were converted to luxury co-ops and had heard tales of amazing deals where insiders had been offered their apartments at half the market price by landlords eager to get things moving. Those kinds of deals were far less common now. But you still occasionally heard stories. To clear out the last four remaining rent-controlled tenants at the Mayflower Hotel,[43] the Zeckendorfs had paid three of them somewhere in the neighborhood of $1 million each. They had then engaged in an epic and protracted set of negotiations with the fourth and final tenant, a 30-year resident named Herbert Sukenik.

Sukenik, according to Michael Gross's book "House of Outrageous Fortune," informed the Zeckendorfs he knew not only how much they had paid for the Mayflower, he had calculated the precise acreage of his block, the taxes, insurance, and the carrying costs of the empty properties — things no developer wants to hear. Sukenik, with the help of legendary tenant lawyer David Rozenholc, was able to extract $17 million from the Zeckendorfs, by far the most ever paid to relocate a tenant in New York.

---

43   Gross, Michael. *House of Outrageous Fortune*. Atria Books. March 11, 2014.

At the Sheffield, the tenants would have to wait until Swig and his team released an offering plan spelling out how much they planned to sell the apartments for and what, if any, insider deals might be offered. But if the tenants needed reason for optimism, all they had to do was look to the press coverage, where Swig, always charismatic with reporters, had worked his magic.

That spring, the New York Sun, in an article headlined "A True Believer in Building Relationships," marveled that Swig could not only discuss Chinese history, and was well-versed in Middle Eastern politics, but that he ran four to five miles every morning, lifted weights, meditated (Mr. Swig has his own "mind-calming mantras") and "regularly takes on 14-foot waves." (Never mind that he surfed in Long Island.) Swig was portrayed as a businessman for whom lucre wasn't the only goal.

"No matter how smart you may be, how good a negotiator, everything ultimately depends on how you approach people," Swig was quoted as saying. "My belief is that the best asset I could create is the people with whom I work. Truly."

As for tenants: "I always say that I'm not really an owner of buildings and properties," Swig explained. "I'm really in the tenant-service business."

The article would serve both as the high-water mark for Swig's image, and, later, an ironic artifact of the times.

In July 2005, when the developers released a preliminary offering plan spelling out the price of each unit at the Sheffield, tenants were disheartened. There were to be no insider deals. Prices, one longtime resident would later grouse to a reporter, "were pretty much off the charts."

Kevin R. McConnell, an attorney for the tenants at the Sheffield, recalled meeting with Swig and his attorney Stuart Saft at Saft's office and handing over a list of inducements and tenant requests that would help those who wished to remain buy their apartments. According to McConnell, Saft and Swig took copious notes and promised to meet again.

At the second meeting, "Mr. Swig and Mr. Saft showed up and handed us a piece of paper and said 'we have reviewed your list and we are not going to make any changes. Good luck to you all.' So 'fuck you!'" McConnell recalled. "There was no willingness to negotiate, no willingness to extend, to these longtime tenants, any kind of concessions. It was all you know, trench warfare."

Offering insider prices, Greg Kirschenbaum, Swig's director of residential operations, would later tell the Times, was "unnecessary in a building so dominated by free-market units, and would artificially depress the asking prices when they hit the open market."

"If there was an insider price, I'd be competing against myself," he said.

There was certainly money to be made. Swig and his partners had borrowed roughly $518 million, $100 million on top of the purchase price, with a senior mortgage secured by the property and several tiers of junior mezzanine financing.[44] In addition, Hoyda and Levy had each contributed $17 million of their own money while Swig had put up $8 million, bringing the total capitalization of the project to $542 million. They planned to use about $38 million to fund the cost of what they would later describe as "largely cosmetic" renovations of the units and common areas.

With an average ask of $1,358 a square foot, the prices were more than $300 higher than the Manhattan average and crept up the higher you got in the building. A one-bedroom on the 30th floor was listed at $877,000. A 550-square-foot studio on the 49th floor cost $1.3 million. A one-bedroom on the top floor then occupied by a rent-stabilized tenant was $1.9 million.[45]

---

44 Affidavit of Kent M. Swig in YL Sheffield LLC v. Wells Fargo. n.d.

45 Healy, Patrick O'Gilfoil. "The End of the Fabled Insider Deal." *The New York Times.* September 4, 2005.

Relations between the Sheffield's new landlords and tenants quickly deteriorated.

Rent-stabilized tenants began to complain of maintenance issues that they suspected were a ploy to get them out. Meanwhile, the exodus of market-rate tenants had already begun, as Swig and his partners declined to renew expiring leases.

Not everybody, however, was willing to go so quietly. And as they watched their neighbors move out, a small, determined core began to form, and fight.

The battle shaping up at the Sheffield was by no means unique. By the winter of 2006, more than 60 condominium conversion projects in Manhattan, encompassing 7,000 units, were filed with the state.[46]

In August 2005, real estate investors Peter Kalikow and Jeremiah O'Connor paid $623 million for Manhattan House, a storied white brick complex on the Upper East Side where Grace Kelly once lived. With 583 apartments, it was smaller than the Sheffield. But after paying a record price of $1 million per apartment, 33 percent more than what Swig and his partners had paid across town, the new owners of the five 20-story towers on East 66th Street were also banking on big returns.

To make their investment work, they too were planning significant upgrades. And they were also heavily reliant on expiring leases—and vacating apartments—to meet the numbers they'd relied upon when they submitted their winning bid.

In the years that followed, the technique became one of the central planks of those pushing legislation to protect tenant rights and rent reform legislation. But back in the easy money days of 2006, with prices for potential conversions spiraling ever upwards, the impact competing

---

46 Barbanel, Josh. "Tenants Stuck as Apartments Become Condos." *The New York Times.* April 30, 2006.

bidders' aggressive profit estimates would have on tenants was only just beginning to become clear, and the battle lines were not yet fully drawn. For decades, Upper West Side cocktail party chatter had featured tales of neighbors and friends who made a mint taking advantage of opportunities offered up by landlords during the condo-conversion craze of the 1980s. Now different kinds of stories began to replace them.

Just like at the Sheffield, Manhattan House tenants, many of them elderly with nowhere else to go, began to mobilize, circulating a list of those who had been forced to move out. They hired counsel and geared up for a fight in the courts.

By the spring of 2006, both battles were coming to a head. A small group of holdouts at the Sheffield hired their own attorneys and argued that conversion laws were designed to protect market-rate tenants, too. At Manhattan House, several hundred tenants had put money into a legal fund and hired McConnell to represent them.

They took grievances to the media.

"These projects, the first large wave of condominium conversions in New York in 20 years, are cutting into the supply of rental apartments, driving rents higher, and ushering in a wrenching period of uncertainty for many existing tenants," the Times noted.

The problem was particularly acute on the Upper West and Upper East Sides, where many apartments were no longer rent regulated, according to McConnell.

"I still contend it was really devastating to those areas," he would reflect years later. "The building is like a small neighborhood, people know each other, and a lot of people, even though not protected by rent stabilization, had lived in their apartments for an extended period of time. They all were neighbors and then, wham-O, these eviction proceedings started coming down and decimated the tenants and the tenant population and indeed the tenant community. Landlords did sweeps and they basically tried to throw out as many people as they could."

But it wasn't just tenants in buildings ripe for condo conversions under pressure. In the summer of 2006, a property would go on the market that would highlight the issue of affordable housing and set the real estate industry and tenants groups at odds like nothing before it. This megacomplex, a bastion of the middle class, would become emblematic of the profit-versus-purpose battle being waged between starry-eyed developers and the city residents they were supposed to serve.

XIV

"The Mama of All Residential Offerings"

Stuy Town

Stuyvesant Town–Peter Cooper Village was a storied housing complex that had long been the kind of community where cops, firemen, and teachers could afford to raise families. With 11,232 apartments, the sprawling collection of 110 red-brick buildings overlooking the East River dwarfed the Sheffield, Manhattan House, and indeed, everything else in the city.

Sitting on 80 acres stretching from East 14th to East 23rd streets and First Avenue to Avenue C, the complex was so vast and the location so prime that every major developer in the city would be interested.[47]

---

[47] Bagli, Charles V. "Harry Macklowe Gambles Again." *The New York Times*. October 6, 2013.

"This was the mama of all residential offerings and you knew it was selling into a piping hot climate for large deals," Doug Harmon, a top investment-sales broker then at Eastdil, would later tell the Times.

The outcome of the auction, expected to break all records, would dovetail in unexpected ways with both Swig's own fortunes and those of Steve Ross and Related. The saga of the complex would also have a lasting impact on New York City real estate, affect the fortunes of tens of thousands of New York tenants, and serve as a rare humbling of market-rate forces.

Built in 1947 by the Metropolitan Life Insurance Company at the urging of Mayor Fiorello La Guardia and Robert Moses, Stuy Town was envisioned as a middle-class residential community that would help relieve the city's already chronic housing crunch.

A plaque at the complex, dedicated to MetLife president Frederick Ecker, said he had "brought into being this project, and others like it, that families of moderate means might live in health, comfort, and dignity in parklike communities, and that a pattern might be set of private enterprise productively devoted to public service."

In the years after its construction, Stuy Town would become an oasis for thousands of white World War II vets and their middle-class families, and a number of prominent figures would call it home, including New York Times columnist David Brooks, President Obama's political guru David Axelrod, and NPR's Robert Siegel.

"When I grew up there, it was a place of window fans and clothes-dryer racks stretched over the bathtubs," Siegel recalled on air after the sale was announced. "A teacher or a fireman or a cop could live there, in Manhattan, in a place with lawns, trees, hedges, and even a couple of fountains... It was an inner city oasis with no rich people and no poor people."

Stuy Town was in fact just one of a number of large middle-class residential complexes MetLife would become famous for building, including Parkchester in the Bronx, the Riverton Houses in Harlem, and Park Merced in California.

For decades, the idea of middle-class housing fit with the ethos of MetLife, which prospered by selling affordable insurance to low- and middle-income families and was famous for the kind of paternalistic corporate culture large American companies were known for in the early and middle parts of the century. It was the kind of company where 19,000 employees ate free meals on white china in the company dining halls.

But that was a different era. In 2000, amid a wave of insurance-industry consolidations, the company had gone public to raise the capital it needed for buyouts. And things changed rapidly.

For decades, MetLife had maintained long waiting lists for its rent-regulated apartments at Stuy Town, and filled vacancies with other middle-class families who needed affordable housing. But with its new emphasis on the bottom line, the company took a different approach. Under state rent laws that went into effect in 1997, landlords were allowed to remove an apartment from rent regulation after a vacancy once its rent rose above $2,000 a month. To get the rents above the threshold, landlords could renovate the apartment and pass the cost of doing so onto future tenants, hiking rents by 1/40th of the cost of improvements.

Soon after going public, the company launched a $50 million capital-improvement program for Stuy Town, spending an average of $30,000 to $40,000 to upgrade each vacant unit prior to renting it out to new tenants. The company also introduced income guidelines, requiring new tenants to demonstrate certain income levels to qualify for apartments there.

The feel of the complex began to change, as 20-and-30-somethings, many with incomes well above $100,000, began to move in.

In a 2001 Times article, State Senator Roy M. Goodman, a longtime champion of tenants at Stuy Town and elsewhere, articulated the rising concerns of many and emphasized that the basic mission for MetLife's project had always been "serving middle-income families."

"I consider MetLife to be one of the best landlords I know of," Goodman said. "But lately, with the demand for more revenue, they seem to have changed their emphasis."

Contractually, MetLife was no longer obliged to keep the two complexes middle-class. But to many, it seemed a gray area. The two complexes would never have been built without generous city incentives. The intent had clearly been to create and preserve affordable housing. And it had tremendous symbolic meaning in New York. Without places like Stuy Town, where would the city's teachers, firemen, and policemen live?

Tensions began to rise. Under the 1997 rent guidelines, MetLife was also allowed to pass on the costs of large-scale capital improvements to existing tenants through rent increases — which the tenant association fought in court. In one lawsuit, typical for the time, the tenants challenged an application for a rent increase to help pay for the rewiring of Stuy Town. In another battle, they challenged the right of the company to institute the use of key cards, suspecting the company was intent on using the system to gather data on the comings and goings of the tenants.

Even so, within a couple years the situation had reached an uneasy status quo.

Then, in January 2005, MetLife announced it was acquiring a large portion of Citigroup's insurance business for $11.8 billion.[48] To help fund the megadeal, MetLife planned to sell real estate assets.

The first big sale came within two months, when the company offered up One Madison Avenue, a 100-year-old complex on 23rd Street and Madison Avenue which, with its 41-story office tower, had served as the company's home for nearly a century. The auction drew more than a

---

48   Bagli, Charles V. "Harry Macklowe Gambles Again." *The New York Times*. October 6, 2013.

dozen offers, and the winning bidder, the mega REIT SL Green, paid $918 million with an eye toward condo conversion.[49]

Less than a week later came word that the company had sold the 58-story MetLife building, at 200 Park Avenue, an iconic rectangular edifice above Grand Central Terminal that had been featured in the movie "Godzilla." At 2.8 million square feet, 200 Park was the largest office building in the world. And the winning bid of $1.72 billion was a new record for an office tower.

The prize went to Tishman Speyer, which already owned the Chrysler Building and Rockefeller Center, and had bid unsuccessfully against Macklowe for the GM Building and Ross for the Time Warner Center site.

But even those huge deals would be dwarfed by the value of Stuy Town, which some suggested could fetch north of $5 billion.

MetLife began homing in on the right broker to handle the sale, and settled on CBRE's Darcy Stacom, the same dealmaker who had worked on Swig's Sheffield and 25 Broad Street buys, as well as Tishman's purchase of the MetLife Building.

Many of the same groups that had bid for Time Warner Center and the GM Building were ready to throw their hats in the ring. And their backers were a who's who of the new sources of capital available to developers in the globalized chase for prime New York City assets. Steven Roth and Michael Fascitelli's Vornado teamed up with the Emir of Qatar. William Mack's Apollo of Time Warner Center fame was also in the mix.

For Ross and Related, the deal seemed fitting. Ross, after all, had cut his teeth on affordable housing and still boasted one of the largest portfolios in the nation. To prepare for the bid, Related spent $500,000 to study coal-tar pollution left behind by a gas plant and storage facilities that

49   Leuck, Thomas J. "$1 Billion Dollar Deal Turns MetLife into Condos." *The New York Times.* April 31, 2005.

once occupied the site. The firm had begun talks with Lehman Brothers to partner up on the acquisition more than a year earlier.

Their primary rival, it seemed, would be Tishman Speyer, the same group they had squared off against for the Coliseum site. Prior to winning that deal, Ross could look to Tishman Speyer as the kind of pedigreed, top-tier real estate company that Related could only aspire to be, steeped in the kind of credibility that only came with owning a truly important part of the city. But with the success of Time Warner Center and the transformation of Columbus Circle an unqualified success, Related was now competing as an equal. Not that Ross was about to admit that.

"I respect them a lot," Ross would later say when asked about Tishman Speyer. "I think we're better than they are but that's beside the point. It's a different kind of organization. We're much more entrepreneurial, they operate more as a fund, and you know, we're all owned by the people who work here. We don't have outside partners."

Tishman Speyer was founded by Jerry Speyer, who had married Lynne Tishman in 1964 and joined Tishman Realty and Construction, the firm founded by Lynne's great-grandfather Julius Tishman in 1898. When the firm fell on tough times, Speyer and his father-in-law liquidated the company and reorganized it in 1977 as Tishman Speyer.

Speyer had built the firm into perhaps the city's most prestigious real estate concern. In addition to the Chrysler Building and Rockefeller Center, the company's portfolio included properties such as the Lipstick Building and the New York Times building. It usually teamed up with outside partners or investors to finance buys, and many of the firm's key assets had been snapped up during downturns. By 2005, the company controlled 120 office buildings around the world, spanning 74 million square feet of space. And Speyer was widely regarded as an industry statesman, serving as vice chairman of the Museum of Modern Art, an owner of the New York Yankees, a member of the Council on Foreign

Relations and chairman of the Federal Reserve Bank of New York. He was a major Democratic-party donor and behind-the-scenes force, one of the most connected men in the whole city.

It was Speyer's son and heir-apparent, Rob Speyer, however, who would lead the firm's bid for Stuy Town. Square-jawed and fit, the younger Speyer had grown up on the Upper East Side, attended Columbia College and then gone to work for two newspapers, the New York Observer and the New York Daily News, where the scion prided himself on his willingness to investigate and report on the seedier sides of New York City. The CBS news show "48 Hours" had followed him around in 1994, as he discussed taking the subway every day to "the worst neighborhood in the city."

"Some of my friends joke that I do the tragedy of the day and it's — somebody has to do it," Speyer said in a voice-over of footage that showed him interviewing a man, and then flashed to a headline that read "Mom burns car, kills 2 tots as granny looks on."

"And I — I'm happy to do it," he added. This is everything to me — I keep every byline I have. I live and breathe my job. There's no greater thrill than being on the front page of the Daily News. I love my job. I love my job."

But the pull of skyline-shaping proved too strong, and Speyer, who had joined the family firm a year later in 1995, took over responsibility for all New York City business in 2001, and, by most accounts, brought the same enthusiasm and drive of his newspaperman career to his real estate dealings.

Being a reporter had been the ideal classroom for someone destined to one day stand atop the New York power structure and play the role of kingmaker. It had left young Rob with a deeper understanding of how both city and state government worked, how power was wielded, and how the media could be used as a tool to influence city and state policy.

Jerry Speyer had served as chairman of the Real Estate Board of New York from 1986 to 1988, just as Rob's grandfather Robert Tishman had from 1972 to 1975. And the family was deeply involved with the powerful group that spearheaded efforts to protect industry interests in both Albany and City Hall.

As it happened, the Stuy Town deal was coming at a high-water mark of sorts for relations between the industry and both the development-obsessed Michael Bloomberg and the development-friendly George Pataki, who was then in his 10th year in the Governor's Mansion. Every year the rent laws came up for renewal. And every year under Pataki, "they'd move to make them more pro-landlord," longtime New York Times real estate reporter Charlie Bagli, whose book "Other People's Money" detailed the Stuy Town saga, would later recall in an interview with *The Real Deal*.

The pro-industry bent and the involvement of industry lobbyists had become so routine that one year, the goateed Bagli recalled, former REBNY president Steven Spinola was "in the Senate office writing the legislation when I talked to him."

"And I was shocked — not that he was doing that — I was shocked that he called me," Bagli said.

What was true in Albany was doubly true in Lower Manhattan, at City Hall.

The industry had also cemented its alliances with city and state politicians by showering them with campaign contributions. The City Council was relatively weak, compared to the mayor. But it did have power over land use, which was why City Council races were awash in almost as much real estate money as Assembly and state Senate races. All told, in the first two decades of the millennium, the industry would pour more than $100 million into state-level elections in New York, according to the National Institute on Money in Politics.

When it came to party affiliation, industry players were pragmatists.

"Even some of the old real estate families, they used to have a designated guy that would go to the Democrats and one that went to the Republicans,"

Bagli recalled. "It was a lot of money that was at stake here."

All of this put ordinary tenants, who paid taxes but weren't usually throwing thousands of dollars at city and state politicians, at a distinct disadvantage.

Even so, the auction of Stuy Town presented a quandary for the Bloomberg administration, which had unveiled a $7.5 billion plan that looked to create or preserve 165,000 units of low-and-middle-income housing by 2013. It was to be the largest affordable-housing initiative the city had ever seen, Bloomberg had boasted.[50] Now, some housing activists warned, the plan was in jeopardy.

"This sale is the perfect illustration of the hole in the bottom of the bucket of the Bloomberg housing plan," Michael McKee, of Tenants PAC, told the New York Sun. "The plan deals only with production. They will never build as much as we're losing."

In response, city officials promised to work with any potential buyers to ensure that affordability would be maintained, and pointed out that rent-controlled tenants were protected under the law.

But some weren't so sure. Daniel Garodnick, a City Council member who grew up in Peter Cooper Village, knew as soon as he heard the news that the complex was up for sale that it could prove calamitous for tenants.[51]

At a meeting with the tenants association soon after the news came out, he warned that only a tenant-backed bid could save the community. With multiple bidders vying for the prize, the sales price was likely to be astronomical. If tenants thought MetLife had become aggressive in recent

50 Gardiner, Jill. "Mayor Announces 'Landmark' City Plan for Middle-Income Housing." *The New York Sun.* October 20, 2006.

51 Bagli, Charles V. *Other People's Money.* Dutton. April 4, 2013.

years, it was nothing compared to what they might face from new owners struggling to meet the kind of overheated projections many of the bidders were likely to rely upon to put forth the highest offer.

Their worst fears seemed to be confirmed when details of marketing materials began circulating among potential bidders. At the time, close to three quarters of the apartments in the complex's Stuyvesant portion were still protected under the rent-stabilization system. The materials suggested that in 2008 alone, 800 apartments could be deregulated. And that by 2018, the percentage of affordable units would fall to just 30 percent, to 2,539 from 6,251. Rents collected could more than double to $519 million. At Peter Cooper, numbers could be reduced to 712 affordable units from 1,734, with rents rising to $170 million.

With "aggressive investigation of potential stabilization violations," the memo prepared by Stacom's team suggested, a new owner could deregulate 1,000 units in both complexes in 2008 alone, "approximately double the current rate." By investing in major capital improvements, a new owner could speed up rent deregulation and win additional rent increases, even in the rent-stabilized apartments.

Tenants were hard at work preparing a bid of their own, which city officials were considering subsidizing.

"From the seller's perspective, they can get the same price," Emily Youssouf, president of the city's Housing Development Corporation, told the Times. "As long as they can make as much money, I think that's probably their primary concern."

But soon, other city officials concluded that the turnover rate in the memo was far too aggressive and unrealistic, and that the projected sales price did not make sense. Bloomberg had then assured MetLife executives the city had no plans to intervene.[52]

Dan Doctoroff would later frame the decision as a choice between protecting old units or creating new ones — the city could either use a limited pool of money to save Stuy Town, or they could use the same amount of money to create more units elsewhere.

"We faced a really difficult choice," Doctoroff would later explain. "You can create many more units in Queens and have money left over. What's the right thing to do? We obviously chose to create more units. It doesn't mean affordable housing has to be perfectly distributed in every neighborhood. Instead, the goal was to make the whole city better so people would have much better choices. I think it requires really aggressive land-use changes, it requires a lot of money, and it requires a recognition that not every neighborhood is going to be the same. But then you can create greater neighborhoods all across the city."

To soften the blow, the city staged a carefully timed press conference two days after the Stuy Town bidder was to be announced. At the press conference, Bloomberg announced the city had purchased 24 acres in Long Island City across the Hudson from the United Nations, and planned to construct the "largest middle-income housing project since Brooklyn's Starrett City was built in 1974."[53] (Inspired by Stuy Town, the owners of Starrett City would two months later announce they were putting the 140-acre, 12,000-resident, middle-income complex up for sale.)

On the same 24-acre site where Doctoroff had proposed to build an Olympic Village, up to 5,000 units of housing for families earning between $60,000 and $145,000 a year would rise.

---

52   Bagli, Charles V. "Harry Macklowe Gambles Again." *The New York Times*. October 6, 2013.

53   Bagli, Charles V. *Other People's Money*. Dutton. April 4, 2013.

Doctoroff told reporters the city subsidy on the Queens deal is "roughly half of what it would have cost" to preserve the housing at Stuyvesant Town.

"We can get two units here [in Queens] for every one [in Stuy Town], plus we get a major increase in the housing stock," Doctoroff said. The city hoped to issue an RFP by 2007 and start construction in 2008. However, the project, which came to be known as Hunter's Point South, would not break ground until 2013, with the second of three phases only kicking off in 2019.

After a high-profile bidding process, Tishman Speyer would emerge victorious in the Stuy Town bid, shelling out a record-shattering $5.4 billion. In the October 17 press release announcing their win, the Speyers promised to protect the legacy of the complex.

"Stuyvesant Town and Peter Cooper Village have provided thousands of New Yorkers a beautiful place to live for almost 60 years," Rob Speyer said. "We are proud to play a role in maintaining its place in our city's future." Jerry added that the firm was "honored to become stewards of the property," and that "no one should be concerned about a sudden or dramatic shift in this neighborhood's makeup, character, or charm."[54]

But the price they paid would make it impossible to live up to that promise.

---

54   Bagli, Charles V. "$5.4 Billion Bid Wins Complexes in New York Deal." *The New York Times*. October 18, 2006.

XV

Miracle on the Hudson

The Chance to Develop a Megasite

If losing the Stuy Town deal stung Steve Ross, he didn't show it. He had plenty to distract him.

The success of Time Warner Center and Related's expansion into other realms had catapulted him to a new level of wealth and influence, exceeding even that of his famous uncle Max Fisher, the gas station magnate and advisor to presidents.

In 1993, Fisher had donated $20 million to his alma mater, Ohio State, prompting the university to rename the business school after him. In December 2003,[55] a few months after the official opening of Time Warner, Ross had returned to his alma mater and asked how much it would take to convince them to rename the business school after him.

---

55   Service, S.N. "Business Education at Michigan: A Narrative History." *States News Service*. March 23, 2017.

A few months later, after Ross ponied up a record $100 million, the University of Michigan announced the renaming of the business school to the Stephen M. Ross School of Business, and the triumphant mogul addressed the student body.

"It seems it was only yesterday that I sat here as a student," Ross said.[56] "Never would I have dreamed that the school would one day bear my name."

Fisher, by then 96 and wheelchair-bound, took the mic and revealed that it was he who, all those years earlier, had lent his nephew tuition money to attend the school. Jokingly, he attributed Ross's $100 million donation to his turning down Ross's attempts to repay him.

"I said, 'Stephen, I don't want your money. But I would like to see you use that money for another fine purpose.' I want you to know that I started all this!"

Ross now occupied the office he had pledged decades before to build for himself overlooking the park, and "commuted" there by elevator every day from his full-floor 8,300-square-foot[57] penthouse in the Southern Tower of Time Warner Center.[58] His beautiful, accomplished, and far younger second wife, the jewelry designer Kara Ross, would later offer Architectural Digest Magazine a look at their palatial home and the lifestyle it afforded them. (Ross and Kara would end up divorcing in 2021.)

"Living above Central Park like this feels like you're actually living in the park," she said. "It's as if you're in a painting that's always changing,

---

56 George, M. "$100 Million for Business School." *The Detroit Free Press*. September 10, 2004.

57 Colman, David. "Jewelry Designer Kara Ross's Home in New York City." *Architectural Digest*. March 2015.

58 Brennan, M. "Stephen Ross the Billionaire Who Is Rebuilding New York." *Forbes*. March 7, 2012.

from green to yellow to red to gray and slowly back to green again. It has a kind of power that most art can only dream about."

In 2006, Ross made his debut on the Forbes 400 list of richest Americans, with an estimated fortune of $2.5 billion. And his firm's future prospects looked bright, too. Just a fortnight before the Stuy Town announcement, the city and MTA had announced a new plan detailing an opportunity that electrified the developer community.

Originally, the city had planned to take ownership of any new buildings in Hudson Yards and lease them back to developers for 30 years, using the payments to pay off the bonds. But now, they planned to offer the rights to a vast 26-acre site to private developers through a competitive bidding process, and use the money to help pay for the planned extension of the No. 7 line. The agreement included time limits, with the MTA aiming to sell the property in about a year.

The largest development opportunity in U.S. history was suddenly up for grabs.

For Ross, the project offered the ultimate blank canvas — and the ultimate challenge. It made even what Related had accomplished at Columbus Circle look puny by comparison.

"I don't think there's ever been anything like this — on this scale," he would later declare.[59]

Like that desolate, windswept expanse of Columbus Circle in the 1990s, the seeming isolation and scale of the railyards struck most observers as daunting — but this was no mere "hole in the donut." The canvas was gargantuan, stretching from 10th Avenue to the West Side Highway, and three city streets from 30th to 33rd. At 26 acres, the site could hold nearly six Time Warner Centers. Or, put another way, 20 football fields, eight

59 Bagli, C.V. "Real Estate Executive with Hand in Trump Projects Rose from Tangled Past." *The New York Times*. December 17, 2007.

and a half baseball stadiums, six and a half U.S. Capitol Buildings. It was nearly a fifth larger even than Rockefeller Center in Midtown with its 19 commercial buildings, ice skating rink, and long plazas.

Like the Columbus Circle of old, Hudson Yards wasn't much to look at. Perched on the very western edge of the city, the sprawling rail yards were visible from the West Side Highway, the main artery running north to south along the Hudson River. And most New Yorkers were used to averting their eyes from the vast, gloomy expanse when they passed it, gazing out instead to the more cheerful shores of New Jersey and the aging, industrial piers of Weehawken directly across the river.

Beneath this train storage yard lay a maze of underground tracks that Amtrak used to maneuver in and out of Penn Station and that connected various points up and down the East Coast. It was a crucial artery, which added to the magnitude of the task — whoever won the bidding would have to construct a huge platform over the existing tunnels, railyard, and 30 tracks. It would be a massive and tremendously expensive engineering challenge, requiring a developer to raise and then shell out hundreds of millions of dollars before they could even begin to think about profit.

The winner would also be bound by a number of conditions hammered out between the city and local community groups. Roughly 14 acres, more than half of the total project area, would be devoted to public open space. There would be space for a cultural component, a large performance space that would be known as "The Shed," just as there had been at Columbus Circle. The city had also agreed the site should include a new public school and a large number of affordable housing units. So it was clear that in order to recoup their costs, whoever won the deal would need to build their buildings tall and luxurious enough to charge a premium.

All told, the developer of Hudson Yards would be permitted to construct up to 13 million square feet. It would be a multibillion-dollar city-within-a-city. (The price tag would eventually top $25 billion, making it the most expensive private development in U.S. history.)

As Ross and his team began to evaluate the opportunity, it was clear that if you could get past the intimidation factor, there was plenty to get excited about.

The city and state had committed to spend at least $4 billion in the area. The $2 billion, 1.5-mile-long expansion of the No. 7 line was perhaps the most obvious contribution for the project.

"The history of the City of New York teaches us that development follows subways," Senator Chuck Schumer had told business leaders a few months earlier. "The Hudson Rail Yards is the last significant developable parcel in Midtown Manhattan and building the No. 7 extension will light a stick of development dynamite under the Far West Side."

Other projects also promised to have an impact. There was the $465 million in upgrades to the Javits convention center, which would sit on the edge of the yards and promise a steady draw of visitors. There was a promised $440 million to build the Hudson River Park nearby along the riverfront, and another $500 million for the expansion of the High Line, which would feed directly onto the eastern edge of the platform.

These were precisely the kind of amenities Bloomberg, Doctoroff, and a whole host of other acolytes of what was known as "the new urbanism" believed would attract the creative class that cities across the world were competing for to revitalize their centers.

And indeed, Chelsea and the Meatpacking District were already among the hottest areas in the city.

"In New York people follow the young," Ross would later explain, "because people in New York have a lot of energy and they think they're young and they follow where the young people are going."

Early on, Ross had mastered the minutiae of tax law, and could navigate a thicket of government regulations to win affordable-housing contracts and raise money through syndication. He had moved on to 80-20 housing, another government program whose byzantine structure dissuaded some developers. He was well-prepared to navigate the complexities of the Hudson Yards bid.

Ross liked to joke that he hired young people with PhDs — they were "poor, hungry, and driven." But in fact, what Ross most valued was young hires who relished daunting projects.

"You want bright people who love dealing with complexity and challenges," he said.

All mixed-use projects were intricate. But Hudson Yards, given its sheer scale and transit challenges, would likely top the list. Ross believed — and could argue convincingly — that his company was ideally organized to take on the challenge. Elite developers tended to specialize — Gary Barnett's Extell, for instance, excelled at luxury residential, while Brookfield Properties, at the time, was best known for shopping malls. For mixed-use projects, they teamed up with other developers whose skills complemented their own.

Ross liked to argue that most of his rivals really only cared about what they were doing and "don't care about the others," which led to battles for resources, at the expense of the overall project. Related, by contrast, he said, had spent over a decade cultivating all the specialties under one roof.

Increasingly, Ross had become an evangelist of the idea that those flocking to cities preferred a specific kind of neighborhood — one where they could live, work, and play.

That idea might not sound radical. But the 20th century's devotion to parkways and federal highways led both to the rise of the suburbs and new urban zoning policies. The middle-class lived in the suburbs and worked in the cities. They shopped in commercial centers. Urban zoning policies reflected that — often segregating residential, commercial, and industrial developments from one another, creating pockets of land inhospitable to multiple uses. This was one of the reasons that Lower

Manhattan had for years been a desolate wasteland at night, why so much land had sat fallow along the Hudson River before the aggressive rezonings of the Bloomberg era, and how you got massive cocoons of housing like Stuy Town and Co-op City.

But there was something at play now. You saw snippets of it at Columbus Circle, where people would step out of their offices and shop and eat in the neighborhood. But that was only the first step, Ross thought.

"People will be looking to live in nodes, which will be more sustainable so they won't have to travel," Ross said. "I think it's the future, what everybody will want to live in."

His Hudson Yards would be the ultimate expression of that vision.

Bidding for the prized Far West Side site opened up in October 2007, more than two and a half years after the crucial rezoning and a few months after Eliot Spitzer, a real estate scion whose family owned some of the city's toniest rental buildings, became governor of New York. And the whole city was now paying attention. Bidders included the city's elite development firms, among them Related, Extell, Durst and Vornado in a joint bid, Brookfield, and Tishman Speyer.

"Hudson Yards is one of the largest land grabs in New York history," New York Magazine opined in an article headlined "West World: Who stands to make a killing as a new Midtown goes up." The article called the project "a developers' bonanza on the scale of Rockefeller Center," noting it was worth as much as $7 billion. It would have an impact on not just the extension of the No. 7 train, the proposed Javits Center expansion, the High Line, and the Farley Post Office transformation into Moynihan Station, but also "the adjectives applied to Bloomberg and Eliot Spitzer in the history books." Some of the developers involved in redeveloping the West Side, the article's authors added, would get "extremely rich."

Late on a Wednesday in November 2007, Ross got the news that Related had 48 hours to put together the materials for a public exhibition of their Hudson Yards proposal. Though the company had spent months laying the groundwork for their plan, they found they had to scramble to meet the deadline of Nov. 17, which is when the MTA and the city planned to showcase the firm's vision for the 26-acre development site, along with those of four other bidders, in a tiny storefront on Vanderbilt Avenue and 43rd Street, directly across the street from Grand Central Station.

At Related headquarters on the 18th, 19th, and 20th floors of Time Warner Center, the deadline set off a frenzy of activity, as assistants raced to print out renderings, unplug monitors, disassemble intricately carved models, and pack everything into boxes to haul across town.[60]

Later, at the East Side exhibition site, representatives for each of the competitors drew lots to determine how to divvy up territory in the cramped space. Brookfield, which owned World Financial Center downtown, drew the lucky first number and chose to set up directly to the right of where the visitors were to enter; Related was relegated to a far side of the room.

Still, as Ross' team assembled their display and prepared for its unveiling, they were confident.

Inside a glass display case on a low-slung rectangular platform the length of a banquet table rose roughly two dozen white model buildings arrayed around a long plaza, fronted by a lush patch of greenery and a grove of tiny model trees that stretched in ribbons around the edges of the development and directly through its middle. But the focal point of the display stood at the back: Rising up from the far end, to tower over the rest of the model, was an oversized rendering of a majestic, two-million-square foot, glass — and-steel skyscraper, backlit by the soft orange, blue, and yellow hues of a sunset over the Hudson.

---

60   Schuerman, Matthew. "Developers Scramble as Spitzer Caps Financing." *The New York Observer*. March 5, 2007.

A few nights after the exhibit went up, representatives from Related would take the microphone in front of the press and public, put up a picture of the same building, and spell out the firm's vision.

The development would mirror the visual diversity of the city at large, with the architecture ranging from masonry to glass and steel, a mix of apartment buildings, hotels and offices throughout, and space for residents all across the economic spectrum, including a significant amount of affordable housing units. (Unsaid, of course, was that the market-rate apartments would mirror Time Warner Center in their opulence.)

And as with Time Warner Center, a media company would anchor the project. Rupert Murdoch's News Corp would be headquartered in the centerpiece skyscraper, at the base of which would sit an all-glass rectangular atrium with retail and open space.

News Corp's presence would bring to Hudson Yards not just the prestige of the Wall Street Journal, the buzz of the New York Post, the energy of its 24-hour cable news channel, but also the glamor of 20th Century Fox, which, Ross noted, promised to hold premier screenings on the plaza out front.

"One of the things it seemed to us about building a space is to make it exciting, to make it active," said Eugene Kohn, one of the principal architects on the project. "And we're very fortunate that a major media tenant has decided to take the key tower — the focal tower."

Kohn then pulled up a rendering of a crowded plaza at night, filled with New Yorkers, all moving in anticipation towards the glowing, multistory, all-glass atrium.

"What's probably most important about the tower is what takes place at its base," Kohn said. "We see it as a great and active exciting place that our major tenant will help to activate as a public space."

As Kohn wrapped up his presentation, Ross had reason to be optimistic. He knew that his deal with News Corp gave him an edge, just as he believed his deal with Dick Parsons and Time Warner had propelled Related to the front of the pack for the Coliseum site.

Neither Extell nor Brookfield offered up tenants, though some of Related's other competitors did. Tishman Speyer had recruited Morgan Stanley as both a development partner and occupier, while Vornado and the Durst Organization promised to build a new headquarters for Condé Nast, already a tenant at their Times Square building.

Ross had another edge. Though the numbers weren't yet public, it would later emerge that Ross had bid $1.049 billion, topping bids of $1.015 billion by Durst-Vornado, Brookfield's $908 million, Tishman's $819 million, and Extell's $598 million.[61]

By then, Ross had restructured his firm in a way that insulated it from the kind of exposure that had almost destroyed the entire company during the downturn of the early 1990s. And he was also in the final stages of closing a deal that would set him up for anything the market might throw at him.

In December 2007, Ross had put the finishing touches on a major financing deal, selling equity and convertible debt which amounted to a roughly 25 percent stake in the company. The deal raised nearly $1.4 billion in investments from Goldman Sachs and MSD Capital (an entity that managed Michael Dell's personal wealth), which bought 7.5 percent equity stakes in Related. Meanwhile, three international companies, including an affiliate of Abu Dhabi's sovereign wealth fund Mubadala Development Co. and Saudi conglomerate Olayan Group, made convertible debt investments. With all of the company's projects at the time already fully financed, it was a hefty war chest.

"It's a combination of having cash on hand and having this investor

---

61   Brown, Eliot. "Related's Rail Yards Triumph." *The New York Observer*. March 19, 2008.

group react quickly to new opportunities," Related's Jeff Blau said at the time. "We're now positioned to have more liquidity when the marketplace has less, setting ourselves up for the future."

The deal allowed Ross to convert part of his stake to cash without giving up any governance power and without having to pay any interest on the debt.

"Everything was priced to perfection and we took out over a billion dollars tax-free," Ross would later recall. "It was probably the best deal I ever did." (In 2020, Ross repeated the playbook, scoring a convertible-debt investment from Saudi Arabia's sovereign wealth fund.)

Of Hudson Yards, Ross was equally confident.

"We had an office tenant, we had this building," Ross would later recall. "And people had faith. We had worked with the MTA on Time Warner Center and we delivered on everything we said we would do and developed a great relationship. Everybody thought we were going to win. The city thought we were going to win."

Unfortunately for Ross, things wouldn't go as planned.

XVI

Could You Spare $1 Billion?

Macklowe's EOP Play

I t was an opportunity to supersize his empire in one fell swoop.

When Roy March casually mentioned the potential transaction to Harry Macklowe, the 69-year-old mogul was smitten — just as the canny Eastdil dealmaker, with his shoulder-length blond locks and signature pocket square, had suspected he would be.[62] While Ross was dreaming about Hudson Yards, it was a collection of Midtown office towers that captivated Macklowe.

More than 7 million square feet of Class-A office space in the heart of Manhattan's trophy business district could be up for grabs, a portfolio that would instantly double the size of Macklowe's empire.

The collection included gems such as 527 Madison, a sleek, 26-story

---

62   Ward, Vicky. *The Liar's Ball*. Wiley. October 27, 2014.

boutique tower on 54th Street; 1540 Broadway, the 44-story glassy skyscraper that was once the headquarters of media conglomerate Bertelsmann; and One Worldwide Plaza, the 50-story office complex built by William Zeckendorf Jr. and designed by David Childs, which occupied an entire city block between 49th and 50th streets on Eighth Avenue, boasted 360-degree views of Midtown, and was second in value only to Macklowe's GM Building.

"These are assets that you never find together in a lifetime," Macklowe would later gush.[63]

It was January 2007, and March's client, the investment behemoth Blackstone Group, was about to pull the trigger on the largest leveraged buyout in history: the $39 billion acquisition of Equity Office Properties Trust, a publicly traded company run by Sam Zell that was the nation's largest office landlord with 543 buildings. But even the mammoth Blackstone was reluctant to absorb outright a portfolio roughly equivalent in value to the GDP of Tunisia.

To make the deal work, Jonathan Gray, the wonkish 36-year-old head of Blackstone's real estate group, hoped to line up buyers for a significant chunk of the properties before he went ahead with it. Then he could unload them as soon as he closed, lock in profits, and keep only a small portion of the properties — and the risk — on the balance sheet.

If Macklowe wanted to pluck the juiciest New York City components out of the mix, he would need to make a bold offer. And he'd need to move fast.

It was the kind of deal only a handful of players would dare attempt. The price, which would have to be somewhere in the neighborhood of $7 billion, was intimidating enough. But in order to pull it off, the buyer

---

63 Koblin, John. "Macklowes Stomping Back Big with Buy." *The New York Observer.* February 26, 2007.

would also have to raise that money in a matter of weeks, unheard of for a portfolio that big. In normal times, only another publicly traded REIT or private equity firm with vast cash reserves could be expected to execute such a massive buy. Few expected to see a lone-wolf developer pull it off.

The short timeframe coupled with the sheer size and number of assets would preclude the exhaustive due diligence on rents and values that most banks would usually require before lending such a large amount. It would also prevent Macklowe from finding other equity investors to put money into the deal prior to moving forward.

But thanks to the booming market for securitized debt, these were not normal times.

To execute the $7 billion deal, Macklowe planned to offer up a mere $50 million of his own money initially, roughly 7 percent. He would attempt to borrow the rest on a short-term basis. Then, after the deal closed, he could seek out additional equity investors — sovereign wealth funds in the Middle East were the most likely partners — pay down the loans and refinance with saner structures.

It seemed a madcap venture where the buyer could be left holding the bag. But Macklowe would be on anyone's shortlist of gamblers who could pull it off.

Everybody in New York City real estate knew "Harry." His relationships with lenders were long and rich. And he was on a hot streak.

His success at the GM Building, where he'd unlocked hundreds of millions in value, had caused him to be seen as among the most creative of developers — a "magician" with his properties, his admirers gushed, who in the tradition of the legendary Harry Helmsley, could spot the "romance" in a property, the place from which to extract hidden gains.[64]

---

64   Dunlap, D.W. "Redefining Public Space at the G.M. Building." *The New York Times.* March 2, 2005.

For years, the vast, windswept plaza in front of the GM Building fronting the southeast corner of Central Park had been the most problematic portion of the property. In what some speculated was a homage to the plaza at Rockefeller Center, the original developers had sunk the tower's frontage 12 feet below the sidewalk, and put in a restaurant. But it added little charm to the neighborhood — in its last days, the concrete pit had housed a lowbrow Houlihan's restaurant franchise. Donald Trump and the Conseco Insurance Company had purchased the property in 1998 and raised the plaza level above the sidewalks. But that only served to keep people off of it. With no tenant, it presented a desolate expanse.

Macklowe's solution was both elegant and transformative. After lowering the plaza to sidewalk level and extending it closer to the street, he dropped a giant glass cube into its center. The sparkling 32-by-32 foot crystalline structure, reminiscent of I.M. Pei's iconic glass pyramid at the Louvre in Paris, was flanked by two shallow pools, surrounded by chairs, tables, and plants, providing for the first time an inviting public space. The biggest business innovation, however, was what he put inside the cube: a circular glass staircase, and a cylindrical elevator, leading down to a new 24,000-square-foot subterranean commercial space,[65] made possible with the zoning expertise of Macklowe's ace land-use lawyer Sandy Lindenbaum, who had argued he had more space to spare under existing regulations.

And then, there was the matter of the tenant.

In the fall of 2003, Macklowe had managed to secure a meeting with Steve Jobs and convinced him to open a huge Apple Store in the space beneath the plaza. (It had been Jobs's idea to build the cube, but in the media Macklowe would get most of the credit.)

65   Dunlap, D.W. "Redefining Public Space at the G.M. Building." *The New York Times.* March 2, 2005.

Macklowe was a master salesman with a unique blend of charm and ruthlessness. The media tended to focus on the ruthless part, starting with the infamous and illegal "midnight demolition" of those SROs in the midst of the homeless crisis. There was, too, his notorious feud with his longtime East Hampton neighbor Martha Stewart. For years Stewart had complained that Macklowe refused to compromise on the size of the hedge lighting fixtures and an unsightly fence at his vacation home, both of which blocked Stewart's view of a pond. The running battles provided tabloid fodder that reached an embarrassing and entertaining denouement when Macklowe's handyman accused Stewart of pinning him against a gate control box with her Chevy Suburban.

But real estate insiders tended to focus more on Macklowe's strengths. He had, according to his longtime attorney Rob Sorin, "a certain ability to influence people to do what he wants them to do."

A big part of this was his sense of humor. On the website "Old Jews Telling Jokes," Macklowe could be seen in action, standing straight-faced before a white backdrop in a dark, immaculately tailored business suit and purple tie, his Groucho Marx–like eyebrows bobbing up and down behind his thick glasses, as he mimicked the intonations of an elderly lady with a Yiddish accent. She is appearing before a judge to answer for the theft of a can of peaches — six peaches, to be precise.

"Sara — you are going to go to jail for six nights," Macklowe, playing the judge, intones. "It's final!"

She says, "Oh my God!"

"Her husband stands up. 'Your honor!...She also stole a can of peas....'"

He could transition seamlessly from wisecracks into a detailed sales pitch. As a young man starting out, what the Times once called Macklowe's "overweening cockiness" had deeply irritated his bosses. But he had later polished that trait into a potent tool of persuasion. He made people believe in his ideas, and he often made people want to help him. Recalled one former collaborator: "He looks very intently at you and he listens very carefully, and he has a vision for things." In the case of the Equity Office deal, it also helped, of course, that he had in his portfolio the most coveted office building in the city, the GM Building, which he could put up as collateral.

To raise the money, Macklowe tapped his contacts at Deutsche Bank, lining up a $5.8 billion loan on a one-year term, collateralized with the seven trophy EOP buildings. The final portion of the loan — the $1.2 billion covering not the actual but projected future values of the properties — would prove the hardest to secure.

Whoever lent Macklowe that money for that last piece would be taking a far greater risk. Their loan would be "junior" to Deutsche Bank, meaning that in the event of default, they would be last in line to get paid. And to snag the buildings, Macklowe had agreed to pay a price that only worked if rents continued to rise. In the meantime, that money would merely be used to pay interest on the other debt.

Rob Horowitz, Macklowe's loan consigliere, suggested he turn to a source of capital that in the months ahead would come to play a far greater role than anyone could then have imagined in the fortunes of not just Macklowe, but his son-in-law Kent Swig, and later the thousands of tenants at Stuy Town and the Sheffield. It was a firm that specialized in high-risk, high-reward deals, and complex, distressed situations that few others would touch: Fortress Investment Group.

Steve Stuart, a managing director at Fortress, was sitting at his desk on the 46th floor of 1345 Avenue of Americas, when Macklowe called. A blond 40-something Goldman Sachs and Deutsche Bank alum who had once been Trump's banker, Stuart knew Macklowe well. The two had golfed and talked business on multiple occasions — in fact, just a few months before, Macklowe had approached Stuart for a short-term $600 million loan he needed for a different time-sensitive deal. Though Macklowe had

DAN DOCTOROFF, *deputy mayor for economic development in the Bloomberg administration, in 2005. Doctoroff oversaw the rezoning of 40 percent of the city, transforming industrial areas into live-work-play neighborhoods (AFP/Getty Images)*

ARTHUR AND WILLIAM LIE ZECKENDORF,
co-heads of Zeckendorf Development and Terra Holdings, in 2006. Their **15 CENTRAL PARK WEST** *project set a new standard for luxury living — and pricing — in New York (Patrick McMullan/Getty Images; Patti McConville/Alamy)*

THE NEW YORK COLISEUM *at Columbus Circle,*
which many saw as a monument to misguided city
planning. The site would later become home to Time Warner
Center (Bettmann/CORBIS/Bettmann Archive)

ABOVE: THE TIME WARNER CENTER *development site at Columbus Circle. The project would make Steve Ross a billionaire and catapult him into the top echelon of developers (Stephen Chernin/Getty Images)*

BELOW: *The completed project is a 2.8-million-square-foot complex with office space, luxury condos, a Mandarin Oriental hotel, Jazz at Lincoln Center, and some of the city's most notable restaurants. Ross would go on to supersize the model at Hudson Yards (Getty Images)*

ABOVE: *Developer* **STEVE WITKOFF,** *whose holdings include the Woolworth Building, with longtime friend Donald Trump at the White House in 2018 (Mandel Ngan/AFP via Getty Images)*

LEFT: KENT SWIG *with then-wife Liz in 2005 in New York City. Swig amassed an empire of holdings Downtown and embarked on some of the city's boldest condo projects before it all came crashing down (Jimi Celeste/Patrick McMullan via Getty Images)*

LEFT: HARRY AND LINDA MACKLOWE. *Macklowe left his wife of over five decades, in what* The Real Deal *dubbed "real estate's biggest divorce," for a Frenchwoman he housed in one of his condo projects (Dimitrios Kambouris/ Getty Images)*

BELOW: *Macklowe declares his love for his new wife,* **PATRICIA LANDEAU,** *in the most New York real estate way possible: with a 42-foot-tall photo on his 432 Park Avenue, as seen on March 11, 2019 (Andrew Lichtenstein/Corbis/ Getty Images)*

ABOVE: *A 19th-century depiction of the freight yards at the*
NEW YORK AND HUDSON RIVER RAILROAD *(Universal History Archive/Getty Images)*

BELOW: *Construction at* **HUDSON YARDS** *in June 2017. The $25 billion megaproject has been criticized for being a totem for the rich rather than a truly inclusive neighborhood and has faced criticism for the nearly $6 billion in tax breaks and government assistance it received (Gary Hershorn/Getty Images)*

MAYOR MICHAEL BLOOMBERG *with* **STEVE ROSS** *at the groundbreaking ceremony for Ross's Hudson Yards, the largest private development in U.S. history, in December 2012 (Mario Tama/Getty Images)*

STEVE ROSS *with* **MAYOR BILL DE BLASIO** *at an event unveiling plans for a Hudson Yards park in September 2016 (Drew Angerer/Getty Images)*

L-R: BUILDING TRADES' GARY LABARBERA, RELATED'S JEFF BLAU, BLAKE HUTCHESON OF OMERS, SEN. CHUCK SCHUMER, RELATED'S BRUCE BEAL, CNN'S ANDERSON COOPER, STEVE ROSS, AND BIG BIRD *at the grand opening of phase one of Hudson Yards in March 2019 (Drew Angerer/ Getty Images)*

Extell Development's **GARY BARNETT,** *a former diamond dealer who went on to build some of the city's most ostentatious luxury condos, including* **ONE57** *(pictured below) (The Real Deal; William Edwards/Getty Images)*

eventually chosen not to pull the trigger on that deal, Stuart's team had already gone through his books, analyzing lease terms and expenses on the GM Building, and Stuart and his team had been willing to lend him the money then. Now Macklowe wanted to know if they would do it again. On a slightly larger scale.

"Look, I've got two weeks to buy these properties," Macklowe told Stuart. "I've got Deutsche Bank lined up for a $6 billion first loan. I need a billion-two equity bridge and I need it in two weeks."

Stuart absorbed the massive ask. It was an absurd amount of money to come up with so quickly. Even in the high-flying world of big-city real estate, this was shylock territory. But both Stuart and Macklowe knew that Fortress was one of the very few players who might consider it.

Stuart said Fortress might do the deal, but only if Macklowe were willing to back the loan by pledging equity from all the other buildings he owned. In addition, Fortress wanted personal guarantees — in other words, the loan would be a "recourse" loan. Macklowe would have to risk his entire way of life — his homes, his yachts, his vaunted art collection. Though they weren't exactly asking for Macklowe's firstborn, they were asking for his firstborn's inheritance.

The interest rate would be north of 15 percent. The loan would be due in 12 months. And if Macklowe failed to pay, Fortress would have the right to come after every asset he owned. Once Macklowe signed, the clock would start ticking and he would have a "gun to his head." Would that be acceptable?

After Stuart hung up, he turned to Chris Linkas, a colleague who would play a major role in structuring the financing.

"You're not going to believe the deal Harry Macklowe wants to do," Stuart said.

When they heard the terms, Macklowe's advisors strongly urged him against it. The developer had done recourse or "hard-money loans" before.

When he had purchased the GM Building in 2003, he had guaranteed the $250 million subordinate loan. But it was far less risky, because the GM Building had strong cash flows, and he had plenty of other ways to raise the money if things went south.

"This was a bet-the-ranch personal guarantee," Sorin would later recall. "My concern for Harry was betting not only the ranch but his personal assets."

Sorin strongly urged Macklowe to limit his exposure. A billion-two was a huge number.

"This was, by any measure, an astonishing ask," Linkas would reflect more than a decade later. "I mean, there never was this kind of loan before."

After his conversation with Macklowe, Stuart rose from his desk, and walked his rough sketch of the deal down the hallway into a capacious corner office with floor-to-ceiling windows overlooking Central Park. To the northeast stood Sheldon Solow's 9 West 57th Street and, looming over it in clear view, stood the majestic glass and white Georgia marble of the 50-story GM Building, the property that would serve as their primary collateral if Fortress were to do the loan. It was the key to the whole deal.

Sitting behind the desk was Pete Briger, a gruff, youthful-looking financier with intense dark brown eyes and a wry smile, who headed Fortress' real estate and credit business.

"We've got the opportunity," Stuart told Briger, "to make the world's largest hard-money loan."

They ran through the details. With just two weeks, there would be no possible way to go through and value all of the new assets Macklowe hoped to acquire and evaluate the wisdom of his deal. (Just adding up and analyzing the thousands of leases with different terms, locked in rates and incentives would take weeks, let alone analyzing local market conditions and doing projections.) And it would be hard to accurately value all the assets, anyway.

Macklowe's projections, like those relied upon by almost all of the buyers in the supernova market, were almost certainly "priced to perfection," assuming both that rents would continue to rise and that vacancy rates would continue to fall. In fact, the average annual rents on the buildings were at the time of the sale somewhere between $55 and $59 per square foot. But in the end, the deal would be underwritten with projections of future rents at $100 per square foot or more.[66] Macklowe would be borrowing money to make his interest payments while he upgraded the properties and waited for the market to rise.

Stuart and Briger were aware such "Goldilocks" expectations seemed to be priced into every new deal, and had agreed on the need for caution. Still, the payoff might be worth it: At an interest rate of 15 percent, Fortress's return on the $1.2 billion loan would come to roughly $180 million, and it seemed likely they could identify $1.38 billion in assets — and a comfortable safety margin — before making the loan.

The duo had always thrived on uncertainty. Almost 20 years earlier, they had started out together as young trainees — Briger out of Princeton, Stuart at Columbia — in Goldman Sachs's analyst training program. Sitting practically on top of each other in a cramped bullpen, the two had been assigned to mortgage and structured finance at an auspicious time.

It was the late 1980s, and the nation's banking institutions known as "savings and loans," or S&Ls, were about to collapse, and the soon-to-be-formed Resolution Trust Company was about to offer up one of the greatest asset fire sales of all time. Amid that wreckage, Briger and Stuart learned some of their earliest lessons. As the government attempted to offload roughly half a trillion dollars in assets taken over from failed S&Ls, the pair became adept at finding gold in the wreckage. They had

66   Pristin, Terry. "A Warning on Risk in Commercial Mortgages." *The New York Times.* March 2, 2007.

snapped up portfolios of credit card loans, delinquent mortgages, empty office buildings, and automobile loans. And crucially, they'd learned to protect themselves.

"Back then, there were a lot of assets with really bad data," Stuart said. "A lot of the stuff traded for pennies on the dollar. A lot of that was due to just really terrible information. So you're making a real draconian assumption on what that information is. But once you did that, there was often a natural buyer for a lot of the stuff. You have to figure it out. 'Now we've got it, now who are we going to trade it to?'"

A comfort for both risk and deals "with hair on them" had given them an edge ever since. It would give them an edge in the months to come.

In 1997, Stuart had jumped to Deutsche Bank to kickstart its commercial real estate lending group. He was the first banker there to do business with Trump, who was emerging from the bankruptcies of several of his properties. (Stuart would become one of his regular golfing partners and would even dine with him and Evander Holyfield in the immediate aftermath of the infamous Tyson-Holyfield ear-biting bout.) Later, Stuart moved to Japan, where he worked with noted opportunistic financier Christopher Flowers, scooping up distressed assets during the Asian financial crisis, before heading to Fortress.

Briger, meanwhile, had remained at Goldman. In 1998, he helped form the "special situations group," a secretive and immensely successful unit that often traded in distressed assets. In rare media interviews, Briger described himself as a financial-services "garbage collector,"[67] finding value in discarded assets. In fact, there was nothing particularly blue-collar about Briger or the crack unit he assembled upon joining Fortress in 2002. He was a sophisticated financier, whose edge came from careful

---

67   Jenkins, Jay. "Peter Briger Jr.: Fortress Investment Group's King of Debt." *The Motley Fool*. March 23, 2015.

modeling and meticulous analyses of the assets he traded in.

The Macklowe loan was indeed a special situation. And Fortress had a huge pool of money set aside for just this type of transaction: an opportunistic fund, marketed to investors as "high risk, high reward."

Briger signed off on the deal, and asked Stuart to move ahead.

In February 2007, the Blackstone-EOP deal closed. Jon Gray's wife, Mindy, arrived at Blackstone's office in New York with an oversized bottle of Veuve Clicquot. Right after a toast, Gray trimmed the "unbelievable golden mane" of his key advisor on the deal, Eastdil's March, who had also dangled part of the portfolio in front of Macklowe. March had promised he'd trim his famous locks if the deal went through.

At $39 billion, it was the largest leveraged buyout ever. Zell, the seller, a billionaire who happened to be a motorcycle enthusiast, advised Gray to also buy a motorcycle, according to the New York Observer, so that the media would have something to focus on when they invariably started writing about him after such a giant transaction.

"I ride motorcycles, so they start every story with me riding a motorcycle," Zell told his much-younger counterpart. "You need to find a hook."

At the same time, Macklowe made his move, scoring the $1.2 billion from Fortress that would allow him to buy the $7 billion EOP portfolio as the bigger Blackstone-EOP deal went through, and the one-year payback countdown started. One person present at the closing would later recall it dragging into the early morning hours. Harry's son, Billy, nodded off on a windowsill, as "Harry basically signed [Billy's] inheritance away."

The reaction in New York to Macklowe's coup ranged from quiet admiration to outright concern and amazement at his chutzpah.

"He's owned a considerable amount of real estate, but this moves him into the top tier of larger owners," Douglas Durst, the major landlord, told the Observer. "It's a big jump for him."

"You've got to give it to Harry; he's got nerves of titanium," Mitchell Steir, CEO of Studley, the brokerage where Macklowe had begun his leasing career, told the Times. "He never ceases to amaze."

In the larger deal that made Macklowe's buy possible, however, some saw an ominous warning signal. If the size of the EOP-Blackstone deal, the magnitude of the leverage, or the assumptions underlying it weren't enough to scare market prognosticators, the name of the seller certainly did.

Since the 1970s, Zell, a short, bald, acerbic Midwesterner, had been nicknamed "the Grave Dancer," for his knack of bailing on the frothiest of markets near the peak, sitting along the sidelines and watching other investors crash, and then moving in to scoop up assets on the cheap.

What was one to make of Zell's move this time? Had he once again called the market's "top"?

Later, Zell would explain that he hadn't been looking to sell.[68] But when Gray asked Equity Office's CEO Richard Kincaid what it would take, Kinkaid had replied: "Sam says it has to be a Godfather offer — too good to refuse."

Gray had called back a few months later to ask what a "Godfather offer" might look like, and Zell suggested $45 a share. Blackstone offered $47.50.

"Blackstone's offer was well north of what we knew was the value of our real estate," Zell would later write.

"While I was certain the market was frothy, I wasn't selling to get out of the office market," Zell would write. "I had simply received a Godfather offer."

By the time the deal was done, Blackstone's bid had risen to $55.50 a share, more than 25 percent higher than what Zell had believed the shares were initially worth. Upon completing the deal, the private equity firm carried $32 billion in debt and a $3.5 billion bridge equity loan. And

---

68   Zell, Sam. *Am I Being Too Subtle?* Portfolio. March 9, 2017.

within days of closing, Gray embarked on a frenzy of flipping the likes of which the market had never seen.

Macklowe's $7 billion New York City buy was followed, within days, by the sale of 19 buildings in Washington D.C., 17 in Seattle, 17 in Portland, 17 in San Diego, and 24 buildings in the L.A.–Orange County area.[69] Sales in Chicago and San Francisco came next. Some of the buyers even tried to flip the flipped properties themselves: Tishman Speyer bought six in downtown Chicago for $1.7 billion, and immediately tried to re-flip three of them.[70]

By June, Gray would unload roughly 100 million square feet of property for about $28 billion. By then, the deal appeared a slam dunk for Blackstone, which had put up just $3.5 billion of its own money to buy the whole portfolio. On paper, the buildings that they still held from it, with a core of prime properties in Boston and L.A., were valued at $7 billion.

Macklowe seemed intent on taking a different approach. At the GM Building, he'd found a way to connect the vast unused space in front to the basement below, built the glass Apple cube on the plaza and created new rentable commercial space out front. On Madison Avenue, he'd also pushed out the retail footage.

Here, too, he hoped to find the romance in his new assets. That would mean studying the properties and evaluating his path forward, after which he would look for equity partners and long-term financing. He decided to take some time to do so.

It was a decision he would come to regret.

Throughout the fall and into the winter of 2007, the subprime contagion had continued to spread. In September, Bear Stearns had posted a 61

---

69   Pristin, Terry. "A Warning on Risk in Commercial Mortgages." *The New York Times.* March 2, 2007.

70   Bagli, Charles V. "Harry Macklowe Gambles Again." *The New York Times.* October 6, 2013.

percent drop in net profits due to its hedge-fund losses. And by October, other banks had begun to admit they, too, had problems. Citigroup, the nation's largest bank, announced it would write off $5.9 billion in the third quarter, causing its profits to drop 60 percent. UBS, Europe's biggest bank, wrote down $3.4 billion in mortgage-backed securities. Merrill Lynch and Bank of America announced losses, too.

Initially, investors cheered the financial news assuming the worst was over, and the crisis was now in the rearview mirror. On October 9, the Dow and S&P set new records, closing at 14,164 and 1,565, respectively. On October 10, the NASDAQ peaked at 2,811. But, in fact, it was just the beginning of a long series of huge loan- and property-related bank write-downs, with the lessening of recorded value of assets on the books, as well as write-offs, where the asset is removed from the balance sheet altogether. On October 11, a decline in stock prices commenced — one that would accelerate to warp speed in the months ahead. (Investors wouldn't see those lofty market numbers recorded on the 9th and 10th again for another five years.)

By winter of 2007, the uncertainty over subprime products had catalyzed a downward spiral for all securitized commercial-debt instruments, particularly those backed by property. Burned by securitized subprime loans, investors began to doubt other kinds of securitized debt, as well. Demand for lucrative CMBS began to dry up. Investors couldn't sell the old ones, and banks got stuck with the new ones. With billions of dollars in loans stalled on the balance sheets of banks that had expected to securitize them and offload the risk to outside investors, banks slowed their lending. The pipeline that had delivered a flood of ready cash to the market was now clogging up.

The extent of the trouble came into clearer focus at the beginning of 2008, when Morgan Stanley announced it was writing down $400 million in commercial mortgage loans from the fourth quarter. Even more alarming, Wachovia, the nation's fourth-largest bank, announced write-downs of more than $1 billion for commercial loans for the second half of the year. The price of the assets underlying many of its securities had fallen, and the company was having trouble offloading them.

Wachovia's losses, one industry publication noted, were particularly startling for the Manhattan real estate investment market. The bank was the home of Rob "Large Loan" Verrone, the top CMBS underwriter in the nation, notorious for quoting lines from "The Godfather" while negotiating deals.

Verrone had emerged as one of the most vocal champions of CMBS, and during the boom years had helped to popularize the kind of "mezzanine financing" that had allowed buccaneering developers like Macklowe to put far less of their own money at risk. His deals included Stuy Town, Swig's 80 Broad in Downtown, and many others. But between December 2006 and April 2007, his shop had slashed the amount it lent by 75 percent. His superiors let it be known that the bank was likely to grow even tighter.

"Many of our competitors were pursuing a strategy of hoping that after Labor Day, after the new year, things were going to get better," Bob Ricci, one of Wachovia's managing directors, told the Times. "But just the opposite happened."

David Lichtenstein, who as chairman of the Lightstone Group had borrowed $7.3 billion the previous April to acquire the Extended Stay hotel chain for $8 billion, lamented the situation to one reporter.[71] Anyone looking for debt was now "in a terrible situation."

"It's like trying to buy a flashlight in the middle of a hurricane," he said. "Wall Street is experiencing the banking equivalent of a hurricane."

---

71   "The U.S. Strains to See Light at the End of the Tunnel." *EuroProperty Magazine.* March 3, 2008.

XVII

Marching to His Own Tune

Swig's Risky Game

K ent Swig walked amongst the guests filtering into the marble lobby of 25 Broad Street in Lower Manhattan and took in the kinetic lights hitting the walls, melting from amber to purple to lime green.

Out front, the building's granite-and-brick façade was awash in purple, the signature color of Swig Equities. Inside, photographs of the model apartment interiors and amenities danced across a large custom screen, including one of the "musician's pad," with a pony skin rug and vintage guitars. Interspersed were images of Swig's other projects, including the Sheffield. Brokers, bankers, attorneys, and friends sipped on cocktails and admired sweeping staircases, ornate 18-foot-high coffered ceilings, and terrazzo marble floors, wandering into a sales office decorated with what one reporter would later describe as "regal portraits of Liz and Kent Swig."[72]

It was February 2007, and Swig was introducing his ambitious vision for his Downtown hotspot to the world. The idea for the light show and videos came from Liz, who told a reporter from Real Estate Weekly that it was "exciting to play with the grandeur and elegance of the building, along with the newness of lighting and video."

"The opening basically mirrors the concept of 25 Broad Street," she added, of the century-old office-building-turned-residential-product, "a successful merger of the new and the old."

Swig touted the building's "horizontal townhouses" with high ceilings, a day spa and screening room, private dining, and a children's playroom.[73]

And he had more such enclaves planned for the well-heeled in the neighborhood. Swig had paid $29 million for 45 Broad Street around the corner, nearly triple what the seller had paid three years before. It was an eyebrow-raising premium, especially given that Swig's new property had a deed restriction that prevented the owner from ever building any structure taller than eight stories on the site.

But Swig had unearthed a game-changing piece of information. The deed restriction stemmed from a 100-year-old agreement the owner of 45 Broad — who had also owned 35 Broad at the time — had inked with a neighboring landlord, at 25 Broad. That neighboring landlord had lent the owner of 45 Broad a large sum of money on the condition that if he was not repaid by a certain date, the 45 Broad owner would forfeit the right to build taller than eight stories on his two properties — which would protect the landlord-lender's views. Sure enough, the borrower had

---

72, 73   Cresswell, Julie. "With Fortune Falling, a 1 Percent Divorce." *The New York Times.* February 1, 2014.

failed to pay back the loan, locking in the height restriction.

But since Swig owned 25 Broad, he could lift the restriction on 45 Broad any time he wanted, immediately multiplying the value of the property. Not only did he do so, he also approached the owners of 35 Broad and convinced them to sell their air rights — which he also controlled — for $10 million.

"I went to the owner of 25 Broad and asked if they would waive the deed restriction on the height limitation," Swig would later quip. "I looked in the mirror. I said 'yes!' And then all of a sudden, through that negotiation, which didn't take long, 45 Broad could go up pretty much infinitely high!"

He planned to knock down the building at 45 Broad, creating a prime development site, and then use air rights acquired through an even more creative gambit.

Though 25 Broad with its grand limestone façade was a genuine historic treasure, the building had a quirk. In the back, a 90,000-square-foot wing jutted out at a diagonal into an enclosed lot, rising some 20 stories.

The design of this odd appendage, which held 20 apartments, seemed to bear little relation to the architecture of the rest of the building and was entirely blocked in, with no views, by the buildings around it. Swig realized that if he could somehow convince the Landmarks Commission to let him knock it down, it would not only open up the views for the lower levels of his planned development at 45 Broad, he could also transfer the air rights and add 12 stories to his 35-story tower.

Swig made an appointment with Lindenbaum, the same land-use wizard who advised Macklowe, and laid out his vision for the site. His first reaction was not what Swig had hoped for.

"Are you nuts?" Lindenbaum exclaimed. "This will never — ever — get done!"

Lindenbaum told Swig he wouldn't take the case.

"If I go in on a bold move like that, they'll be so angry at me, that I'll lose all my credibility," Lindenbaum said.

Swig convinced Lindenbaum to at least hear him out. For one thing, no one could see the wing he wanted to knock down — you'd need a helicopter. Then, Swig pulled out a thick folder that contained all the documentation that had gone into the original landmark case. Out of the hundreds of pages with tens of thousands of words written up by the landmarks commission, they had devoted precisely 16 words to the structure in the back — and in those 16 words they had called it "secondary." Swig told Lindenbaum he had also gone through the entire borough and there was no similar structure in a rear yard, so this would not set any precedents. Finally, Swig said that after he knocked the structure down, he would build a park there, and noted that a park had been there before that wing was built.

Eventually, Lindenbaum relented. And after researching the case, they were able to find evidence from the building's original architect that he had tacked on the structure in question as an afterthought, because he had extra square footage he hadn't known what to do with. The Landmarks Commission considered the case and, after Swig at their urging won the consent of the Landmarks Conservancy and the Municipal Arts Society, they finally approved his plan.[74] It was a decision that could be worth tens of millions of dollars to Swig.

The site at 45 Broad could catapult Swig to the next level, he thought. Here, perhaps he didn't have to choose between residential, office, and hotel. Maybe he could do all three.

His Uptown ambitions had also evolved. In the wake of Time Warner Center, the market was on fire, and Swig was thinking accordingly.

At the Sheffield — which he had renamed Sheffield57 — Swig had

---

74   Glassman, Carl. "Part of Downtown Landmark Proposed to Be Demolished." *The Tribeca Tribune*. April 5, 2007.

convinced his partners to tear up their original business plan for "cosmetic upgrades" and instead shoot the moon. Prices for luxury condos had skyrocketed throughout 2005 and the first half of 2006, allowing Swig to argue that the project had the potential to be far more profitable than they had originally anticipated if they invested more money in transforming the complex from a "Class B" condominium to a "first-class luxury condominium."

He proposed adding high-end finishes to the apartments and common areas, overhauling the mechanical systems, replacing the street-level façade, adding a gym and spa, and combining smaller apartments into "family-size" units.

Swig also sold his partners on his plan to move the driveway out, put glass on it, and transform a "dingy exterior space" into a "magical interior space, lit with natural light." He wanted to extend the lobby outwards, and redo the plaza and park area out front. The Sheffield had 856 units. Swig proposed gutting everything, combining them and getting to 572 larger units.

"I saw, to me, a very unique opportunity to re-envision a building completely and bring it into the condo market," Swig said.

Such boldness did not come cheap. To finance this new vision, the team would need to recapitalize the project, borrowing an additional $86 million to be repaid two years later, in July 2008. The new money would come with onerous terms: The lenders demanded more personal guarantees and required the partners to contribute an additional $12 million of their own equity.

Neither of his equity partners, Yair Levy and Serge Hoyda, wanted to put up more cash or more guarantees. But Swig was undeterred. He felt so strongly the new plan was the right way to go that he agreed to put up their shares of new equity as a loan, and even offered more personal guarantees. In fact, Swig even agreed to release Levy and Hoyda from backup indemnity clauses they had provided him as part of the initial financing, ensuring they would share in whatever pain he might experience should the project go south.

In exchange, Swig demanded more control over the day-to-day affairs of the project, and wanted a free hand to make decisions unilaterally. Levy and Hoyda assented.

The stakes for Swig had risen considerably. He was all-in.

The project was to move in three phases. Condos would be marketed from the bottom up, with the "momentum" building as the more desirable and expensive apartments with better views came online.

By the spring of 2007, Swig had mostly completed Phase 1 and sold 15 percent of the units, with prices averaging about $1,500 a square foot, well above the $1,388 originally projected. Swig had also inked a lucrative deal to net lease the building's 105,000 square feet of office space, street-level retail, and basement parking garage to the Hearst Corporation, which occupied an office tower next door. The company had also purchased the option to buy their space at the Sheffield for $95 million at a later date.

Not everything, however, had gone to plan.

Over the course of the winter, hundreds of Sheffield tenants had moved out, just as the new owners had projected. But the holdouts had mobilized, and tensions were rising. Around Christmas time, tenants had received letters that read "Merry Christmas. We have opened up the relocation office on the third floor. Please come by and we will see if we can relocate you," their attorney, Kevin McConnell, recalled. That letter had not been received well.

The tenants began complaining about the renovations being done. Construction crews had begun knocking down walls with "very little protection to tenants that were actually living there," they said, throwing up dust and debris, occasionally knocking out services like elevators, electricity, and water.

In court, the tenants started to score some victories that promised to delay the pace of Swig's plans. The core opposition consisted of a group of 23 market-rate holdouts, who had refused to leave even when their leases expired. Swig had taken them to housing court and attempted to evict them, yet they had won an improbable victory. McConnell had argued that the condo plan Swig had filed with the state had implied there would be no evictions, yet Swig's refusal to renew the expiring leases constituted eviction, thus violating the offering plan.

That March, a housing-court judge ruled in their favor. Swig vowed to appeal, but the tenants could stay put in the meantime.

McConnell was also representing a larger group of the Sheffield's rent-stabilized tenants, who had begun documenting what they claimed as incidents of "harassment," "stalking," "floods," "cut phone lines," and "workers barging into apartments without permission."

By the spring of 2007, the media and New York politicos were beginning to pay attention. City Councilwoman Gale Brewer, State Senator Tom Duane, Congressman Jerry Nadler, and Assemblyman Richard Gottfried all either attended or sent representatives to a tenants' meeting. The bad press was beginning to tarnish Swig's golden-boy image. And if it resulted in problems with permitting or any other governmental approvals that slowed down the process, it could get expensive very fast.

"Swig Equities is running an extraordinary campaign of tenant abuse and harassment," Gottfried said to the New York Observer in April. "It's pretty shocking. City agencies and the courts really need to step up their actions to protect the tenants."

Swig downplayed the problems. "It is tough to live through construction," he told the paper. "However, the faster we get it done, the better off everybody is. And frankly, the residents have hit the lottery — they are going to end up with one of the finest buildings in New York City, and the rent-stabilized tenants are going to be able to stay in the building with regulated rents."

Things came to a head on a Sunday in late April when Brewer organized a demonstration outside the Sheffield.

On the plaza in front of the building, about two dozen protestors gathered, waving oversized posters and chanting. One man held a color placard depicting someone in a white hazmat suit taking asbestos readings in the Sheffield hallway. Swig's face, with his bushy blond eyebrows, sun-chapped surfer lips, and pearly whites partially obscured behind a huge red X in a circle on the sign, grazed several posters. One featured a close-up of him with the words "Golden Boy Hits Bump."

Midway through the protest, a high school marching band from Brooklyn arrived on the scene. The two-dozen-piece brass ensemble, later identified as "the Steppers Marching Band," was led onto the plaza by a baton-waving man, wearing a white suit and yellow headband, and blowing a whistle, and four buxom dancers in tight white jumpsuits, who swiveled their hips as the band burst into song.

The band was there, it turned out, at the "invitation" of the man whose face was on the posters: Swig. Belting out soul classics such as the Isaac Hayes theme from "Shaft," Stevie Wonder's "Signed, Sealed, Delivered" and "Ain't No Stopping Us Now," their songs reverberated across the plaza.

If Swig's gambit was meant to overshadow the protest, it backfired. Cameramen were gathering footage, and the protestors soaked up the attention.

"You really have helped our side so much. Thanks, Swig!" one tenant organizer, standing on the sidewalk in front of a metal partition, said into a camera. "We thank you for making this a big, big news day for us and for the cause of people living in this city, working people, people who have to deal with condo conversions, getting kicked out."

By that summer, Yair Levy had grown frustrated by the slow pace of progress at both the Sheffield and the project on 92nd Street,[75] which also involved Swig. Uptown, Levy and Charles Dayan had felt sure their original plan to build a nine-story luxury condo on steel stilts would make the deal a home run. The team had proposed renting the 134 existing apartments and selling 56 luxury condos, for a total projected sellout of more than $145 million.

Yet two years after the deal, construction had yet to start, and the necessary approvals were still held up. To make things worse, Levy had a friend who ran a restaurant on the ground floor of one of the buildings on 92nd Street. That friend had shared some alarming news about how tenants saw Swig.

"Yair, look, they don't like him and they're very upset with the way he's talking to them and the way he has handled everything," Levy recalled him saying. "He doesn't even come himself. He sends people to talk to them, and they don't offer them any reason to cooperate. Maybe you should talk to them."

By then, according to Levy, the partners had begun to hear from bank officials who were alarmed at the slow pace of the development.

"Swig said, 'Leave it to me, I talk to the tenant, I do this, I do that, I'm the manager,'" Levy would later complain. "So we tried not to be involved, and it took two years. Then the bank started to get upset. They wanted to know why we hadn't started."

Levy began setting up meetings of his own in the restaurant and talking with the tenants, which seems only to have fueled the opposition further. The tenants told the media and local politicians that they didn't believe the landlords really meant to protect their rents. And they had recruited a wide array of local activists and politicians to their cause, delaying the project's start further.

---

75 Barbanel, Josh. "Big Deal." *The New York Times.* July 6, 2008.

Levy "tried to sneak around Swig and tried to make a deal with the tenants themselves," Assemblywoman Linda Rosenthal, a leading critic of the 92nd Street conversion, later told *The Real Deal*.

Down at Sheffield57, meanwhile, Swig determined that adding additional floors to the top would be impractical. But it had been a costly diversion. The reserves needed to service that project's loan had begun to run low, and he needed more money to keep construction moving.

Swig was not particularly alarmed by this circumstance, considering it simply the cost of doing business. But his partners were not so merry: When Swig approached them for further capital, they instead complained about the slow pace of the project and accused him of failing to stay within the budget.

"'We don't put any more money in because you're not controlling the expenses, not controlling the costs!'" Levy said. "We're not putting any more money."

Privately, Levy had started to feel that he had badly overestimated Swig's development capabilities. He had been under the impression, he said, that Swig had run the entire Macklowe organization, but had since learned that was not the case — and he blamed Swig for the misunderstanding.

"I used to tell him, 'let's move! The market is not forever. Timing is very important,'" Levy would later claim.

Levy concluded that not only did Swig's firm lack the infrastructure to pull off two huge, complex projects, he was also not focused because of his background.

"You have to understand, the guy came from money," Levy, who hadn't, would later complain. "He didn't fight out or suffer to make this money, so everything came easy. He was spending the money very easy, like, it's no feeling for the money. He tried to get very fancy. And he thought that the market is forever!"

Swig would dispute that characterization. What set him apart from his partners, he would say, was the willingness to do what needed to be done to make the vision work. Unable to procure money from them, he found it elsewhere, securing a $21 million loan from Square Mile, a hedge fund run by the investor Jeffrey Citrin.

Like Briger and Stuart at Fortress, Citrin had cut his teeth during the early 1990s. A former debt and restructuring attorney, he had joined the firm Cerberus — later famous for its acquisitions of the military contractor DynCorp, Safeway grocery stores, and Chrysler — starting their real estate practice and running it until 2005. Though his new firm was smaller than Fortress, he too looked for "special situations" that might spook other players. By putting the work into understanding situations, he promised to both protect his investor's money and offer high-interest, hard-money loans.

Citrin's loan to Swig for the Sheffield came with a steep 24 percent annual interest rate, due in the spring of 2008, with an option to extend into 2009 under certain conditions. Citrin had also insisted on the same kind of personal guarantees that Harry Macklowe had agreed to for the Equity Office deal. Should Swig default, Citrin's Square Mile would have the right to go after his personal assets.

Swig saw his deal as less risky than the one inked by his father-in-law, however, because unlike Macklowe's Fortress loan, Swig's deal with Citrin included a provision that allowed his creditor to convert the loan into an equity stake in the Sheffield. Swig would later insist that he had always expected Citrin to convert the loan into an equity stake — a process that required Swig to first get the blessing of all his lenders.

Citrin disputes he ever made such a commitment.

"We had no intention of converting anything," he said. "We had every intention to enjoy a negotiated high rate of return. We were essentially a mezzanine lender."

Whatever the intention, the two struck a deal, and Swig said he set to work getting the lenders' permissions to convert the loan to an equity stake.

"The project needed it," Swig later said. "And I wanted to get it done quickly. When I looked at the Sheffield and I looked at the numbers that we were going to make, it made sense."

XVIII

Stood Up on Prom Night

Hudson Yards Heartbreak

At the same time Harry Macklowe was racing to take on $7 billion worth of debt, Tishman Speyer and its main equity partner in Stuy Town, BlackRock, were racing to sell stakes in the giant complex. Though their winning bid had come to $5.4 billion, in the end the companies had actually needed $6.3 billion, because of $240 million in acquisition costs and the lender-dictated need to create a $650 million reserve fund. About $3 billion of that money came from a 10-year, interest-only mortgage from Wachovia and Merrill Lynch. (The two financial behemoths, of course, had no plans to actually carry that loan on their balance sheets — they planned to package it into CMBS, and then sell it off to investors). After $1.4 billion in secondary "mezzanine" loans, BlackRock and Tishman Speyer had put $1.89 billion of equity into the deal.

They weren't comfortable with that much skin in the game. Through late 2006 and the first part of 2007, the companies worked furiously to sell off large equity stakes and whittle down their own exposure. Buyers included the California pension funds CalPERS ($500 million) and CalSTRS ($100 million), the Church of England ($75.7 million), and a wide array of others, according to Bagli's book "Other People's Money."

In the end, Tishman Speyer's own exposure to the $5.4 billion deal, the largest and most audacious in the city's history, was just $56 million, a little over 1 percent of the value.

When the Equity Office deal had been announced in early 2007, Tishman Speyer had correctly figured that Blackstone would immediately try to reduce its exposure by putting a bevy of trophy buildings on the market. That would soak up liquidity and crowd the field with the very same kind of assets that Tishman Speyer owned.

The Speyers were "very long" at the time, company sources would later say, "particularly in New York and London."[76] It was time to bank some profits and reallocate.

By the summer of 2007, Tishman Speyer had unloaded $10 billion worth of assets, including three of its most coveted office towers in Manhattan, accounting for $3 billion (the firm sold another $1 billion in assets in the first half of 2008).

The first of these deals would be the same trophy office tower where a young Steve Ross had taken space all those years earlier in an attempt to dazzle potential clients: 666 Fifth Avenue. And in the years ahead, the building would become an item of international media fascination thanks to the rising prominence of its then-obscure new owner: the 26-year-old scion of a New Jersey real estate dynasty and future husband to one Ivanka Trump: Jared Kushner.

---

76   Piore, Adam. "Mort Zuckerman Gets the Last Laugh." *The Real Deal*. September 2008.

Still, despite the ominous economic signs appearing on the horizon, even the Speyers couldn't resist Hudson Yards. In December 2007, they bid $819 million for the project, then hiked their offer to north of $1 billion, on top of the more than $2 billion they would need to shell out to build a platform over the yards.

As the new year rolled in, many believed the competition would come down to Tishman Speyer and Related, and the MTA was going to have to make a tough decision.

In the end, Rupert Murdoch would make it for them.

On a Sunday evening, just hours before a second round of bids for Hudson Yards were due on February 26, Ross received a phone call from his contact at News Corp. The economy was shaky. There were too many uncertainties. They could no longer commit to the project. Murdoch was pulling the plug — News Corp was out.

Ross hung up, stunned. In a single moment, months — years — of carefully laid plans had been upended. The next morning, he slunk into work and informed his team they'd have to change the proposal, though there was no way they could fill the hole blown through them. The heart of their plan had been ripped out, and with no time for Related to come up with something new.

"We were basically in brainstorming mode," Blau recalled of the frantic few hours that followed. "We had eight different ideas. We said we'd do this, we said we'd do that. But we were just kind of throwing around ideas because we had had this great bid and it died at the very last moment."

In the end, Ross and his team cobbled together a bid for just one half of the rail yards,[77] an approach likely to place them at a great disadvantage since everyone else would likely bid on the full project. But there was

---

[77] Brown, Eliot. "Related's Rail Yards Triumph." *The New York Observer*. May 19, 2008.

simply no time to completely rework the bid and put the pieces together in a way they were certain would work. Plus Ross was unsure of how his investors would react to the News Corp withdrawal.

On March 26, the MTA and city announced that Tishman Speyer had offered the highest overall bid.[78] Durst/Vornado continued to make counter offers until the last moment, but the firms still bid about $40 million less than Tishman Speyer. In the press the next day, Related's bid was hardly even mentioned — most had dismissed it as a capitulation.

In announcing the news that Tishman Speyer had won, Mayor Bloomberg invoked the same lodestar that had guided Ross's vision for Time Warner Center: Rockefeller Center.

"Just think how that transformed Midtown Manhattan," Bloomberg said. "This is going to do the same thing for the Far West Side."

Almost immediately, Ross regretted not bidding for the whole site.

Ironically, the winning bidder would also be haunted by the outcome. Although Related didn't know it at the time, Tishman Speyer's partner in their bid, Morgan Stanley, had also decided to pull out of the bidding. Unlike Ross, however, the Speyers had decided to move forward anyway. In the weeks following his coup, Rob Speyer began to worry. Was his firm taking on too much?

---

78   Bagli, Charles V. "At 11th Hour, Rivals Vie for Deal on West Side Railyards." *The New York Times*. March 25, 2008.

XIX

Harry's Reckoning

Macklowe Loses His Shirt

S oon after agreeing to terms for the $1.2 billion hard money loan in February 2007, Pete Briger, Steve Stuart, and Fortress co-founder Wes Edens descended the elevator from their office tower on Avenue of the Americas and walked the couple blocks west to Macklowe's office at the GM Building to discuss the deal and the repayment plan. Despite the tough terms of the loan, it was in everybody's interest for Macklowe to pay it off as soon as possible. No one back then had reason to expect trouble.

Still, the team made sure to impress upon Macklowe that the loan was a "ticking time bomb," Stuart would later recall, and suggested that the developer quickly sell some assets or recapitalize some of his buildings.

Everyone, it seemed, was on the same page.

But Macklowe needed time to do it right. He had suddenly doubled his property holdings and become one of the largest office landlords in the city. Indeed, the extent of Macklowe's particular challenge had become clear to some of the guys at Fortress in those frenzied days leading up to the deal's signing.

After Stuart had spelled out the terms for the Macklowe-Equity Office loan, and Briger signed off on the idea, Fortress had had 10 days to make sure they were protected. Chris Linkas was tasked with evaluating the assets that would collateralize the loan. It had been a nightmare.

The first thing Linkas and Stuart had done was assume all the equity in the EOP office portfolio was "vaporized," since Deutsche Bank held the senior portion of the debt and, if things went south, would have to be paid first. Instead of spending time on those assets, Linkas's team had dug into the credit documents of Macklowe's other legacy assets, so he could get a sense of what kind of loan obligations Macklowe had already placed on them, when those loans would be paid off, and how much equity Macklowe had in each building — how much money, in other words, Fortress would be able to go after if Macklowe defaulted on them.

But as is the case with many New York developers that own some of the most expensive buildings in the world, Macklowe's operation was akin to a mom-and-pop shop.

Most of his modest staff were in accounting, leasing, legal, and operations. Only his son Billy and a protégé named Noah Leonard were empowered to take any real decisions, and Macklowe still signed off on most things. It was Leonard who was in charge of rounding up spreadsheets with projections and anything else Fortress might need. And Macklowe's rapid decision to raise $7 billion had left no time to prepare for the kind of forensic analysis Fortress now intended to perform.

"They weren't ready to do a billion-two bridge loan with a big credit fund in two weeks," Linkas would later recall. "Macklowe had run his business very lean and grown his staff as needed. Then all of a sudden, we're demanding all this information in an organized fashion. It was a nightmare in the amount of time given."

Linkas was on the phone several times a day with Rob Horowitz, Macklowe's loan broker, who helped stitch together a picture of the exact financial situation. They had all worked nights and weekends, and together, they had managed to pull it off.

But now, Macklowe's same skeletal staff was tasked with getting a handle on a portfolio of buildings comprising 7 million square feet of office space. In this case, Macklowe's creativity wouldn't be enough — he needed more time and more people.

"This is a guy who grew his portfolio literally building by building," Linkas said. "Suddenly, he's bitten off a huge chunk of Manhattan in an instant to become one of the biggest office landlords in the city. I think it takes time to process that."

It soon became clear that time was the one thing Macklowe did not have. By the spring of 2007, the credit markets had begun to turn.

"Things started to feel very, very uncomfortable," Sorin said.

Macklowe didn't hire an investment banker to put together a "book" with an offering for new equity investors until late spring and early summer, according to Stuart. And the offering contained what many saw as a major flaw: it asked investors to put equity into the seven Equity Office buildings (in the end Macklowe ended up buying seven buildings, not eight), but excluded a stake in all the other trophy office towers Macklowe owned, including the GM Building. To Stuart, that seemed a tough sell.

"He owned a ton of other New York City assets," Stuart would later recall. "If you're an investor, and if there's vacancy, are you going to lease the stuff you own 100 percent first before you lease the stuff that's owned 50/50 with a sovereign wealth fund from the Middle East? I think that part of the ask was just a bridge too far."

As midsummer approached, Macklowe still didn't have the money to pay back Fortress. By then, highly leveraged loans had become rare. And a number of building sales had been postponed, canceled, or restructured. Investors were widely reported to have begun "shunning" the CMBS market that had been feeding the frenzy for so long.

Highly leveraged loans "are not being made or are very rare now," Robert O. Bach, of brokerage Grubb & Ellis, told the Times. "Some people would say, there's been more of a return to sanity."

In late August, the publication Commercial Mortgage Alert sounded the alarm. With $3.4 billion coming due in six months, it "seems unlikely that Macklowe would be able to raise anywhere near enough to refinance," it noted.

"If Macklowe can't pay back Fortress...they can take his world," one source familiar with the situation told the publication.

Soon after, the Times ran a story on the front page of its business section noting the "widespread talk in the industry" that Macklowe was in "deep trouble."

Macklowe's grand coup, the article noted, was coming to be seen "not just as a feat of financial derring-do but also as a watershed that ended two years of frenzy in the commercial real estate market." The article raised the possibility that Macklowe, who had been steadily collecting plaudits for his reimagination of the GM Building, might actually lose the trophy tower.

"If you're looking for a poster child for what's been going on, it could well be that deal," Mike Kirby, a principal at research firm Green Street Advisors, told the paper. "It had all the elements of the froth in the market — assets flipping left and right at ever-higher prices and excessive amounts of debt at ultracheap prices."

In the article, Billy Macklowe, speaking from his "sleek corner office at the GM Building," had shrugged off the concerns, and said he was in advanced discussions with three groups to line up permanent capital.

"That's how we always looked at the deal," he said. The company's next steps may also include "one or two divestitures" of some of its buildings, he said.

Nonetheless, the article set off copycat follow-ups in the city's real estate press, quoting experts around the industry speculating about the fate of the Macklowes.

Macklowe continued to "live his usual life," according to Vicky Ward, whose book "The Liar's Ball" chronicled the deal. He went sailing on his 112-foot yacht, Unfurled. He and his wife, Linda, closed on a $60 million seven-unit spread at the Plaza. And he invited a group of bankers out to East Hampton to golf.

"On the helicopter ride out there one of the bankers quipped, 'Harry knocked down a building in the middle of the night. Do you think he'll kill his bankers on a plane?'" Ward wrote.

Everyone survived. And the noose continued to tighten.

"The mortgage market has changed," Billy Macklowe told a Bloomberg reporter in early September. "We're in advanced discussions with several groups to refinance the purchase, to achieve several outcomes with respect to the portfolio." These might include an equity infusion or asset sales, he said.

By then, Macklowe had fired the Deutsche Bank team tasked with raising equity, and replaced them with Perella Weinberg Partners, a privately owned investment bank with offices in the GM Building and strong ties to Middle Eastern financiers known to be actively looking for Manhattan investment opportunities. (Perella Weinberg's Tarek Abdel-Meguid sat on the board of Kingdom Holdings, and was an influential advisor to the company's boss, Saudi Prince Al-Waleed bin Talal, the 13th-richest person in the world.) Macklowe had also increased his mortgage on the GM Building by $500 million, a move many speculated was done to help service the crushing debt he had accrued on the megadeal.

"In buying the EOP properties at such a premium — nearly $1,000 a square foot — Macklowe bet he would be able to flip some buildings at a higher price or refinance the debt at similar terms," the New York Post noted. "But now, with the global credit markets virtually shut down, Macklowe is having trouble finding lenders for such highly leveraged buildings at a time when many believe Manhattan office rents are about to fall."

In September, the Macklowes traveled to the Middle East to score investors. They returned empty-handed. And Macklowe's advisors convinced him to retain a firm specializing in corporate turnarounds to help restructure and potentially negotiate with Fortress.

Smelling blood in the water, Macklowe's competitors began circling. Vornado bought a stake in loans collateralized by four of Macklowe's buildings, a move observers noted might put them in position to repossess some of his real estate should he falter.

Soon it became clear that Macklowe was going to lose the EOP buildings. He was probably going to lose a lot more than that.

In meetings, Linkas would later recall, Macklowe began to grow increasingly quiet. Missing were his ribald jokes and loquacious charm. Billy was "in tears," as time ran out, according to Ward.

In February 2008, just as Ross and his rivals were preparing their final Hudson Yards bids, Macklowe defaulted on his loans. Deutsche Bank took back all seven Equity Office buildings, and planned to sell them.

Briger agreed to a four-month extension on the Fortress loan, but with a key condition: Not only would Macklowe's interest rate go up, he would have to put the GM Building up for sale.

In March 2008, Bear Stearns collapsed, selling to JPMorgan at the bargain-basement price of $2 a share. The downfall of the mighty investment bank pulverized global credit markets and put a big question mark on the health of the entire American financial system.

By May, Macklowe had struck a deal to relinquish his beloved GM Building and three other Manhattan trophies to an investor group led by

Mort Zuckerman's Boston Properties. And the media was reporting that Harry's relationship with his son Billy had deteriorated to the point where Billy might try to oust him from his own company.

The most spectacular high-wire act in New York real estate history had gone horribly wrong. Macklowe was in free fall.

XX

Ice Ice Baby

Swig and the Ice Bucket Incident

Despite taking a few blows, Kent Swig was still wheeling and dealing. But fate was gearing up to land a knockout punch. He'd watched the downfall of his mentor and father-in-law with sadness. But later he would insist he saw little connection to his own situation. It was still easy back then to dismiss Macklowe's misfortune as the result of the sheer size and audacity of his crazy bet — though, of course, the business climate had grown unquestionably more challenging.

"Did I hear, read about it, and see it from both the inside and outside? Of course," Swig said when asked years later about the crisis and any discussion involving the rising tensions with his in-laws. "That was a personal thing of family, but it didn't impact my business."

Downtown, Swig was still following his plan, pushing to take business to an entirely new level, one that would place him in the pantheon of real estate moguls.

In May 2008, around the same time his former mentor was handing over his most prized asset, Swig publicly unveiled his grand vision for 45 Broad Street, just around the corner from the New York Stock Exchange. On the site of the former eight-story building, Swig would construct a 62-story glass tower, the nation's first "Nobu Hotel and Residences." The complex would include a 128-key five-star hotel, 77 luxury condos, and the city's fourth Nobu restaurant, granting the project all the cachet of the trendy sushi eatery and its co-owners, the actor Robert De Niro and restaurateur Drew Nieporent.

The previous October, Swig had acquired Helmsley-Spear, another former piece of the vast empire once controlled by Harry Helmsley. Founded in 1866, the commercial brokerage had hundreds of full-time and freelance employees, and managed millions of square feet of commercial and manufacturing space.[79] The deal prompted trade publication Real Estate Weekly to ask, "Is Swig the next Harry Helmsley?"[80]

Behind the scenes, however, the business was throwing up several hurdles for Swig. And relations with his partners had deteriorated steadily.

The team had finally won preliminary approval from the Department of Buildings to begin constructing their luxury addition to the six-story buildings on Amsterdam Avenue and 92nd and 93rd streets. But by then, the lender that had initially financed the partners with a $52.5 million loan, Fremont Bank, had collapsed beneath the weight of its residential subprime loans, and sold off many of its assets. The bank's commercial real estate portfolio was acquired by iStar Financial, a juggernaut in the industry. In January 2008, iStar filed to foreclose after the team defaulted on mortgage payments.

---

79 "Swig Maps Out Big Plans for Helmsley-Spear." *Real Estate Finance and Investment*. October 5, 2007.

80 Geiger, Daniel. "Is Swig the Next Harry Helmsley?" *Real Estate Weekly*. October 10, 2007.

What little hope remained for the ambitious project was snuffed out in April 2008, when the buildings department issued a stop-work order, citing building code and zoning issues.[81] The reversal was prompted in part by tenant opposition — which Levy and Dayan blamed on Swig.

The Sheffield, meanwhile, continued to fall behind schedule.[82] Though by May 2008, the condos were 50 percent sold, closings were delayed by up to one year. The partners had hoped to sell the units through March 2008, use the proceeds to pay the loans down to about $250 million, and then refinance approximately $200 million, which was set to mature on July 9. But with credit frozen in the wake of Bear Stearns' collapse, a refinancing now seemed highly improbable. What's worse, the sales market had slowed considerably.

As the July deadline approached, Swig warned his partners of a domino effect. Should they default on their Sheffield loans, the company would then have to allow 30 purchasers who had executed contracts but not yet closed the right to withdraw. And since the market was declining, it was "foreseeable that the majority of purchasers would accept such an offer, potentially decimating the project" and their chances for a profit, he would later say.

Even so, Swig convinced most of his lenders to "extend and pretend," executing a series of agreements which allowed him to extend the maturity date of the loans until April 9, 2009. With 25 Broad Street proceeding apace Downtown, he was confident he could pay his debts.

In an interview with a reporter a few days after the Nobu announcement,

---

81 Geiger, Daniel. "Uncertain Market Causing Real Estate Tempers to Flair." *Real Estate Weekly*. May 13, 2009.

82 Acitelli, Tom. "At the Sheffield." *The New York Observer*. September 27, 2007.

in fact, Swig seemed ebullient.[83] His desk was piled high with mounds of papers, merging into one another, mixed in with miniature rubber Gumby and Pokey figures, a couple of green pins that said "Waiting for Gore," and, in deference to the Passover holiday, an oversized Ziploc bag of whole-wheat matzo. A bottle of unopened Dom Perignon sat on the top of a cabinet behind his desk, above a bulletin board with "[Anthony] Weiner for Mayor" stickers.

He played down the troubles Uptown and focused on the momentum Downtown, which he believed would provide the capital he needed to fix any looming loan deadlines.

He was still the same good guy who'd jogged through the streets of China followed by a man on a bicycle, he insisted, and stressed that there was so much more to life than business.

Above all, he said, he hoped for "peace of mind" and "a nice happy work environment with financial stability."

Underneath his cufflinks that day, Swig wore a red string from a bottle that contained the tequila he'd used to toast his late best friend Jim Runsdorf, after the 43-year-old financier's untimely death. Runsdorf had been hit by a boat in 2005 on the Hudson River after an early-morning rowing session.

"I'm running around all the time, I'm looking at my watch," Swig explained. "This sort of reminds me what I should be thinking about when I'm running around trying to get to meetings: friends, family, good times."

Then Swig got to talking about his passion: surfing.

"It's that one second," he said. "It's absolutely perfect. You're timing it. You can just feel it. Then when you hit it, it's just incredible!"

It was an apt metaphor, Swig acknowledged with a smile, not just for

---

83   Piore, Adam. "Mort Zuckerman Gets the Last Laugh." *The Real Deal*. September 2008.

dropping in on a wave, but also for real estate development, where timing was also everything.

"If you make a mistake, it can be rather punishing," he added. "There's that thing about being held down and drowning."

Yes, the waters of the market were a little choppy right about then, he conceded. But he was ready to ride the wave. What came next, however, was more of a tsunami.

By early September, tensions with his Sheffield partners had reached cinematic highs. A meeting to discuss the team's problems led to one of the more infamous episodes in industry history: the "ice bucket incident."

The exact sequence of events that day remains murky. Levy and Swig tell different versions.

But their accounts have some commonalities, and court records tell part of the story. Everyone agrees that in July 2008, the partners had finally managed to sell the buildings on Amsterdam Avenue for $63 million. It was a far cry from the $145 million the partners had once dreamed of getting for their luxury condos, and well below the $90 million price tag the team had initially placed on the two buildings when they first had tried to offload them. Levy and Dayan had blamed Swig, and were still seething.

That same month, four contractors at the Sheffield had placed mechanic's liens on the building claiming they were owed $2.77 million. By August, S&P put the building on an investor watch list, warning that the partners might have trouble refinancing the property when their loans came due.

Swig had still not succeeded in convincing all the lenders involved in the Sheffield to allow him to convert Square Mile's loan — personally guaranteed by him — into an equity stake. As a result, Swig was still on the hook, and his assets were exposed. Though in April 2008, Square Mile had agreed to restructure the loan, it had pushed the due date back just a few months, to September 30. Under that agreement, Swig still had the option to push it back to the spring of 2009, under certain conditions — but one of those conditions was that he not default on any of his other loans. And now that was in danger of happening.

The September 11 partners meeting was prompted in part by demands from another lender, which had issued a capital call, asking that the partners put $60 million more into the project before they would agree to extend the loans any further.

Everyone agrees that when Swig asked Levy and Hoyda to cough up for the capital calls, they refused. Levy said the two felt they had spent enough, and that they had already come to believe the project was doomed.

"Kent tried to save it, but we felt like there's nothing to save," Levy recalled. "We didn't want to put additional money in because we felt he's not controlling the deal the way he should control it as far as deadline, as far as budget."

Swig then got upset, stood up and "started to scream" at his lawyer, Levy would claim years later.

"Sit down," Levy claims he told Swig — at which point Swig swiveled around and charged at the diminutive 5'6" Levy. According to Levy, that's when he reached for a nearby ice bucket and struck out in self-defense.

Swig remembers things differently, and described Levy as a "pathological liar." It's true that Levy's version varies from anything reported at the time. In Swig's version, he was calmly seated. When Levy's attorney informed Swig that neither he nor Dayan would add any more money to the project, Swig assumed it was because they didn't have it, and stated calmly "I understand. I'll put up money for them."

According to Swig, Levy and Dayan were worried that he was offering to do so to "squeeze them" out of their share of future profits, and their attorney began to raise those concerns.

"I've been putting up money for the past year because your clients haven't put up money," Swig recalled, telling their attorney. "I'm not intending to squeeze you down, otherwise you wouldn't be sitting in this office."

However, when Levy's attorney told Swig his clients were unhappy with the way Swig was running the project and wanted control over the spending, day-to-day activities, and budget of the project, Swig was less conciliatory.

"I'll make it very simple," Swig responded. "The answer is no. You can have no control over this, because one, I already have it, and two, I've just put in another $60 million. I'm not giving you control."

It was at that point, according to Swig, that Levy, who had gotten up to get a glass of water from the drink cart, went "nuts."

"I'm talking to his attorney, and the next thing I know, I look up and he's got an ice bucket and he slams it into me," Swig recalled. "I blocked it. But he broke my finger. Then he hit me again, right after my shoulder surgery, smashed all over it. I'm soaking wet in there, and then he went berserk. I was sitting there, but nobody stood up, nobody did anything. I was just calmly sitting there. He went nuts."

Whatever the case, the administrative staff at the lawyer's office called the police, who, according to Swig, hauled Levy away in handcuffs.

Levy "snapped," as per a police report.

He "went into a fit of rage and his behavior was intolerable," a Swig spokesperson later told reporters.

Swig had been recovering from the incident and was still trying to find a way to save the Sheffield when the news that would change everything broke four days later.

XXI

High Tide

Lehman Collapses and Takes Real Estate with It

On September 15, 2008, Lehman Brothers filed for bankruptcy, with a mind-boggling $613 billion in outstanding debt, the largest insolvency in U.S. history. At the same time, insurance giant American International Group sought a $40 billion lifeline from the Federal Reserve, warning that it too was about to go under. Meanwhile, Merrill Lynch, with 60,000 employees, agreed to sell itself to Bank of America for the fire-sale price of $50 billion.

These seismic events followed the decision by the federal government to place the Federal National Mortgage Association (Fannie Mae) and the Federal Home Loan Mortgage Corporation (Freddie Mac) into conservatorship to prevent them from failing.

The simultaneous fall of all these giants, along with the realization that Uncle Sam had no intention of bailing out the nation's fourth-largest investment bank, sent world financial markets into a free fall. Many wondered which bank would be next — indeed, many feared the entire financial system might be on the verge of collapse. The situation would be a body blow for Macklowe, Swig, and every other highly leveraged wildcatter in New York real estate.

That Monday, the Dow Jones Industrial average dropped 504 points, more than 4 percent — its largest decline since 9/11. It was just the beginning of the carnage. The stock market would fall another 778 points just two weeks later, dragging down markets around the globe.

Stories circulated of hedge-fund titans hoarding gold bars in basement bunkers, and financial commentators speculated as to whether the U.S. might spiral into an abyss to rival the Great Depression.

Not only was a deep and painful recession now all but assured, but the events of that September put an end to any illusions that the credit crunch that had plagued New York's real estate markets would end anytime soon. Indeed, the immediate impact was to make it far worse.

Many attributed Lehman's collapse in part to its role as the real estate industry's ATM. Now, what precious little financing possibilities had remained available to developers dried up. Lenders refused to finance projects that had been all but certain bets, even trophy skyscrapers with blue-chip tenants. Deals stopped or fell apart. Investors with money watched and waited, unsure just how much further there was to fall, aware it was unwise to try to catch a falling knife.

"Everything's frozen in place," Steven Spinola, then-president of the Real Estate Board of New York, told the Times.

Many who owed money were likely to lose their buildings, especially those who had bought at the top of the market.

As if to drive the point home, in late September, S&P downgraded the bonds used in Tishman Speyer's $5.4 billion purchase of the Stuy Town complex, noting an estimated 10 percent decline in the properties' values and the rapid depletion of reserve funds.

In an October 1 article, meanwhile, the Times catalogued a growing list of aborted deals and troubled developments caused by the collapse: HSBC, the big Hong Kong–based bank, had torn up an agreement to move its U.S. headquarters to 7 World Trade Center after bids for its existing home at 452 Fifth Avenue came in 30 percent lower than the $600 million it wanted; a 40-story Times Square–area office tower under construction by SJP Properties for the past 18 months still did not have a tenant; law firm Orrick, Herrington & Sutcliffe pulled out of what "had been an all but certain lease of 300,000 square feet of space at Citigroup Center." Tishman Speyer aborted a $400 million deal to buy the former Mobil Building, a 1.6 million-square-foot tower near Grand Central Terminal. Overall, the number of residential sales in Manhattan plummeted by nearly 50 percent in the months following Lehman's collapse, with the market largely paralyzed. At the top end of the market, for apartment sales above $10 million, activity dropped by a staggering 87 percent year over year in the first quarter of 2009.

More than half of the new office towers built since 2000 had been for financial firms, including the Midtown headquarters of the now-shuttered Bear Stearns and Lehman Brothers.

"The crisis on Wall Street does not bode well for the proposed towers designed for financial firms at some of the city's most important projects, including the rail yards on the West Side of Manhattan," one article noted.

"The speed at which this has flip-flopped has been stunning," Green Street Advisors' Mike Kirby told a reporter of the Manhattan market.

For residential developers, even those without too much leverage were likely to feel some discomfort. Buyers looked for any and all loopholes to get out of their contracts. An analysis by *The Real Deal* found buyers asking for their deposits back on nearly 400 units within 20 buildings. One novel strategy, pioneered by real estate attorney Adam Leitman Bailey, was to sue on behalf of buyers wanting their deposits back if developers had neglected to meet filing and registration requirements mandated by the Interstate Land Sales Full Disclosure Act. Related's buildings were a key Bailey target.

The uncertainty was so great that even those used to preparing for the worst were terrified.

"I wonder how many years that has cut off of all our lives," Pete Briger, sitting around a polished conference table at Fortress Investment Group's office, would recall years later.

Fortress was an opportunistic fund built to capitalize on trouble. But this was bedlam.

"There were government agencies that were going out of business — Fannie and Freddie," Briger said. "There were banks that were trading for a dollar or two — household names. Lehman Brothers looked like it hadn't been marked correctly. It was a full-on change in actual risk and perceived risk. Anybody that wasn't frightened at that time was just a dope."

Doing the homework, even the kind of exhaustive homework Fortress did before entering any deal, was "not so scientific."

"You were sort of trying to put things together and understand what your margin for error was, and we had done a lot of due diligence on these situations, but we felt in all the situations that we had a big margin for error," Briger recalled. "But if the world ended, and there were definitely days when it looked like the world could end, some of the stuff might not be worth what we invested in it. There was no precedent for that."

Swig's initial reaction to the Lehman collapse was one of shock and wonder.

"No one knows what is going to happen," he told one reporter.

"It's a bloodbath," he told another. "It's extraordinary."[84]

In fact, he was now underwater. And his charm, creativity, and connections wouldn't be enough of a life raft.

Years later, Swig would sit in another conference room, this one at 770 Lexington, look back on those weeks immediately after the fall of Lehman and shake his head. Up until that day — the "ice bucket incident" notwithstanding — he could see a path forward. He just needed a little more time.

By July 2008, Swig insisted, he had finished 25 Broad, to "the point where I had little towels on the workout machines with '25 Broad' on them." He had almost a third of the units under contract with deposits, and the buyers had begun to move in — $138 million worth of sales were on the books. All he needed to do was begin the process of closing them. The money was there. He was ready.

But when Swig had called his bankers at Lehman in the weeks before its collapse and asked for permission to close — as stipulated by the terms of his loan — he claims his bankers came back with a curious answer.

"We can't give you permission," one told him. "We have to reevaluate everything."

"What do you mean 'reevaluate'?" Swig said in response.

Swig was still anxiously waiting for the situation to be resolved when Lehman declared bankruptcy. And in the subsequent weeks, he insists, he repeatedly attempted to reach his bankers to secure permission to close and convert. No one even called him back.

Meanwhile, the money in Lehman accounts used to service his loans was no longer being transferred to 25 Broad. There was no one there to do it. Swig also lost access to the funds he needed to pay his contractors for

---

84 Weiss, Lois. "Lehman Carnage Harming NYC Real-Estate Projects." *The New York Post*. October 22, 2008.

construction on his Nobu project at 45 Broad.

Swig realized he had no choice but to temporarily shut things down. He was devastated. By late October, the Nobu project had ground to a halt and the sales office at 25 Broad was closed. Swig filed legal summons against Lehman accusing them of "commercially unreasonable conduct and deliberate delay."

And then, the New York Post got wind of the ice bucket incident. The absurdity of the attack provided much needed comic relief amid a deluge of suddenly apocalyptic headlines.

The incident went viral. The real estate blog Curbed seized on the incident, declaring that the fair-haired mogul so used to being lionized in the media would hence forever be referred to as "Buckethead."

As 2009 dawned, the vise around Kent Swig tightened further. Lawyers for Lehman declared Swig in default of his loans on the two projects, totaling well in excess of $200 million, and prepared to foreclose. By spring, Swig had shuttered the Nobu project, returned all the deposits at 25 Broad, and walked away. Both projects were functionally dead.

The bad publicity, meanwhile, prompted some of Swig's other creditors to take action.

Square Mile's Jeff Citrin had been watching the Sheffield debacle closely, and by the end of 2008 had concluded it was time to protect his investors. The chances of Square Mile getting repaid from the proceeds of the project seemed increasingly slim. With the project way over budget and not close to finished, with liens placed on the property, the partners publicly feuding, and the sales market virtually frozen, it seemed likely that the owners of the senior debt on the project would soon foreclose and wipe out Square Mile's position.

"The project," Citrin said later, "was a disaster."

Eager to be first in line for the personal assets Swig had used to guarantee the loan, Square Mile declared him in default on his Sheffield loan (which they had the right to do once he was placed in default on his Downtown projects by Lehman). Then seeing no path to a negotiated outcome, they filed in court to collect. A court date was set for the summer.

Others soon followed. In April, Citibank declared Swig in default of a $5 million personal loan and filed a lawsuit. That same month, some 100 Sheffield condo owners filed a complaint with the New York Attorney General's office alleging Swig and his partners had failed to pay $5.4 million in common charges over 20 months, and had improperly withdrawn tens of thousands of dollars from the Sheffield's reserve funds.

By then, contractors had placed $6 million in mechanics liens against the units. Andrew Cuomo, then the state attorney general, ordered sales suspended, after Swig failed to update the condo offering plan with financial disclosures. In May, the Times declared that the Sheffield57 was "already well on its way to being one of the most disastrous condominium conversions in city history."

To add insult to injury, after pleading guilty to harassment and receiving a sentence of two days community service, Levy sued Swig, accusing him of "siphoning off" $50 million in construction funds for "personal or unrelated purposes" instead of putting it into the Sheffield.[85]

In late spring, Swig learned that Guggenheim Partners, which held a $76 million piece of the debt on the Sheffield, planned to put that debt up for sale. Swig learned that Steve Ross and Related were considering buying the note (a rumor Ross would later confirm had been true). It was the worst possible scenario, since that particular piece of debt, given its position in the "debt stack," could be used as a tool to gain control of Swig's beloved development.

The procedure by which this could happen was byzantine. Suffice it to

---

85   Bagli, Charles V. "Assault Accusations, a Lawsuit and a Notorious Condo Deal." *The New York Times*. June 10, 2009.

say though that under the laws of real estate finance there were countless ways for sharks to go after the assets held by wounded fish like Swig, and one of the most effective was to obtain possession of a strategic piece of the debt on a property insiders called "the fulcrum loan," because it could be used as a lever to gain control.

Swig couldn't understand why Guggenheim planned to sell its piece, though he would later learn that JPMorgan had foreclosed on the fund and planned to liquidate it. Since Related's speciality was residential, they would have little use for Swig if they acquired the loan. They would have every incentive to use it as leverage to prevent Swig from doing any closings, force the project into default and take it over.

After weighing his options, Swig made a decision that would sound shocking to many. Swig turned to the same company that had lent Harry Macklowe the catastrophic $1.2 billion loan on the Equity Office deal — the deal that nearly ruined him.

Swig decided he needed the guys at Fortress.

Swig had known Dean Dakolias, who co-headed the real estate group, since the early 1990s. And though he had never done business with Fortress before, he had socialized with a number of the other guys there, including Steve Stuart. He had met them through the same late friend who Swig thought about every time he looked down and saw that red tequila string tied around his wrist: Jim Runsdorf.

Dakolias and Runsdorf had rowed together when Dakolias was at Columbia, while Swig had met Runsdorf soon after moving to New York City, when the two had both worked on one of Cuomo's early campaigns. All three had gone into real estate, with Runsdorf serving as a partner at Pantheon Properties.

Swig knew the Fortress guys to be tough. But he also trusted them, and knew he could speak frankly.

"They had lots of money and lots of brains," Swig said.

As they convened one morning, Swig told Dakolias and other Fortress executives that what he was about to discuss was very sensitive. That was why Swig was asking them to sign confidentiality and non-circumvent agreements, which would prevent them from discussing the information he was about to reveal or use it to do a deal without him.

"Kent, we never, ever sign non-circumvent agreements," Dakolias responded.

"I need you to do that, Dean," Swig replied. "Because I'm going to open up all this, it's a great opportunity and I want to be part of it because I control it, and I need you to do this."

Dakolias shook his head.

"We can't do that, Kent."

"Okay I appreciate it," Swig said. Then he stood up, packed up his bag, and walked to the door.

"Kent, come back," Dakolias said. "Okay, why would we sign that? Explain it to me."

"Two reasons," Swig said. "One, I'm going to make you very happy, and two, it's going to be the most successful deal that you will probably ever do."

"We understand the success part. What's going to make us happy?"

"I'm going to let you be rough with me and push me over," Swig told Dakolias. "I know you like to play rough. You can knock me out of the way, and you're going to make a ton of money."

Dakolias laughed. Finally, he took the paper and signed it. Swig sat back down and explained why he was so bullish on the Sheffield, and then explained how Fortress might step in, foreclose on Swig and his partners, wrest away control of the project and set themselves up for hundreds of millions of dollars in profits.

Swig had paid down the $400 million first mortgage from KeyBank to "nothing" through condo sales — only $32 million remained to be paid, he told them. There was still some work to do on the renovation: The health club still needed to be finished and there were some other common areas that needed to be built out. Yes, some angry tenants remained — they would have to be managed. Even so, the unsold units would eventually be worth far more on the open market than what it would cost to acquire the piece of the mezzanine loan Guggenheim was shopping around.

"Guggenheim, for whatever reason, we don't know what it is, is putting out their loan and selling it into the open market," Swig explained. "Something must be going on in their company, because in probably 90 days, they'd be fully paid. I have $65 million of signed contracts already sitting ready to close. Plus I have a bunch of contracts about to be signed."

Swig said he wasn't in a position to bid for it on his own, but if Fortress were to step in, buy the Guggenheim debt and allow him to retain a piece of the future profits, he would do everything in his power to help them win control of the property and extract the value.

He needed a team used to fighting things out, in court if necessary, a team that could move fast and decisively.

"I want to do it in a venture with you where I'm protected by you inside — I want to be in the Fortress," he told them. "I don't want to be on the outside."

The gambit would rely on a complicated set of procedures laid out in the Uniform Commercial Code. Swig and his partners had bought the building with a total of $400 million — which had been paid down to $32 milion — in a first mortgage, $70 million in equity, and $240 million in mezzanine debt, and had thus sunk roughly $710 million into the property. In the depressed market, of course, the property would never recoup that amount. But Fortress could get it at an extreme discount.

If Fortress were to buy Guggenheim's $76 million senior stake in the mezzanine debt, which it could likely get at a discount, and then help Swig pay off the remaining $32 million on the first mortgage, it would become the next in line to get paid. If Swig were then to default on that debt, Fortress would be the senior remaining lender and be in a position to foreclose on the Sheffield. It would look bad for Swig — he would get massacred in the press. But he was willing to be the fall guy.

Assuming Swig did not put the asset into bankruptcy — which he would pledge to Fortress not to do — the property would then be put up for auction. If Fortress were outbid, any proceeds from the sale of the Sheffield would go to pay off their $76 million senior stake first. Only then would any leftover money go to pay off the next in line in the mezzanine-debt stack — which consisted of seven more tranches totaling roughly $170 million in additional debt.

The math was easy for real estate wonks to do: If they bid and won the auction, they could obtain a property Swig claimed would still eventually yield hundreds of millions of dollars in condo sales for a fraction of the $710 million Swig and his partners had already put into the project. All the debt junior to them would be wiped out. Any other bidder would have to pay Fortress and all the other mezzanine debt holders in front of them, up to $240 million. Therefore the most likely bidders were JPMorgan, which held a $78 million loan just behind the Guggenheim piece in seniority, and Gramercy Capital, which owned the next tranches in the mezzanine-debt stack, and were thus motivated to at least bid as much as they were owed to protect their investments.

But Fortress had another edge. Only they would know that Swig had promised not to put the asset in bankruptcy. Swig would also voluntarily hand over his condo plan, which would allow Fortress to avoid having to come up with a new one (a process that could take up to 15 months). Swig would not reveal the deal in the media, allowing the perception that the property had been wrested from him to stand.

In exchange, Swig would be granted a portion of any future profits — but only after Fortress had made back its money, and then some.

Dakolias and his partners were intrigued. They promised to look over the numbers.

Within just a few days, Swig had a deal.

XXII

Class Warfare
Troubles at Stuy Town

The Lehman bankruptcy would also signal the death blow for Tishman Speyer's ambitious efforts to convert Stuy Town.

In the months leading up to the crash, Stuy Town tenants had begun to mobilize. They had seen a war coming even before the sale, and had tried to stave it off with their own bid. Once the Tishman Speyer sale had gone through, many had seen their worst fears being realized. They could see that the only way for the firm to make its massive purchase price work was to turn over rent-stabilized units.

"The recovery of rent-regulated units quickly became a preoccupation at weekly staff meetings [at Tishman]," Bagli wrote in "Other People's Money."

To reach their numbers, the company was projecting turning over rent-stabilized apartments at the rate of 15 percent the first year and 12 percent the second year, according to estimates its executives presented to bond-rating agencies in December 2006. Behind the scenes, at an early staff meeting in Rockefeller Center, however, Adam Rose, whose firm had been managing the complex, warned Tishman Speyer that those numbers would be impossible to meet.

"We've been screening the rent-stabilized tenants for years," he said. "You'll get four to five percent."

"This is my experience, this is what I believe," he added when challenged.[86]

That didn't sit well with the new owners, who promptly replaced Rose and his management firm. To expedite evictions and weed out illegal sublets, Tishman Speyer put three law firms to work and hired private detectives to investigate the background of rent-controlled tenants whose leases were up for renewal, hoping to find evidence their apartments were not a primary residence — a condition of being eligible for a subsidized apartment.

By the spring, dozens of tenants had received eviction notices. Others received letters informing them their rents would rise, some more than sixfold. The offensive was so sweeping that City Councilman Daniel Garodnick set up legal clinics to explain to the scores of terrified tenants — many of whom had been accused falsely of breaking the law — what their rights were.

"These are scary letters to get," he told the New York Post.

In June of that year, a crowd of up to 7,000 gathered at Stuy Town for a raucous rally. Among them were more than two dozen elected officials, including State Senator Tom Duane, who led chants of "More control! Less rent!" while demonstrators waved signs that said: "SOS Help Me. Don't let me lose my home, Mayor Michael Bloomberg, what's wrong with you!" and "Vote them out."

---

86   Bagli, Charles V. *Other People's Money*. Dutton. April 4, 2013.

"If the trend continues, we're quickly becoming a city of the very, very wealthy with enclaves for the very poor and nothing in between" Manhattan Borough President Scott Stringer said in a speech.

Meanwhile, across town, Rob Speyer's doubts about the Hudson Yards deal had only grown. The Speyers had been unable to find a tenant to replace Morgan Stanley and had tossed out the architectural renderings on which they had based their winning bid for Hudson Yards. The MTA had told reporters to expect a deal signing in early April 2008. But Speyer had postponed it. Then he'd started asking the MTA for assurances. What would happen if the extension of the No. 7 line exceeded the projected $2.1 billion price tag? Either the state or the city, he argued, needed to promise that they would provide additional financing if that happened. He then brought up the fact that the 2005 rezoning of Hudson Yards had only covered the eastern half of the railyards, and the rezoning of the western portion was pending. He then dropped a bombshell: Speyer told MTA negotiators he wanted to delay the closing until both sides of the yards had been rezoned and delay making payments until the process was complete—which could take up to 18 months.[87]

Gary Dellaverson, the MTA's chief financial officer, had been shocked. The agency wanted to lock in their developer immediately. Speyer's new demand would dramatically slow the flow of money to the MTA and introduce new uncertainties. The Speyers would be able to walk away at any time, and the MTA would be right back where it had started.

By early May, negotiations had collapsed.

"We were unable to reach a meeting of the minds," Dellaverson told the Times. "At this point, there is no agreement between Tishman Speyer and the MTA. The MTA remains committed to the development of the West Side yards."

87　Bagli, Charles V. *Other People's Money*. Dutton. April 4, 2013.

In retrospect, it would prove the right call. After Lehman went under, the Speyers had plenty of other problems to worry about.

By the end of 2008, Stuy Town had lost $2 billion in value — if "it had ever been worth $5.4 billion," according to Bagli's account.

"It appeared that the $3 billion first mortgage was safe," he would later write. "But Rob Speyer and his partners figured that the fourteen firms — ranging from Hartford Financial to the Government of Singapore's GIC, SL Green, and Allied Irish Banks — that had lent the partners a total of $1.4 billion in junior loans would have to agree to major concessions. As for the hundreds of millions of dollars poured into the deal two years earlier by the Church of England, GIC, CalPERS, and the other pension funds, it was gone. All gone."

At the time, however, for Tishman itself, there was still hope. Back then, Speyer was still hopping on the phone speaking "on background" with reporters to try and spin the story (he declined to be interviewed for this book).

Then in March 2009, the appellate division of the state supreme court handed down a surprise decision that sent shockwaves through the city's real estate market.

Years earlier, tenants had filed suit, arguing the owners of the complex were barred from decontrolling the rents on a number of apartments, because they had taken $24.5 million in tax breaks from the city's J-51 housing program, designed to spur the creation and preservation of rent-stabilized apartments.

The court sided with the tenants and reversed a lower-court decision. It ruled that the owners of Stuy Town had indeed illegally deregulated thousands of apartments.

Tishman Speyer and its partners had been assured by their lawyers that the case was all but certain to be dismissed. Now, in addition to their exorbitant interest payments and host of other problems, they might potentially be forced to repay the residents of somewhere in the neighborhood of 4,400 apartments.

Speyer learned the news from his attorney while in a taxicab from the airport in Mumbai, India, he would later recount to Bagli.

"Speyer's response," Bagli writes, "was a roar: 'Shitttttt!'"

Over the course of the next six months, the property lost nearly $85 million after debt service. It was such a calamity that in July, Larry Fink, chairman of Tishman Speyer's equity partner, BlackRock, the world's largest asset manager, traveled to the West Coast to take the highly unusual step of personally apologizing to the board of CalPERS for endorsing their investment in the deal.

The New York Court of Appeals upheld the lower-court ruling. On November 6, 2009, CWCapital, the nation's second-largest special servicer, took control of the $3 billion first mortgage on the property. Special servicers specialize in distressed securitized loans to make sure bondholders are paid off. It was the first step toward foreclosure.

Tishman and BlackRock officially defaulted on a monthly debt payment in January, and CWCapital initiated foreclosure proceedings. In June 2010, a judge ruled that CWCapital could start preparing to auction off the 80-acre complex.

The next month, CWCapital itself would go up for auction, and the company would be snapped up by a new owner.

The buyer was by then a familiar name in the market: Fortress Investment Group.

PART THREE

XXIII
Diamond in the Rough
Gary Barnett and One57

T he aerial shot of the construction site that appeared in the media just before Christmas 2008 looked as if it could have been snapped back in the bad old days, when the city was bankrupt. Walled off from the street by a flimsy wooden fence, and the worn, exposed brick of the buildings surrounding it, sat a debris-filled L-shaped lot, with a grimy yellow bulldozer parked in the middle of the dirt. It looked like it hadn't moved in months.

Yet the photo wasn't from the South Bronx of the '70s. It depicted a site on West 57th Street in the golden shadow of Time Warner Center, owned by Gary Barnett's Extell Development. Prior to the subprime crash, many observers saw it as among the most valuable assemblages in the city.

The photo could have been the metaphor for the island as a whole. Across the city, cranes and bulldozers sat idle. Construction workers waited in vain for the phones to ring, and banks had closed their lending windows.

The only people who were busy, it seemed, were the legions of attorneys trying to save their clients from financial ruin.

"I wake up worrying," Phil Rosen, co-head of Weil Gotshal & Manges' real estate practice, said at the time. He estimated he was working 80 hours a week, serving clients as both attorney and therapist. "Real estate restructuring experts will be very busy for the next 12 to 24 months," he said.

By the end of 2008, about $106 billion in commercial properties were distressed or potentially troubled, according to research company Real Capital Analytics. The credit markets remained on ice and there seemed little hope of a recovery.

By the following year, the list of stalled projects in the city would grow to 500. In a year-end column, the New York Post's veteran real estate scribe Steve Cuozzo summed up the sentiment.

"YES, the new year will be a stinker," he wrote. "Even if relatively few pessimistic market-watchers (like this column) are right to say that the world isn't ending, it might feel that way."

After ticking off a number of depressing stats (office vacancies at 10 percent and rising), Cuozzo highlighted four development sites he felt were in "urgent need of a prayer."

Two sites were owned by Harry Macklowe, whose empire had continued to crumble since losing the GM Building to Fortress. The first was at 510 Madison on 53rd Street, where Macklowe had in better times built a 350,000-square-foot office tower on "spec," starting construction before a tenant had been secured. Even as Macklowe had been forced to sell off much of his portfolio, he had managed to hold onto the project, expecting hedge funders to flock to the Class-A building with swanky amenities tailored to them. But, Cuozzo noted, the opening "couldn't come at a worse time." Few hedgies were eager to move into luxurious new digs.

Macklowe's prized development site on the southwest side of Park Avenue at 57th Street, meanwhile, was in such ominous shape that

Cuozzo had dubbed the area "Midtown's Most Miserable Corner." Since acquiring the Drake Hotel in 2006 for $440 million, and demolishing the building, Macklowe had been applying all of his considerable talents to buying up air rights and townhouses on surrounding lots and building an assemblage, bringing his total costs to date, according to some estimates, to $724 million — even before construction. The location seemed ideal for an ultra-luxury condo, a project that could be immensely lucrative in the distant future. But Macklowe would first have to survive the punishing downturn.

Deutsche Bank had foreclosed on a $559 million loan, and within just a few months, iStar Financial, which owned the largest portion of the loan, $224 million, was preparing to sell their note. Demand for it, however, was tepid, because attempting to wrest control would likely result in years of negotiation and litigation.

Cuozzo then turned his attention to Barnett's vast assemblage across from Carnegie Hall where that lonely yellow bulldozer sat.

Way back in 2006, when 15 CPW was breaking records nearby, and the owner of the Plaza, Elad Properties, had announced plans to sell the triplex at the top of the building for $32 million, Barnett had told Cuozzo he still had not decided what to do with his project.

"We will one day do something but nothing is imminent," he said. "We hope it will be within this decade."

Now, the future of the site, which Cuozzo described as "Extell's abyss," seemed even murkier. But Cuozzo had discovered a series of puzzling construction filings that indicated Barnett was gearing up to build a 750,000-square-foot hotel-and-condo tower that would rise to a height of 1,000 feet. Even more improbably, as the headlines proclaimed the unraveling of the American financial system, Barnett planned to do so without a construction loan in place. It was so out of character with the general doom and gloom that many found it hard to believe. Could it really be true? Was Barnett really going to do something that seemingly risky? Many were skeptical.

Yet years later, Barnett would look back on those dark times and insist that it had been true. In the immediate aftermath of the worst financial meltdown in more than three quarters of a century, at a time when hedge funders were stockpiling gold and banks around the world were hoarding cash, Extell's enigmatic and famously media-averse leader had made up his mind to do something so audacious that his peers would later shake their heads in wonder: Barnett would build a gleaming tower so high it would cast a shadow over Central Park, and so luxurious that only the top 1 percent of the world's 1 percent could even contemplate buying an apartment there.

While many wondered if Barnett was ever going to get going, he was ready to begin excavating and digging down to build the foundations. And when Barnett's building began to rise above the ground some months later, the site would become the first major new construction project the city would see since the crash.

The tower would come to be known as One57. And it would spark the creation of a new block in town that would take the luxury boom for the ultra-rich to a new level — a place called "Billionaires' Row." In 2011, Michael Dell would buy an apartment there that would be the first to ever break the $100 million threshold in New York.

It would also bring more press scrutiny to Barnett, outrage many who saw the tower as a symbol of New York's pandering to the ultra-wealthy, and prompt a huge sigh of relief from the real estate industry, as many would later credit Barnett with leading the development community back into action.

"It had an enormous impact," the developer Steve Witkoff said. "When we watched him go live, and we watched him take that risk and later sign a construction loan and put a completion guarantee, we said, 'Wow. Maybe we should be thinking like that.' That's what a project like that does. It galvanizes others to also build. That got us focused on building. It's 100 percent that they changed the way we thought."

One57 would also be patient zero for the next big trend driving development of Manhattan real estate — the arrival of and wholehearted dependence on foreign money.

Today, it's still easy to overlook Barnett amid the larger-than-life personalities that dominate the industry. Though he has long since earned his seat on the dais at the annual REBNY banquet at the Hilton in Midtown that is real estate's biggest shindig of the year, he lacks the swagger of a Steve Ross, the braggadocio of a Donald Trump or Larry Silverstein, the charismatic bonhomie of a Steve Witkoff or a Jerry Speyer, or the connections of a Joe Rose or a Zeckendorf. He's a quiet, intense man, partial to turtlenecks and boxy suits, a family man who'd rather spend the evening at home in his modest two-story Queens home with his wife and some of his 10 kids than at a cocktail party schmoozing with fellow VIPs.

In a 2010 profile of Barnett, New York Magazine dubbed Barnett the "anti-Trump," and noted that his "lone-wolf style hasn't exactly endeared him to his peers."

Born Gershon Swiatycki, Barnett was raised as one of 10 children of a respected rabbi and Talmudic scholar in an insulated Orthodox Jewish community on the Lower East Side, and later in the Jewish enclave of Monsey, in Rockland County.

His move into real estate was born out of romance.

While holidaying in Florida in 1980, Barnett met Evelyn Muller, the daughter of a prominent Antwerp-based diamond dealer. The two wed, and Barnett was invited by her father, Shulim Muller, into the family business, S. Muller & Sons. Barnett spent a decade in Belgium learning the craft and led the Mullers' expansion into the U.S., which is today the world's largest diamond market.

"He developed the American market for us," Jean Claude Muller, one of Shulim's sons and current CEO of the firm, told New York Magazine.

Barnett helped the Mullers and other Belgian diamond families diversify, moving back stateside to invest their money in U.S. real estate. For a time, he partnered on projects with two other young strivers, Ziel Feldman and Kevin Maloney, who were also attempting to make their bones as developers.

"We had a little tiny office with no heat and Home Depot card tables for desks," Maloney said of that period. "We were just guys cobbling deals together, begging and borrowing to try to get deals closed."

After starting with Midwest shopping malls, Barnett made his first splash in New York with the 1994 purchase of the Belnord, a magnificent block-long limestone rental tower on West 86th Street and 87th Street, bound by Broadway and Amsterdam Avenue.

"[The Belnord] was like a 100-carat diamond in the rough," Barnett reportedly recalled telling his Belgian investors.

Meanwhile, in 1995, under the aegis of his own real estate firm, Intell Management and Investment, Barnett purchased Nynex Properties Company, a subsidiary of the telephone corporation that was founded six years earlier to invest in real estate projects. By the late 1990s, Barnett had built Intell's portfolio up to 3.5 million square feet in places such as Louisville, Kentucky; Wichita, Kansas; Manchester, New Hampshire; Westchester, and Staten Island. (The company was later renamed "Extell," an amalgam of "excellence" and "intelligence.")

Barnett then decided to zero in on his hometown, and in 1998, sold the bulk of his holdings for $350 million to Canadian developer Paul Reichmann (former owner of Olympia & York). One of the first things Barnett did with the proceeds was buy his partners out of the Belnord. He also went into development.

In 2005, Extell bested Related, the Durst Organization and Vornado to win the development rights to a gargantuan 77-acre tract of land running from 59th Street to 72nd Street along Riverside Drive fronting the West Side Highway. On the site, with its coveted Hudson River views, a young Trump had once talked up plans to build a 16.5-million-square-foot development for NBC he called "Television City," that would have included the world's tallest building at 152 stories. In the face of financial woes, however, Trump had instead abandoned those plans and sold a 70 percent stake in the site to a group of Hong Kong investors.

When those investors had put the site up for sale in 2005, Barnett hadn't hesitated. While far bigger bidders chewed things over, Barnett bought a plane ticket to Hong Kong, huddled with a representative of the sellers on the 16-hour Cathay Pacific flight, and, after landing and showering, proceeded directly to meet the principal for a marathon negotiation.[88] The deal, for a record $1.76 billion, was announced in New York City in June, shocking the other bidders. It incensed Trump, who excoriated the pact in the press and sued his partners, alleging they had sold the property to Barnett on the cheap and received kickbacks of $19.8 million as part of a tax-avoidance scheme, according to New York Magazine. Trump lost the case.

Barnett's ambitions for the Far West Side site and others nearby would lead to years of wrangling with community groups and politicians.

In June 2005, he appeared before a local community board on the Upper West Side. As if the Riverside project was not controversial enough, in another development planned farther uptown he revealed a pair of needle-thin luxury towers across the street from one another on Broadway between 99th and 100th streets. The neighborhood was then dominated by utilitarian mid-sized brick and stone buildings, and had scarcely seen

---

88   Sherman, G. "The Anti-Trump." *New York Magazine*. September 26, 2010.

new construction in three quarters of a century. When Barnett unveiled his renderings, "people shrieked," Sheldon Fine, chair of the community board, would later tell a reporter.

At 37 and 31 stories tall, the all-glass towers would stick up and out of the rows of squat buildings around them like a jagged pair of shiny goalposts. When completed, condos in these glassy monoliths would cost far more than most people living in the neighborhood could afford.

For months, Barnett's team had been quietly acquiring the unused "air rights" on properties contiguous to his two lots. The idea was to take advantage of what some considered loopholes in the zoning code that allowed owners to exceed height limitations for one building, by adding the unused square footage that belonged to the buildings next to it. The code allowed developers to add the unused square footage from one site to any other site connected to it by as little as a tiny sliver of land, or through other contiguous properties where the owners had agreed to grant air "pass through" rights.

In the years that followed, Barnett would become renowned for his skill at the byzantine but lucrative development practice of assemblage — amassing a development site piece by piece, buying out neighboring owners, while keeping a low profile and hiding the master plan to prevent owners from recognizing their leverage and raising their selling prices. It was a process that required finesse and patience — one that Barnett's former acquisitions czar, Dov Hertz, compares to "getting a cat to come out from under the bed and drink from the bowl." Barnett would then use the assembled air rights to build to dizzying and sometimes controversial heights.

In the case of the Upper West Side towers, Extell had chosen its site the same way it chose the location for its other projects: Barnett, Hertz, and others had driven up and down Broadway looking for blocks where buildings appeared to be shorter than zoning permitted. They then checked the records to make sure none of the properties were owned by another developer likely to squeeze them for big money, and finally, began approaching people.

"What happens is, you're knocking on the doors of people who aren't interested in selling, and you're not interested in telling them that you're doing a development," Hertz said. "You have to start a conversation."

It was an art form, requiring patience, finesse, and just the right mix of desire and feigned apathy. Hertz would often start by saying he likes to buy buildings, or he "likes five-story buildings," or he likes "this block" — anything but his true intentions. Those conversations, he said, could sometimes take years.

But all of this was just a teaser for what was to come. By the time Cuozzo wrote about "Extell's Abyss" on West 57th Street, Barnett had been operating in the area for more than a decade. He had acquired his first piece of the assemblage in 1998, around the time he was raising funds and liquidating his non-New York holdings. It was Feldman, his Belnord partner, who introduced him to the property. Feldman told Barnett he was planning on acquiring what was then a 49-year ground lease on a 94,000-square-foot site at 157 West 57th Street. He offered to flip it to Barnett. A few months later, the deed hit city records, which shows Barnett paid a mere $10 and undisclosed "other good and valuable considerations" for the 49-year lease, which back then didn't strike either one as particularly valuable. Years later, Barnett would have trouble remembering why he even agreed to purchase the site from Feldman.

"I think I was thinking that we could tear down what was there and build a residential building," Barnett said.

There was no reason to rush. Back then, Columbus Circle was still moribund. The idea of a gleaming luxury tower was the furthest thing from Barnett's mind.

To put together the site that would become One57, Barnett took years.

Initially, he figured he could get the air rights to go up to about 300,000 square feet. And back then, assemblage was an easier game.

"In those days, nobody really kind of had big eyes and said, 'Oh my gosh, they're going to get a zillion dollars for stuff with a view of the park, right?'" Barnett said. "People were more rational about what they owned. It wasn't easy. We had to get a bunch of tenants out of the buildings. All these walkups, there were tenants in there, we had to get them out. But it was easier."

Even Barnett's ambitions were initially far more modest.

"I wish I could claim to have the foresight that this would become One57, but it was really step-by-step," he said. "I'm not by nature a big gambler, so it was, 'oh okay, we can get the air rights. Okay, let's get the air rights. And well, we need the footprint really to do that, so we have to buy some of the buildings, and we have to vacate some of the buildings. And then we have the opportunity to buy this.'"

In the end, Extell would complete 20 transactions. It owned seven contiguous properties, surrounded by 13 buildings on West 57th and West 58th from which it had acquired the air rights, broken up by three lots that had no air rights attached to them; from those owners, Barnett had negotiated "pass through" authority.

The costliest deals came late in the game. In the early 2000s, Barnett acquired the building on the corner of West 57th and Seventh Avenue housing the Briarcliff Condominiums. In 2006, he was able to trade it to the owners of 157 West 57th Street and convert the ground lease into ownership there. In exchange for the air rights he needed on a 58th Street condo building owned by investor Ezra Chammah, he agreed to give Chammah a stake in the project — one full-floor apartment that Chammah would later sell for $30 million.

Some property owners caught on and hiked their demands so high, Barnett had to modify his plans. He had intended to acquire the

4,000-square-foot lot next to the large parcel on 58th Street that housed the Park Savoy Hotel, realizing it would allow him to "square off" his parcel and turn his L-shaped footprint into a rectangle.

Barnett had already acquired the air rights from the owner of the site, which Barnett figured was worth about $10 million, though he was willing to pay more. But when the owner demanded $80 million for the property, Barnett decided he would have to build around it.

"He kicked away tens of millions of dollars," Barnett said.

By that time, Barnett's ambitions for the site had ballooned. He had watched the price escalation at 515 Park Avenue, then Time Warner Center, 15 CPW, and the Plaza, and he realized he could think of getting as much as $5,000 to $6,000 a square foot for apartments there.

Then came the real estate crash. Barnett had sensed the market beginning to turn. He knew it was time to "sell down and get more liquid." But he, like Briger — like everybody else — was not prepared for the speed and depth of the collapse.

"Usually there's a gradual diminution, sharper, but not everything falling off the table, which is what happened," Barnett recalled. "I saw this market getting ready to turn, and I should have just done whatever I needed, but I didn't do it with as much urgency as I should have. I never thought it would go like it went. I mean, everything just stopped. I'd never seen that."

In the weeks immediately after the crash, Barnett couldn't sleep at night for the first time in his career. Starting construction was the last thing on his mind. As he lay awake in those early morning hours, he thought about how much debt he had on assemblages — those that were midway through, or projects under construction, like 535 West End Avenue, where it was too late to stop.

"When the market crashed and I was on the 15th floor of West End Avenue, one of my projects, and I had no construction loan, and I was pouring concrete every week, and running out of money," he would recall, "that was nerve-racking."

Barnett had been far more careful than some of his competitors and had some cash. His leverage, at 75 to 85 percent, was relatively low for those heady times: He'd never done business with Lehman, and had never felt comfortable taking the kind of high-interest loans that had undone Harry Macklowe and now threatened everybody else. But now he wondered if he had been conservative enough.

Finally in November 2008, Bank of America, Helaba Bank, Capital One, and New York Community Bank agreed to finance a two-year $135 million construction loan at 535 West End, but only after Barnett agreed to put up 40 percent equity. It would be among the last construction loans in New York City that anybody would get for months.

"Thank God, the good God is showing me his grace," Barnett recalled thinking back then.

In the end, he would lay off 15 percent of his staff, and turn over the deed for a parcel on Tenth Avenue and 30th Street, where he had planned on building a hotel. He would put two of his most ambitious projects on ice. One was his high-profile plan for what was then slated to be a 40-story tower in his old stomping grounds of the Diamond District. The other was an assemblage on 45th Street between Broadway and Sixth Avenue, where he had poured the foundation for a $300-million 476-room Hyatt Times Square.

But on West 57th Street, Barnett felt he should proceed, if he could.

If he paused there for a couple years, it would mean tens of millions of dollars in extra carrying costs. He would also be restarting at the same time as everybody else, which meant that his units would have a lot of competition. If he took the plunge and started early, he could be the first back on the market, poised to cash in when the world emerged back into the light.

"When you pause, all you're doing is adding money to the pot," he would later explain. "It's not productive, because it's just interest. You're not doing anything with that money, you're just paying to carry."

"When you really think about it," he said, "what choice did I have?"

The challenge was monumental. If Barnett wanted to begin building, he would have to do so "naked," using cash from his investors, and hope to get the loans he needed after he had already begun. It was a prospect most developers blanched at — which is why no one else in the city was doing it — and one that Barnett was not particularly eager to embrace.

But Barnett did have an ace in the hole: a deep-pocketed foreign investor committed to the project and seemingly flush enough to weather the storm.

Barnett had always relied on foreign money, and many of his European investors had been with him for years. A few months prior to the 2008 crash, however, Barnett had gone to Abu Dhabi, the capital of the wealthy gulf nation the United Arab Emirates, and had secured a major new investment from the Tasameem Real Estate Company, a government-controlled entity.[89]

In early 2009, he had found an additional source of funding in Abu Dhabi, tapping Aabar Investment, another government-linked fund. Both Tasameem and Aabar were controlled by the International Petroleum Investment Company (IPIC), a $70 billion sovereign wealth fund led by Khadem Abdullah al-Qubaisi, a flamboyant and connected Emirati businessman who would acquire stakes in companies such as Barclays, Daimler-Benz, and Virgin Galactic. While the rest of the world contemplated financial Armageddon, oil prices remained high and things were still relatively good in the Middle East.

---

89 Bagli, Charles V. "Building a Tower of Luxury Apartments in Midtown as Brokers Cross Their Fingers." *The New York Times.* May 26, 2010.

To head Aabar, Al Qubaisi relied on Mohammed Badawy al Husseiny, a short, bald former accountant who held American citizenship and was known for flashy suits, expensive watches, and frenzied fitness workouts. In 2009, in the depths of the abyss, Al Qubaisi and Al Husseiny agreed to pony up $133 million more to buy a majority stake in Barnett's 57th Street project. And when Barnett later traveled to London to meet with Al Husseiny and asked him to provide money for another tranche in the midst of the slowdown, he did not miss a beat.

"This is the best location in New York City," Al Husseiny told Barnett. "Of course we're moving forward. We're funding our obligations."

In the end, that lifeline from Abu Dhabi gave Barnett just enough cushion and confidence to proceed. In May 2010, the Times broke the news: Barnett was ready to start construction on a $1.3 billion tower, the first major new construction in New York since the fall of Lehman.[90]

In the end, Barnett's Middle Eastern investors would provide three quarters of his initial financing. And later, looking back, many could point to Barnett's reliance on foreign funding for One57 as a harbinger of things to come. With banks and other traditional capital sources sidelined, developers would have to look elsewhere for the funds they needed, both to finance their buildings and buy properties.

The go-go easy days of low-interest CMBS-backed money on demand were over. In their place another capital source would move to center stage — capital that brought to developers a different set of expectations and pressures.

Foreign money, from private investors, sovereign wealth funds, and others, would become more important than ever before. And with the money flowing in from abroad, it became even harder to track its origins

---

90 Bagli, Charles V. "Building a Tower of Luxury Apartments in Midtown as Brokers Cross Their Fingers." *The New York Times*. May 26, 2010.

— both Al Qubaisi and Al Husseiny, for example, were later sentenced to long prison terms for their central roles in the multibillion-dollar Malaysian 1MDB sovereign wealth-fund scandal.

XXIV

If You Love Something, Let It Go

A Second Chance at Hudson Yards

S potted around town during that winter of 2009, Steve Ross seemed to be in a remarkably good mood, considering he was sitting atop an estimated $15 billion of real estate projects in the midst of an industry-wide meltdown.

Clad in a dark tuxedo, a white rose boutonniere just above his left breast pocket outside an industry event one evening, he looked into a camera and announced, facetiously, when asked about his plans for Related, that he no longer had any.

"Being a real estate developer today is like an oxymoron," he quipped. "When there's no money, there's no business. So, today, to say you're going to go out and develop something, I think anybody who told you that is smoking dope or something."

In fact, there were a lot of people in City Hall and at the MTA very much counting on Steve Ross to continue to be a real estate developer. The previous spring, Ross had finally won the coveted right to develop Hudson Yards.

At Related, it was Jeff Blau who received the news that Tishman Speyer had walked away from Hudson Yards. Ross was in China at the time, and Blau, Ross's protégé and chief deputy, was getting ready to leave his office for the weekend when a call came in from the MTA's Dellaverson. The Hudson Yards deal with Tishman Speyer was falling apart. Was Related still interested? Blau didn't need to check with Ross before answering.

Blau had torn his ACL while skiing the previous New Year's Eve, underwent surgery in March, and still walked with a pronounced limp. He limped as quickly as he could to the law offices of Paul, Weiss, Rifkind, Wharton & Garrison, where Meredith Kane, co-chair of the firm's real estate development team, was representing the MTA. After meeting with her, Blau promised to return the following day with Related's attorneys to see if they could hammer out a deal.

Dan Doctoroff, the architect of the entire West Side redevelopment plan, had left City Hall in December and was heading Bloomberg LP, the mayor's financial software, data, and media empire. But he'd been following the developments closely. He was at a beach house in Spring Lake, New Jersey for an annual high school friends reunion when his Blackberry went off. It was Dellaverson, who told him Tishman Speyer was out.

"The dream for Hudson Yards could get destroyed here," Doctoroff recalled telling Dellaverson. "What do we do?"

Doctoroff's first move was to call Ross.

"Look," he told his friend when he finally reached him in China. "You have a chance to step into Tishman Speyer's shoes!"

Doctoroff urged Ross to reach out to Dellaverson directly. Ross, who'd already heard the news from Blau, obliged. This was the project that would define him, he felt, and he wasn't going to let it go again.

"The first words out of Steve's mouth after he heard the Tishman deal was falling apart was something like 'I've regretted not being chosen every day for the past seven weeks,'" Dellaverson would later recall. "All three of the remaining proposers reached out to us in probably like a nanosecond."

Dellaverson promised his MTA bosses that he'd have a backup deal in place within a week. Few believed he could pull it off but Blau and Ross were also determined to move quickly. Blau spent the following weekend cloistered in the Paul Weiss offices with a team of attorneys and bankers from Goldman Sachs. (He recalls being told the other bidders were in the other rooms also attempting to hash out the deal, but wasn't sure whether to believe it.) And while both Extell and the Durst/Vornado partnership balked at signing the designation letter hammered out between Tishman Speyer and the MTA, the Related team was willing to agree to almost every provision — including Tishman Speyer's winning bid price of $1.054 billion.[91] (Years later, in an unrelated incident, Ross and Tishman honcho Rob Speyer would reportedly have to be physically separated when their argument at a REBNY meeting looked like it might escalate.)

Ross returned to New York from China on May 16 to finalize the deal, and signed an agreement the following day, just 10 days after the Tishman Speyer deal had collapsed. He put up an $11 million deposit, which he would follow up with an $18.8 million payment at the closing on the eastern portion of the railyards and an additional $24.7 million for the western portion once environmental and land-use reviews were completed.

Even as the sky was crumbling on the financial world and Ross's

---

91   Brown, Eliot. "M.T.A. Board Approves Related West Side Yards Deal." *The New York Observer.* May 22, 2008.

counterparts like Harry Macklowe were going up in flames, Ross had made the deal of his life.

Related had agreed to a total of about $1 billion in regularly scheduled payments. In addition, they would have to raise an additional $2 billion to build platforms over the rail yards — all of this before they could even start construction of the buildings that would make them money. But now it was almost eight months later, and Ross and the MTA still had not closed on the deal.

Not that Ross had been sitting idle. He had somehow managed to raise hundreds of millions of dollars to complete the $1.1 billion purchase of the Miami Dolphins football team, realizing a long-held childhood dream.

"When I read the paper, the first section I go to is the sports section," Ross told the AP at the time. "Since I wasn't going to make it as a player, it was a dream to become an owner."

The MTA had reason to be nervous about Hudson Yards. The deal they had reached with Ross in May was set to expire on January 31, if no one signed the documents.

Finally, as the deadline approached, Related told officials it was unwilling to proceed with the initial schedule proposed for the 26-acre development site. It was simply impossible to line up financing for a $15 billion speculative development in the current credit climate, Ross argued. Some in the media noted that Ross had just completed the purchase of a billion-dollar football franchise, but Ross was unmoved.

The MTA had little choice but to grant a one-year extension. In exchange for the delay, Related agreed to pay $8.6 million, money which could help pay for efforts to rezone the western half of the property.

"Today's agreement acknowledges current economic realities without derailing our partnership on this important site for New York's future," MTA CEO Elliot Sander said at the time. "The development team made their commitment to the project clear and this new understanding keeps us on the path to obtain the funding critically needed for the MTA's current capital plan."

"When the markets rebound and with zoning in place, New York City will be poised to build a vibrant new mixed-use community at the rail yards," Ross said.

XXV

How to Steal a Building in Broad Daylight

Fortress and the Sheffield

The Sheffield auction was held on Thursday, August 6, 2009, at the Midtown offices of Fortress's attorney Kevin O'Shea.

In the months following Kent Swig's decision to approach Fortress, his situation had only worsened. One associate remembers Swig looking like he had been "sleeping on couches," and continually changing cellphone numbers.

By June 2009, Lehman Brothers had filed suit for a $50 million judgment against Swig after he defaulted on $100 million in mezzanine loans at 25 Broad Street, which by then Lehman had foreclosed on and sent into receivership. News reports suggested Swig had personally guaranteed $50 million.

In July, a New York State Supreme Court judge granted a $28.4 million judgment against Swig in the Square Mile case. If Swig and Square Mile couldn't reach an agreement, all of Swig's personal accounts would likely be frozen. By then, Square Mile was claiming to have made a shocking discovery in court filings. Swig, they said, had told them he owned 30 percent of the Sheffield, but they had learned from court filings that his stake amounted to just 9 percent. Swig claimed it was a misunderstanding, but Square Mile seemed to be raising the specter of criminal prosecution.

Swig's marriage, too, appeared wobbly. Still, Fortress's Linkas said, he put on a brave front.

"A lot of human beings would've cracked," Linkas said. "In his position, at a really important time, he was clear-thinking. He demonstrated a lot of grace under pressure."

To prepare the auction, O'Shea, who had just done a similar auction in Boston for the John Hancock Tower, cleared two large, low-ceilinged, adjoining conference rooms in the Hilton on 55th Street and Sixth Avenue, filled them with rows of banquet chairs and a podium, and hired a fast-talking professional auctioneer used to selling farm equipment, to lead the proceedings. Prior to the auction, O'Shea also instructed the caterers to scour his offices for empty ice buckets, which he lined in formation at the back of the room in a not-so-subtle homage to the infamous Yair Levy–Kent Swig clubbing.

Interest in the auction was high and it drew some 75 people, including Yair Levy's son-in-law, possible buyers, reporters from the Wall Street Journal and Bloomberg, and a number of industry looky-loos (neither Swig nor his partners on the deal were present). In order to qualify for actual participation, interested parties were required to post a refundable $1 million deposit. And as the proceedings kicked off, it seemed clear that Fortress had only one serious competitor for the spoils, JPMorgan. The auctioneer, David Maltz, was so enthusiastic, O'Shea had to tell him to speak slower so people could understand the rules.

As soon as the auction started, Linkas raised his paddle and offered up an initial bid of $20 million, gearing up for what he expected would be a spirited back-and-forth. But when he looked over at JPMorgan's man, his potential opponent just sat there and "stared straight ahead," and the paddle remained in his lap. When the auctioneer announced that Fortress's bid had won the day, Linkas was "stunned."

For less than $100 million, Fortress had just purchased a building that had sold less than three years earlier for $418 million — a project that Swig was still predicting might eventually yield north of $800 million.

Linkas would eventually speak with JPMorgan and learn that the mezz debt was held by two separate funds, and the fund managers could not agree on an auction strategy in time to counter the Fortress bid.

"We stole a building in broad daylight," Pete Briger would later say.

Swig was relieved — ecstatic even. But he wouldn't see any money for years, and in the meantime, his problems multiplied.

Just a month after the Sheffield auction, Swig filed an affidavit in court admitting that he did not have access to $28 million in cash or liquid assets he had been ordered to pay Square Mile, and he warned that enforcing the judgment might cause his business to "collapse and force him to file for personal bankruptcy."

"This will entail severe financial consequences not only for me but for my family, my business, and my employees," he wrote.

A judge nevertheless rejected Swig's entreaties. All of his credit cards and bank accounts were frozen, and the tabloids were soon reporting that Swig was close to bankruptcy.

"We are exploring all options," one of Swig's advisers told the Post. "No one wants to do it, but it's certainly a play on the chess board that we are considering at this time."

The article also suggested Swig might "be on the hook for fraud," for possibly misrepresenting his financial assets and ability to repay loans.

The idea that Kent Swig — real estate royalty, heir to a hotel empire, man of the year, resident of 740 Park Avenue — might be forced to declare bankruptcy was seen with a mixture of fascination and incredulity: What had happened to the $3 billion in real estate he owned?

As if to answer the question, more creditors filed suit: Deutsche Bank won a judgment for more than $11 million in December, then Signature Bank for $5 million, followed by judgments for Capital One, East West Bank, and others.

Even his prized nest at 740 Park was in jeopardy.

Never in the exalted history of the so-called "tower of power" had a resident faced foreclosure. At some point in those dark weeks around the time of the court judgment, Swig admitted some hard truths to his wife, Liz: Unbeknownst to her, he had taken out mortgages on both the 14-room co-op and their luxury Hamptons estate.

By early October, the two were suffering "severe strains on their marriage, and their financial and legal interests had diverged to the point that each had hired separate matrimonial counsel," court filings show.

"Friends and associates say she blamed him for everything: the financial losses, the social embarrassment, the smashed Murano Vase," the Times would write.

Harry Macklowe, still reeling from financial setbacks of his own, was said to be incensed by revelations of the mortgages on personal properties meant for his daughter and grandchildren, the tabloids would later suggest. (At one point, the Post had felt compelled to run a graphic displaying both Mackowe and Swig's debts and suggesting they might make for good family dinner conversation.)

Nonetheless, it was to Macklowe that Swig would turn when he needed $200,000 to continue to pay his restructuring lawyers. Macklowe agreed to lend his protégé the money, but his terms were tough. The same day the loan deal was signed, Swig also signed a postnuptial agreement with

Liz. In the event of divorce, Swig would retain sole ownership of his business ventures. (Macklowe later went through his own acrimonious split in 2016 with his wife of nearly 60 years, Linda Macklowe, in what *The Real Deal* termed "the industry's biggest divorce," given all the prime assets at stake.)

With Swig keeping his companies, Liz would pretty much get everything else. She'd keep the homes on Park Avenue and in the Hamptons, while Swig would assume responsibility for any debt on the properties. She'd get nearly $12 million in artwork, including the Andy Warhol Mao painting and the Jeff Koons hanging in Swig's office. She'd keep $1.8 million in jewelry and $11 million worth of furnishings including, according to the Times, "a $1,000 pig-shaped ashtray in the cigar room and a pair of Albert Cheuret sconces, circa 1925, which were valued at $100,000."

The agreement also had a telling line about how frayed the relationship between mentor and acolyte had gotten. The Macklowes, it stated, would "neither encourage or support any attempt to push Mr. Swig into involuntary bankruptcy."

It wouldn't be long until the document was put to use. One night in December 2009, Liz found her husband lying drunk on the floor in one of the apartment's bedrooms, the Times would later report, citing now sealed court filings. An altercation reportedly ensued. By March, the couple had filed for divorce.

At one point in those days, Swig would recall years later, he was sitting in his office when he received a phone call from one of his lenders, whose bank had received a $9 million judgment against Swig in the summer of 2010.

"Kent, you've got to come down to Sixth Avenue and 22nd Street — you've got to meet me on the corner right now," the banker told him.

"Shit, now what?" Swig thought. Back then, he recalled, "every call was a bad call."

281

When Swig got there, the banker handed him a credit card.

"Look, we know you're having a tough time," he said. "You don't have any money. This is the bank's credit card. Trader Joe's is here. Go buy yourself as many shopping carts as you need of food and we'll take care of this so we know you're going to have some food for the next couple weeks."

XXVI

"From Russia with Love" Meets "Crazy Rich Asians"

Foreign Money Invasion

For the Zeckendorfs, the recession had been remarkably gentle and brief — a blip. Long after their 15 Central Park West — dubbed the "Limestone Jesus" in the blogosphere — had sold out in 2007, it continued to hog market headlines.

Indeed, if Gary Barnett's Abu Dhabi–financed One57 marked the beginning of a new era in post-crash building, to many the 2011 supersale of a 15 CPW pad would serve as a watershed for a new era of international buyers setting the tenor for the market.

In the fall of 2011, former Citigroup CEO Sandy Weill put his 7,000-square-foot penthouse on the market for a princely sum: $88 million. At the time, there was no precedent for such a number, which penciled out to an astounding $12,571 a square foot.

"It looks like he literally just picked a price out of the air that doubled what he paid for it," the appraiser Jonathan Miller would later recall.

Yet in less than a month, a mystery buyer stepped up and paid full ask.

The buyer, it would soon emerge, was Ekaterina Rybolovleva, the college-aged daughter of Russian fertilizer billionaire Dimitry Rybolovlev. He was the same man who had purchased Donald Trump's Palm Beach estate three years earlier for $95 million.

The record-setting condo deal would reverberate throughout the luxury market, not just in New York but globally.

"That number was so shocking," Miller said. "That sale triggered a new thinking in New York — it was the catalyst that sort of lit the fuse."

Just seven years after people had ridiculed the Zeckendorfs for aiming for $2,000 a foot for real estate on the west side of the park, a condo at their project had sold for more than six times that.

But if the price was a shocker, the nationality of the buyer wasn't.

A few months before Lehman's fall, the Wall Street Journal had called attention to the growing presence of fabulously wealthy Russian buyers, many of whom arrived by private jet with bodyguards in tow, to be squired around Manhattan by luxury brokers. Just as soaring energy prices had insulated Barnett's Abu Dhabi investors from the credit crunch, they had fueled boom times in Russia. And buying in Manhattan had suddenly become all the rage.

Russians had come to "represent an important but little-known demographic group for U.S. real estate," the article stated. In New York City, where foreign buyers were said to make up about 15 percent of the market, Russians had suddenly become "the largest contingent."

Though most Russian buyers valued discretion, the sums they paid for some properties, along with their often-colorful backgrounds, generated plenty of headlines.

The most notorious early Russian buyer was Andrei Vavilov, a trim, well-tailored hedge-fund magnate. With his wire-rimmed glasses and a salt-and-pepper buzzcut, Vavilov appeared straight out of central casting, with a passing resemblance to the Soviet General Orlov in the James Bond classic "Octopussy."

Vavilov had risen to become deputy finance minister under former Russian President Boris Yeltsin in 1992, helped push through privatizations and other reforms, and had even survived a Bond-esque assassination attempt in 1996 when someone blew up his car in a Kremlin parking lot. He later joined the board of the Russian energy firm Gazprom, bought a controlling stake in a smaller oil company with a $25 million loan, and sold the company just four years later for $600 million in cash, according to news reports.

Vavilov was dogged by allegations of insider deals and, in the late 1990s, Russian federal prosecutors investigated whether he embezzled $231 million during the sale of MiG fighter jets to India. He denied the accusations, and the case was later closed.

In 2008, Vavilov sued the Plaza Hotel developer Elad Properties after making a purchase there, complaining that two penthouses he'd committed to buy for a cool $53.5 million had been ruined by ugly architectural features including narrow windows that "make the space more closely resemble an attic than a luxury penthouse living room," according to the lawsuit. He would later find a penthouse more to his liking at Steve Ross's Time Warner Center, shelling out $37.5 million for the unit in 2009.

Fellow high-profile Russian buyers included the metals oligarch Len Blavatnik, who paid $27.5 million for a Fifth Avenue apartment and then another $50 million to Seagram heir Edgar Bronfman Jr. for his townhouse. (In 2018, Blavatnik would pay $90 million for yet another townhouse, at 19 East 64th Street, once destined for purchase by the government of Qatar.) Other buyers included Bolat Nazarbayev, an oil magnate and brother of Kazakhstan's president, and Oleg Baibakov, a Moscow-based construction mogul.

And just like the Zeckendorfs had predicted, this new wealth was drawn not to co-ops, with their extensive disclosure requirements, but to condos, with their ask-no-questions ethos.

"They come from a very different culture, and you have to understand that," Victoria Shtainer, a Russian-born broker with Douglas Elliman, would later explain.

Russia, she pointed out, is "not the land of opportunity — it's cutthroat." Those who made it to the top are "always on the defensive."

"They don't talk about who and what they are," Shtainer added. "You have to win their trust. You find that information out later rather than sooner."

"Normally, with buyers in New York, you need to know upfront what's in their bank, in terms of liquid cash, but I would never dream of asking that question," said Dominique Punnett, a half-Russian broker at Stribling & Associates, of a Russian client who was looking for an ultra-high-end apartment. The buyer had made it clear to Punnett, without explicitly saying so, that "price is not an issue."

Sotheby's International Realty's Elizabeth Sample, who had brokered $1.5 billion worth of real estate in her career, noted that in the insular world of Russian buyers, referral business was paramount. She had met her first Russian clients while selling a penthouse at the Pierre near Central Park in 2006. That led to a flurry of referrals, through which she had sold over $125 million worth of product.

"It's not always the price that is the most important, it's more the prestige of the property," she said. "Many Russian clients know what the buildings are, they know what the top condominiums are."

The new New York, with its brand-name condos like the Mandarin Oriental at Time Warner Center and the Plaza, was ideal for these buyers. After showings, Sample, an Alabama native and member of Daughters of the American Revolution, would often meet her clients for dinner —

Cipriani and Thomas Keller's Per Se were client favorites — or breakfast where she could receive her marching orders. Most of the deals, Sample said, closed quickly.

The $88 million Rybolovleva paid at 15 CPW smashed the $48 million condo record set by Russian music impresario Igor Krutoy, who had paid the sum for a 6,000-square-foot apartment at the Plaza just months earlier.

(Soon after, Krutoy, who owned record labels and music TV stations and produced Russia's American Idol–esque "Star Factory," would shell out another $23.9 million for a mansion on tony Gin Lane in Southampton — then tell his brokers he planned to demolish it and build a new one.)

Though the "Russian invasion" began before the 2008 Lehman crash, the recession that followed fueled an even greater infusion of foreign money. It was a simple question of supply and demand. With American bank windows effectively shut, and flashy Wall Street buyers pinching pennies, many in the industry looked for new markets — and found them.

That's at least what Nikki Field did. Field, a trim blonde who was a Pan Am flight attendant before breaking into real estate, headed a Sotheby's brokerage team dealing with the city's toniest product. In the wake of the 2009 financial crisis, Field, along with her partner Kevin Brown, had set out to methodically reinvent her office. She had done so using the same approach Barnett had used — she had gone abroad.

In the weeks immediately after the 2008 Lehman bankruptcy, sales had ground to a standstill. At the same time, she recalled, the phone started ringing off the hook with calls from wealthy clients suddenly out of a job or in financial distress, and eager to offload second homes — or, if they had worked at Lehman or Bear — sell their Manhattan apartments.

"Now, we had to take these properties that they were leaving and sell them quickly," she recalled.

Field had plenty of connections to draw from. She had helped her husband launch a marketing firm, and when she'd landed at Sotheby's in the early 2000s as a broker, she had applied her marketing chops to exploiting the brand, which to her mind implied old money as well as discretion, and carried a certain cachet with the monied classes. Always impeccably put together, Field herself carried an Upper East Side aura.

Soon, she says, the higher-ups had noticed and began tapping her to help sell visiting foreigners considering opening up new Sotheby's affiliates around the globe.

"Most of these places — Buenos Aires, Rio, Mallorca — they've never heard of Sotheby's," she said. "So I would often be the poster girl to go and tell them how you talk about the brand, and how you use it to attract the upper-tier luxury market."

By the first week of October, a little more than two weeks after Lehman, Field was in Moscow, where Sotheby's had just opened a branch. From there it was on to Hong Kong, where the firm's weeklong fall auction house confab was under way. The event was at the time the largest draw of high-net-worth wealth to any art sale annually, filled with newly minted Chinese millionaires buying art, according to Field. Her goal was to meet as many as possible.

She then went on to mainland China — Beijing, Shanghai, Wenzhou — then Singapore and Taiwan.

"We didn't know where the money was going to be coming from," she said. "We had a feeling it might be coming from China."

Before each trip, the New York head office readied the ground with phone calls or emails to local affiliates. Field also did some prep work of her own, using her own local banking connections to secure meetings with private wealth advisors and introducing them to real estate opportunities in Manhattan and elsewhere.

"They're moving a lot of money to the U.S," she said. "They get the comfort level of being able to say to their client, 'I know you're going to buy in Miami or New York or Washington. We're introducing you to a Sotheby's agent that will give you all the information and help you. They have our confidence and endorsement.'"

Her movement would put her in an ideal position to help Barnett when he was ready.

By the fall of 2011, when the $88 million deal at 15 CPW was made public, Barnett had already opened "pre-sales" on the project he was now calling One57, and marketing it as the tallest residential tower in the city, rising 90 stories. Some buyers were already plunking down deposits even though the building wasn't slated to open until at least 2013.

By then, the building was 40 stories out of the ground, and Barnett was promising to create an "unprecedented level of luxury living in the heart of Manhattan," surpassing even 15 CPW. His bold decision to begin construction in the depths of the recession had come to seem prescient.

That fall, he had finally closed on his $700 million construction loan, which came from a consortium of lenders led by Bank of America, but including the likes of Banco Santander and Abu Dhabi International Bank.

Barnett would later call the financing on what he says was the largest construction loan in the country at the time, "extraordinarily conservative," given the amount of equity in the project and the "super low" basis for the assemblage — since he had acquired most of it in a different time.

He was confident that if he planned it right, he could match the success of 15 CPW, and he was making the case to anyone who would listen. While that building had lateral views of the park, some partially blocked by Trump's building, Extell's assemblage was dead center at the bottom of the park — a location Barnett planned to take full advantage of.

"I didn't decide to make the building tall," Barnett would later explain. "The building had to be tall because I had a 750,000-square-foot building, and given the zoning constraints, the only place to put the [floor-area ratio] was to make it tall."

But its vertical audacity would draw howls of protests. And there was another reason to expect controversy: David Childs had designed Time Warner Center with the intent of drawing New Yorkers into Columbus Circle — he sought to merge the streets, and create the sense that Central Park South continued west.

In designing 15 CPW, Robert A.M. Stern had looked to the great prewar buildings that surrounded it, and sought to create a grand limestone edifice that blended in with the neighborhood.

Barnett delivered a different mandate to the man he eventually hired to design his building, the French architect Christian de Portzamparc. Exterior architecture and the building's fit with the skyline were secondary — if that. Barnett's priority was making the inside space ideal for the captains of the universe who would live there.

"A lot of architects want those beautiful art objects, and they design it from the outside in and you wind up with unusable or not such beautiful internal residences," Barnett explained. "And the first thing we look at is, 'how do people live, and how should the floor plans be?' So we gave Christian de Portzamparc our designs and said, 'We want these to be the layouts. Now you go to make it beautiful.'"

In addition to maximizing the interior spaces, Barnett wanted "gracious-size rooms," plus high ceilings. He wanted large kitchens and family rooms. He wanted top-of-the-line finishes. But most of all, he wanted sweeping, unobstructed views to take advantage of the tower's prime location.

It was an approach likely to delight his exclusive clientele — at the risk of enraging everybody else in the neighborhood. De Portzamparc's tower would be sheathed in a glass exterior, designed to create an "illusion of movement," the shading of its glass and steel exterior alternating in thin, neat dark and light lines on one side, and broken up into a cascade of smaller, shimmering squares on the others.

"I thought he came up with a beautiful design, creatively not getting stuck with the wedding-cake type New York zoning requirements, [where] you've got all the little setbacks," Barnett said.

Not everybody shared his opinion.

Some saw Barnett's towers in Manhattan as urban McMansions in the sky, totally out of context with the character of New York. One57 was just the most prominent.

"Look at Gary Barnett, these ugly fucking buildings that he's built," Related's Steve Ross would later grumble from his Time Warner Center office, casting a derisive nod in the direction of One57. "These guys are driven by dollars and they have no sense of taste."

In the years following the crash, however, it would become clear that however distasteful some true-blue New Yorkers found Barnett's aesthetic, the man was perfectly in tune with a new group of consumers who were to become the most prominent new entrants into the city's high-end real estate market. Rich foreigners who liked everything shiny, big, and new.

Right before the 15 CPW penthouse sale, Barnett had priced his 95 units at One57 starting at $6.4 million and going all the way up to $98.5 million for an 11,000-square-foot, six-bedroom penthouse. But after the 15 CPW sale, Barnett upped the penthouse price to $110 million. Next to the $12,571 a square foot that Rybolovleva paid, Barnett's new price of $10,000 a square foot for his penthouse was practically a bargain.

To sell his new building, Barnett rented a full floor at the Fuller Building at 41 East 57th Street and Madison Avenue, and spent, according to Field, somewhere in the neighborhood of $2 million to outfit it and create promotional materials. Visitors to the sales office saw all the spoils that would be available to new residents: herringbone floors, corridors with silk wall coverings and asymmetrical entryways, hand-crafted kitchen cabinetry with built-in wine racks, marble bathroom fixtures, steam showers, and a 24-foot aquarium. The interiors were to be designed by the Danish architect Thomas Juul-Hansen.

"In terms of quality, in terms of the kind of level of finishes that we were delivering, you know, [it was] super-high quality," Barnett said. "Everything slab, different choices, different bathroom finishes. The kitchens were imported from England. So nobody had really done that yet."

"At 15 CPW, a lot of the finishes were throwaways," he continued. "Almost everybody changed out the finishes. So what we did is, we said we're going to make it really nice, we don't want people building for the next 10 years and disrupting everything. So I think it took it up a notch there." (Barnett said the approach was adopted and eventually brought up another notch at Vornado's 220 Central Park South nearby.)

Barnett also played up the views from the top, which he referred to as "the money shot." To do so, he chartered a helicopter and used drone footage to take shots from the levels of the apartment, then paid for the production of a slick video.

For brokers like Field, One57 was just what they had been waiting for. When she stepped into the building's sales office for the first time to see Barnett's presentation, she was in awe. Stepping off the elevator, she saw massive double doors rising up to extra-high ceilings in a cavernous room. The lights went down, and on a huge screen at the front of the room, a movie started. With thunderous music blasting through surround sound — the room actually shook with the bass — a cultured voice discussed what living well meant in Manhattan.

Then came the stunning vistas of Central Park, and a camera zooming in on a model of the sleek glass and steel building. Barnett also positioned the five-star hotel at the base as the ultimate amenity, "a place for your guests if you have people over that you don't have room for or don't want them in your house."

"It was supersized real estate on steroids — a full floor before people really spent that kind of money," Field recalled. "It's one of those great ones that you've seen that everybody else now does but it was the first one of its kind. It was really spectacular for all of us."

By the time One57 opened, Field had positioned herself to make a number of the first big sales. Barnett had previously tapped her to "close out" a couple of his buildings — she had sold the final full-floor unit at the Stanhope to a Goldman Sachs partner, and the final three units at Lucida.

So, in the fall of 2011, Field was back with one of her longtime clients, the Canadian fashion magnate Lawrence Stroll (Field would not reveal the names of her clients but they were later widely reported in the press). In the 1980s, Stroll, along with his partner Silas Chou, a native of Hong Kong, had backed Tommy Hilfiger, and would later take the fashion label Michael Kors public, becoming a billionaire in the process.

Stroll was serious enough about buying that when Field brought him back for a second visit, Barnett was waiting in the showroom to deliver the presentation personally. The sales office had been open about three days, Field said, when her client announced he would take a 6,240-square-foot, four-bedroom, full-floor unit on the 85th floor.

Even with a discount for being the first big buyer, the price was just shy of $50 million.

Soon after, Field received a phone call from Chou, who related that Stroll "says it's great."

"Get me one too!" he told her.

Field called Barnett and negotiated the deal over the phone, agreeing that Chou would pay a little more than $50 million for the 82nd floor.

"It literally took like three minutes," she recalled.

"We had a diamond to sell," she added. "I was in there three days a week for about eight months."

Field would eventually sell 12 units, with three buyers from Russia, one Brit, the Canadian and his Hong Kong partner, a Singaporean, and two from Texas. (All told, foreign buyers would account for roughly 50 percent of the units, with the Chinese making up a full 15 percent, according to the Times.)

Chinese money would flow in not just at the individual level. The nation had a huge trade surplus and big ambitions for the future, and in the years following the subprime crash, the government there was urging its companies to invest overseas, in order to diversify its assets and improve the country's leverage on the international stage.

Between the summers of 2010 and 2011, Chinese banks would quietly pour more than $1 billion into the New York City real estate market,[92] Chinese companies would sign major leases at the Empire State Building and 1 World Trade Center, and begin to invest in construction projects. The investments would occur with little fanfare, but would soon grow so significant that when a Times reporter decided to investigate the trend in the summer of 2011, even veteran market watchers were surprised at the overall impact. When the reporter asked Dan Fasulo of Real Capital Analytics to quantify Chinese investments, Fasulo had run the numbers and then remarked, "It's truly amazing how much they have been able to do without being highlighted in public."

The marquee Chinese deal of the decade came in 2015, when Anbang Insurance Group paid $1.95 billion to purchase the iconic Waldorf Astoria hotel. The firm had gone on a debt-fueled spree from 2014 to 2016, snapping up trophy assets across the country. To explain the company's reasoning, then-chairman Wu Xiaohui invoked some homespun wisdom.

"If you choose to stay in rural villages, you can only meet common village girls," Wu told students at Harvard in 2015. "Yet if you come to Paris, you will have the chance to lay your eyes on the Mona Lisa."

---

92 Semple, Kirk. "As Investors, Chinese Turn to New York." *The New York Times*. August 11, 2011.

Individual Chinese investors would offer another source of manna for developers through a little-known federal visa program known as "EB-5," which offered green cards to foreigners who agreed to invest $500,000 or more in U.S. job-creating projects.

Congress had originally created the EB-5 immigrant visa category in 1990 to allow the entry of immigrants seeking to enter to engage in commercial enterprises that would directly create at least 10 American jobs.[93] Though the required investment amount was $1 million, $500,000 was deemed sufficient if the business was set up in specially designated rural or high-unemployment urban areas. Two years later, Congress added a provision that allowed foreigners seeking green cards to take a more indirect route — they could bypass the requirement to create the jobs themselves, by simply investing their money with a government-accredited "regional center," defined as public or private entities that then funneled the money into projects that promoted economic growth.

By 2003, the program had generated an estimated $1 billion in investment, but was still nowhere near generating the $5 billion a year allowable under the visa quotas. In the years after Lehman, however, it became such an important part of the new ad-hoc financing system for real estate development that market players referred to it as the industry's new "crack cocaine."

One of the first hustlers to see the potential the program held for development was Nicholas Mastroianni II, a Long Island–born developer with a checkered past who heard about it from one of his bankers in 2009. Mastroianni was complaining over lunch one day in South Florida that he couldn't get a construction loan to finance a long-planned $127 million mixed-use waterfront development, when the banker mentioned that one

---

93 Testimony of Stephen Yale-Loehr. Hearing on Promoting Job Creation and Foreign Investment in the United States. July 22, 2009.

of his clients had found a creative solution: That client had convinced scores of investors in Ireland, Scotland, and China to cough up millions of dollars in exchange for green cards through the EB-5 program, and used those funds to restart a stalled project in Vermont.

Not only did Mastrioanni eventually manage to tap the program for enough funding to get construction started on his Jupiter, Florida, project, word of his success quickly spread — all the way to Manhattan.

"So we went out and we did a capital raise and we raised enough money in a weekend, you know, two days, and from that point forward, you know, I saw the opportunity," Mastrioanni recalled. There were 150 projects that were stagnant and couldn't get any financing. And I said, 'We will be the largest lender in this space in the New York market."

XXVII

City Within a City

The Hudson Yards Masterplan

R elated had won the right to develop a project that could net it billions. But to get there would be a yearslong high-wire act.

In May 2010, the developer announced it had brought on an equity partner at Hudson Yards: Oxford Properties Group, the real estate investment arm of giant Canadian pension fund OMERS. The deal would allow Ross to spread the risk of what was being billed as the largest private development in U.S. history, and also let him tap into Oxford's extensive network to help fund the project, which would need billions of dollars in capital over the next few years.

"Their investment in the West Side Yards is an unequivocal show of confidence in the future of New York," Ross said in the announcement.

In an indication of just how large the job ahead would be, the joint venture blanketed the site with more than 30,000 square feet of new construction signage — said to be among the largest installations of such signage ever created.

It was an intimidating challenge. If Time Warner Center had been large, Hudson Yards was gargantuan. The sheer size of the development would require a different kind of thinking. But there were reasons to be bullish. Ross could make a strong case that Chelsea and the area around the High Line were already the hottest neighborhoods in the city. Related had several buildings in the area, and they were getting higher rents than anywhere else in Manhattan.

In order to convince New Yorkers to move farther north and west into the empty space of the railyards, however, Ross would first need to provide the kind of infrastructure that could support them: restaurants, shops, grocery stores. But it was a bit of a catch-22: how could you entice restaurants, shops, and grocery stores to commit to this huge empty space when no residents were in sight?

The key, Ross and his team had always felt, was the early recruitment of blue-chip office tenants. If Related could promise a critical mass of free-spending office workers in the area — and he and his team were eventually expecting to house 40,000 white-collar professionals — it would have no trouble inking the retail and hospitality tenants to serve them. Residential would then follow. That was part of why losing News Corp on the eve of that first round of bidding back in 2008 had been so devastating. Without the right mix of companies committed to the area, the project might well fail.

"If we found office tenants, then we would then get retail because they'd see the office was there, and if we had retail, then residents would want to live there," Ross said. "So that was the whole concept of what Hudson Yards was. We wanted to create a great, great place."

Ross knew there was demand for premium office product. Some 70 percent of Manhattan space was 60 years or older, and the city was lagging behind other global capitals in adding top-tier office properties. The idea of building the facilities needed to serve them on the Far West Side had long been a popular one.

"New York faces stiff economic competition from other U.S. cities and major cities across the globe and we need to invest in our own economic future," Senator Chuck Schumer had told business leaders a few years earlier, arguing for the West Side expansion shortly after the stadium plan had been defeated. "We must push ahead with our long-term goals, unlocking the potential of the less developed parts of the city like the Far West Side while continuing the most vital work of rebuilding Downtown. We can and we must do both."

The first major office tower Related would build was 10 Hudson Yards, an 895-foot-tall building that would rise on the southeast corner of the yards, at 10th Avenue and 30th Street, abutting the High Line. The tower would form the southern edge of a planned three-building, 5.5 million-square-foot "superblock" running from 30th to 33rd streets and 10th and 11th avenues that would include a sprawling indoor retail and restaurant complex in the middle, and, eventually on the other side of that, the largest skyscraper in the complex at 30 Hudson Yards.

Privately, Ross said, he and his team had concluded early on that they were unlikely to make money on their first two office buildings. They were prepared to offer major concessions to recruit the kind of tenants they were looking for to provide a "critical mass to start the project."

The name of their anchor tenant would surface publicly for the first time in November 2010: The New York-based luxury goods maker Coach,[94] which sold its handbags and wallets at 400 stores and had $1 billion in cash on its balance sheet, was considering the move, the New York Post reported.

---

94   Cuozzo, Steve. "These Vacant Eyesores Are Piggy Banks for the Global Elite." *The New York Post*. March 10, 2018.

Coach already owned a 265,000-square-foot headquarters on West 34th Street and a smaller building just a block down, but was said to be in the market for up to 600,000 square feet of office space in the area. It would be months before they finally agreed on terms, but when the deal was signed and announced in October 2011, it was hailed as a major step forward. Under the terms of the deal, Coach would purchase 600,000 square feet in the first tower to be built in Hudson Yards — the bottom third of what would be a 1.7 million-square-foot, 51-story skyscraper. In the end, Ross said, Coach got the office space "at cost," with Related also agreeing to buy the land on which their previous headquarters had sat.

In exchange, Coach planned to move 1,500 employees into the building and create "a vertical campus with an atrium serving as the visual anchor for the High Line."

The mother of all engineering, construction, and sales jobs was underway.

Amid all this, Ross would thrust one of his key deputies, Jeff Blau, into the spotlight. Even back in college at the University of Michigan in the late 1980s, Blau was all about doing deals.

As a sophomore, he'd set up his own business producing course packs and selling them to his classmates. He convinced professors to let him hire their teaching assistants to take notes in their classes, and sold those too. He also teamed up with a local contractor to buy single-family homes in Ann Arbor and subdivided them into student apartments.

Blau's father was a contractor and Blau had spent his summers in his hometown of Woodbury, Long Island, working on job sites. So, in 1988 when Blau signed up for a graduate-level real estate development class as a junior, he was hardly a noob. There were 49 other students in the class, most seeking MBAs, or master's degrees in urban planning, architecture, or construction and engineering. But Peter Allen, the local developer who taught the class, was so impressed by Blau's final project — a proposal for a mixed-use development — he offered him a job at his firm.

"He just naturally understood the field," Allen would later recall. "He was so good — not just at the financials, but the big picture. He could quantify all these issues of mix and density and quality and architecture. That is a hard thing to do."

Blau turned down Allen's job offer, citing a desire to return to New York. But soon after, a Michigan alumnus, Steve Ross, arrived on campus to deliver a keynote address. After the speech, Ross asked Allen for the name of his best student.

"We have one of the brightest kids I've ever seen come here," Allen told Ross. "He wants to come to New York. You've got to hire him."

That had been the start, to quote Humphrey Bogart in "Casablanca," of "a beautiful friendship." And a lucrative one, too.

Now some 24 years later, on a Thursday evening, Allen, Ross, and his longtime deputy were back in Ann Arbor. By then, Blau and Ross had been working together so long, they resembled father and son. Both sat with legs crossed, with near-identical posture, Ross in a gray suit, turquoise tie, and glasses, his oxford cuffs poking out of the sleeves; Blau in a navy blue suit, pink tie, and glasses, looking much the same. The name of the venue itself was a testament to their partnership: the panel was at the Ross School of Business, in the Blau Auditorium.

It was only appropriate that Allen, the man who first introduced them, moderated the event that night. And in the midst of fielding questions from students, Ross made an unscripted but momentous announcement.

"I'll be the first to tell you that next week, we're announcing he's the CEO and I'm just the chairman — you'll read about that next week, I'm sure," Ross said, pointing to Blau, during an exchange about the future of Related. "Just don't tell the press." Related then rushed out a statement confirming the succession plan: Steve Ross was stepping down as CEO of his company. Jeff Blau, 44, would step up. And Bruce Beal would take over Blau's old position as president.

Though Blau would oversee much of the dealmaking, and Beal would focus on bringing the deals to life, Ross had no plans to retire. In addition to remaining chairman and majority owner of the company, Ross would be freed up to throw himself into projects of his choosing. And for the foreseeable future, he intended to immerse himself in Hudson Yards.

A couple of weeks after Ross unveiled his succession plan, the public would get its first detailed look at the vision for the project. Ross invited New York Magazine's architecture critic Justin Davidson to attend what he described as a "high-octane conclave" of architects and real estate executives.

With the groundbreaking for 10 Hudson Yards just weeks away, Davidson took in a high-resolution presentation of the yards and reached for the adjectives to prepare New Yorkers for what would soon fill the gaping hole on the city's Far West Side.

"A chain of glowing towers garlands the skyline, and tiny figures stroll onto a deck hanging nearly a quarter mile in the air," he would write. "Architects discuss access points, sidewalk widths, ceiling heights, flower beds, and the qualities of crushed-stone pathways. You could almost forget that none of this exists yet — until one architect points to a lozenge-shaped skyscraper and casually, with a twist of his wrist, remarks that he's thinking of swiveling it 90 degrees."

There were two ways to conceive of a monster project, Davidson noted. The first approach was to choose an architectural overlord to ensure a unified vision. This was the approach the creators of Rockefeller Center had taken back in the 1930s, with Raymond Hood conjuring limestone-clad Art Deco towers that transformed the Midtown skyline.

Ross chose the second option. He would bring together "the great architects of the world," he explained, and create a "collection like no other place." The overall mix of the development would be designed to mirror the diversity of the city at large — with the architecture of its many buildings ranging from masonry to glass and steel, a mix of apartment buildings, hotels, and offices throughout. The choice liberated Ross from the risk of "oppressive uniformity," but exposed the project to the risk of an un-unified product, a "jumble," Davidson warned.

Still, it was hard not to be impressed by the names who would be involved. Present in the room that day were William Pedersen, co-founder of the high-rise titans Kohn Pedersen Fox; David Childs, partner at the juggernaut Skidmore Owings and Merrill, who had designed Time Warner Center; Elizabeth Diller, from the "cerebral boutique" Diller Scofidio + Renfro, whose visions had informed the High Line; David Rockwell, a "virtuoso of showbiz and restaurant design"; Howard Elkus, from the high-end shopping-center specialists Elkus Manfredi; and landscape architect Thomas Woltz.

Other architects later tapped to design buildings for the more residential Western Yards would include Robert A.M. Stern, Frank Gehry, and Santiago Calatrava, creator of the World Trade Center Oculus.

The schedule, too, was beginning to come into focus. Following the anticipated 2016 completion of 10 Hudson Yards, KPF's 55 Hudson Yards was slated to be finished by 2019. That same year, the million-square-foot seven-level retail-and-food complex designed by Elkus Manfredi would open, along with Diller's "architectural griffin."

At the base of this residential behemoth would sit Hudson Yards' answer to Jazz at Lincoln Center, a 170,000-square-foot cultural facility called "the Shed," fronted by an open-air plaza. The plaza could be covered with an eight-million-pound retractable "shed" — a fanciful roof — that could be opened and closed within 15 minutes. The space would eventually host everything from musical performances to art shows to New York Fashion Week. It would be followed by the mammoth 30 Hudson Yards and a 1,000-foot-high mixed-use tower at 35 Hudson

Yards, designed by David Childs.

Yet for all this fancy architecture, the overall success of the project, Davidson opined, might very well depend on the "most delicate, crucial, and treacherous design problem at Hudson Yards" — a design problem that was still unsolved: the way that Ross and Related chose to handle vast public space, particularly the five acres in the middle. Success could produce "the most vibrant gathering spot on the West Side, a New York version of Venice's Piazza San Marco," failure "a windswept tundra populated only by office workers scuttling between the subway and their desks."

"In the end, how tightly the new superblocks are woven into the city fabric, how organic their feel, and how bright their allure will depend on the judgment and taste of a billionaire whose aesthetic ambitions match the site's expanse, and who slips almost unconsciously from we to I," Davidson wrote.

Those five acres of public space were very much on Ross's mind, too.

With open space, the plaza would be bigger than London's Trafalgar Square, New York's Bryant Park, even Rockefeller Center. Rome's Trevi square had its famous fountain, and beautiful sculptures, to draw legions of tourists and onlookers and render it one of the most vibrant parts of the city. Rockefeller Center had its Christmas tree — a must-visit for both residents and tourists.

Woltz's firm, Nelson Byrd Woltz, had pitched an elaborate design that included a lawn, a man-made stream, and a reflecting quarter-inch skim of water in front of the cultural shed that could be drained whenever the Shed's canopy needed to be rolled out. It also had six-story lookout towers composed of a pair of ramps spiraling in a double helix and wrapped in a perforated screen of rust-colored, weathered steel.[95]

Ross hired the firm. But he wanted changes. He recounted, to New Yorker writer Ian Parker, one of his first meetings with Woltz.

"Throw those plans out!" Ross told him.

Ross then took Woltz to a window in Time Warner Center overlooking Columbus Circle.

"Look at Columbus Circle, how hard it is," he recalled telling Woltz.

"There would be no grass on his plaza," Parker would later write. "Ross, however, had clearly absorbed the idea of an ornament."

The creation of the new business and shopping district envisioned by Doctoroff and Bloomberg was always going to be expensive. Whoever won the bidding for the 26-acre development site at its heart would have to first construct a $2 billion platform over the railyards, that would allow the trains to continue to operate. In addition, the city wanted 12 acres of public open space, a cultural component, a 750-seat public school as well as 10 percent of the units to be reserved for affordable housing.

It was true that municipal and state officials in the mid-aughts had offered up a long list of incentives, committing to spend at least $4 billion in the area, extending a subway line to the Far West Side, constructing a series of new parks, and offering tax abatements valued at upwards of $1 billion over 25 years for commercial and retail buildings, a number likely to rise higher in the years ahead.

But in order to make all its money back — and to then maximize the kind of profits that would draw institutional investors — Ross and his team were always counting on the fact that they could build disproportionately for the 1 percent. The have-nots could look elsewhere.

Related would fill one of the buildings with a luxury shopping mall.

---

95   Parker, Ian. "Stairmaster." *The New York Times.* February 26, 2018.

Rising over it would loom five gleaming glass and steel skyscrapers, with luxury condos priced from $4.3 million to $32 million, and offices fit for Manhattan's Masters of the Universe.

At the time, few questioned these decisions.

"It was a reasonable deal," Kathryn Wylde, president of pro-business group Partnership for New York City, would later say. "If anybody looks at what Related has invested and compares it to 50 years of vacant, dead space, creating no jobs, and contributing nothing to the tax bills, it's hard not to see the benefit."

As 2010 drew to a close, Bloomberg's new economic development czar, Robert K. Steel, made his first speech. A former Goldman Sachs executive and treasury official, Steel chose the New York offices of Google a few blocks south of the Hudson Yards site to highlight his strategy for the next phase of New York City's economic evolution.

The city, Steel warned, had fallen far behind San Francisco, Boston, and other metro areas in the competition to attract new technology companies — a coveted metric of the "creative city" long since highlighted by Richard Florida and other urban planning gurus. To catch up, Steel announced, New York was planning a new initiative to attract a top-tier graduate school of engineering capable of competing with the likes of Stanford and MIT. To attract the institution, the city was willing to consider locating a new facility on one or more of its properties.

The competition proved to be a popular one: In the months that followed, a wide range of institutions that included Carnegie Mellon, Stanford, and Columbia University would throw their hats in the ring.

In December 2011, Bloomberg announced the city had chosen Cornell University to create a new graduate program on Roosevelt Island, a $2 billion campus with as much as 2.1 million square feet of space. The university promised to have its first classes running by the following September. To get the deal done, the city had provided land and agreed to contribute $100 million in infrastructure improvements.

In its announcement, the New York City Economic Development Corporation projected that the new campus would generate more than $23 billion in overall economic activity over the course of the next three decades, as well as $1.4 billion in total tax revenue. It stated that the campus would create up to 20,000 construction jobs and up to 8,000 permanent jobs, and nearly 600 spin-off companies that would create up to an additional 30,000 permanent jobs.

"When people look back 100 years from now, I believe that they will remember today as a signal moment in the transformation of the city's economy," Steel said. "This is an inflection point in an economic renaissance that will position New York City for outsized success in the decades and centuries to come."

The support was bipartisan.

"Job creation is a top priority for the City Council, and with the selection of Cornell University, we're one step closer to bringing new jobs to New York City and becoming the technology capital of the world," said City Council Speaker Christine Quinn.

With construction of millions of square feet of new cutting-edge office space in Hudson Yards finally underway, and plans for a new tech hub in place, the potential for the city's continued evolution seemed limitless.

XXVIII

Redefining Rich

The Rise of Billionaires' Row

G ary Barnett was not the only developer to recognize the megabucks to be made by building tall, thin, and park-facing. In fact, the first half of the 2010s became an ultra-luxury arms race, with each new project trying to outshine and outspend its predecessors.

Plans for what came to be known as the second "supertall" — a skyscraper rising to heights in the range of 1,000 feet or more on 57th Street — were revealed in October 2012.[96] The project, east of Barnett's rising tower, had a familiar name attached to it: Harry Macklowe.

In late 2009, the wily developer had managed to convince L.A.–based private equity firm CIM Group to buy up the distressed debt on his

---

96 Barrionuevo, Alexei. "Another Tower for the New York Skyline." *The New York Times*. October 4, 2012.

prized development site and partner with him to bring his original vision to fruition.

"Is this a comeback?" he cheekily told the Times,[97] feigning "astonishment" to have heard that word employed in connection to what the paper called "his latest, and probably his final, resurrection."

"I never really went away," he said.

The building, 432 Park Avenue, would rise just shy of 1,400 feet, besting Barnett's One57 by 400 feet. Slated for completion in 2015, Macklowe was touting it as the tallest residential structure in the Western Hemisphere. Designed by the Uruguayan architect Rafael Viñoly, it would present a distinctive matchbox silhouette. It would include 147 condo units, with 122 pads starting at $5 million and an additional 25 studios on sale for use of "service personnel." The crown jewel would be an 8,255-square-foot six-bedroom penthouse on the 95th floor, priced at $82.6 million, or about $10,000 a square foot. The building would feature a private restaurant on the 12th floor. There would be four floors of amenities including a fitness center, pool, whirlpool, sauna, steam room, library, and conference and screening rooms. There would be 18 wine cellars, 12 office units, 3 retail spaces, and a porte cochere modeled after the one at 15 Central Park West, so the wealthy could arrive discreetly.

A few months after construction began, a pinstriped suit–clad Macklowe, by then 76, took a Times reporter on a tour of the project, leading him up some 30 stories to the most recently completed floor. This "is a once-in-a-lifetime opportunity," he said. "There'll never be another job like this one. It's going to live on for a very long time after I'm gone."

Though designed by Viñoly, the Times noted that Macklowe had "engaged, almost manically, with its minutiae, going so far as to

97 Bagli, Charles V. "Harry Macklowe Gambles Again." *The New York Times*. October 6, 2013.

commission showers with drains free of grates (so as not to disturb the book-matched marble floors) and designing the lobby as a reference to the Pantheon in Rome."

"Unlike any other new building, the architectural gesture here is one of total and complete integrity," Macklowe said. "There is nothing jarring in the building, nothing that takes you away from its shape. In my career of 50 years, this is the true distillation of everything I've learned. This is it." (Viñoly would later see it slightly differently, saying that the tower "has a couple of screwups, but it has integrity.")

Macklowe would later reveal that the building was actually inspired by a trash can, one designed by Josef Hoffmann and based on the perfect geometrical pattern: the square.

"If you look at it very carefully you see a rhythm, you see a pattern, you see what we call push-pull between negative and positive. So that was very inspirational to Rafael Viñoly and I," he said.

Macklowe also acknowledged that in the race to build the tallest building, "there's a certain amount of penis envy."

Overall reaction was mixed. While some praised it as sleek and elegant, others found it jarringly out of context with everything around it — a giant middle-finger to the legions of New Yorkers who could never afford to live there, and now could see Macklowe's phallic trash can every time they drove in from Queens. Many New Yorkers would come to hate it.

Macklowe's precise stake in the project was not public — and certainly was not anywhere near what it had been on the Equity Office deal. The key force was most certainly CIM.

Founded 15 years earlier by an American banker and two former Israeli paratroopers, CIM, which had a nearly $10 billion war chest with major U.S. pension funds among its investors, had initially been looking to buy three rental properties from Macklowe. But after meeting with the developer, the firm's principals decided instead to take a chance on him by paying off Macklowe's 10 creditors, who held a total of $510 million of the debt on the project, some at severely discounted rates.

"It felt like the world was coming to an end," Savills Studley's Woody Heller, who brokered the deal, would later say. Yet CIM was prepared "to put up a lot of money, all cash," and "at the time it wasn't clear how they were going to be able to finance construction of the building."

To build what would eventually become the $1 billion-plus condo and retail tower, CIM would score $400 million from a British hedge fund, the Children's Investment Fund, which would lend the money at a steep interest rate of 10 percent.

The Drake site would be CIM's entry into New York. The firm liked to partner with local operators in new markets, so they were happy to keep Macklowe in the mix, but his place in the pecking order was clear.

Macklowe, CIM principal Avi Shemesh told the Wall Street Journal, is "involved with the thought process and decision-making, but the final decision is ours."

By the end of 2011, CIM would complete 11 deals across the city, valued at more than $1 billion. Like Fortress, it would emerge as one of the biggest winners in the wake of the financial crisis. Those properties would include an office building in Soho it acquired with Jared Kushner. It also became a lender on one of the city's most prominent projects: Trump Soho.

By 2014, Macklowe and CIM had sold more than half their units at 432 Park and listed the penthouse for $95 million (it would later be bought by Saudi retail magnate Fawaz Al Hokair for $88 million). The project's website offered details in Russian, Chinese, Italian, Portuguese, French, and Spanish, among other languages. And at least one third of the buyers came from overseas.

Ads for Billionaires' Row projects were found in international media, targeting the world's oligarchs and other assorted supperich. And with one of Barnett's One57 penthouses under contract for $90 million, the city's clan of elite developers sprang into action, unabashedly targeting billionaires. No fewer than five more supertall, ultra-luxury buildings were planned near One57 and 432 Park.

Though homes asking north of $5 million constituted just 8 percent of the market, about half the new projects launched in this period targeted that price point. The tighter mortgage standards that remained in the wake of the credit bubble had little relevance to these new condos: About 80 percent of the buyers were paying for their new digs in all-cash.

"They love this asset class," David Friedman, then-president of global wealth data aggregator Wealth-X, said to *The Real Deal* of ultra-high-net-worth individuals.

Though banks still remained risk averse, Wall Street, sovereign wealth funds, and private capital "had all this money burning a hole in their pockets," the appraiser Jonathan Miller noted. Interest rates remained at historic lows, yet investors wanted high returns. They were looking for high-yield investments.

It was unclear how deep the market actually was for $10 million-plus apartments, but the thirst to cash in on it pushed the price for potential development sites, particularly those that could tap into Central Park's global cachet, into the stratosphere. Monied Manhattanites preferred to live on the Upper East Side or further Downtown, but wealthy foreigners loved 57th Street. By the end of 2013, bidding wars drove land prices so high, the winners had no choice but to go supertall to recoup their costs.

The Times' Bagli harkened back to the first gilded age, when the 843 acres of Central Park had inspired another boom in ultra-luxury housing along Fifth Avenue, with the Astor, Vanderbilt, Frick, and Whitney families all building mansions along a stretch of Fifth Avenue north of 50th Street — a stretch known as "Millionaires' Row." Now, a new row of opulence was rising, dominated by tall, slender cigarette buildings, so tall and so skinny that to some longtime New Yorkers, it seemed almost absurd.

"Taken together, the seven high-rise buildings promise to remake the skyline and to redefine what it means to be rich in a city that is a cradle of capitalism and not so long ago was an emblem of urban poverty," Bagli wrote.

Bagli referred to the stretch by its new nickname: "Billionaires' Row."

The planned projects included a 950-foot-tall residential tower to be built by Steve Roth's Vornado between Central Park South and 58th Street, and between 7th Avenue and Broadway.

To make way for the project that would come to be known as 220 Central Park South, Roth had managed to get rid of the rent-stabilized tenants of the 20-story building on the site so he could knock it down, prompting a legal battle. In 2009, the court had sided with Roth — who had cited laws allowing such evictions if the developer planned to demolish the building in question. But the developer still had to settle accounts with those leaving, and paid millions to buy out the tenants who were still present in the building. After demolition had been completed in early 2013, Roth had hired 15 CPW designer Robert A.M. Stern to design another limestone tower, and the developer hoped to top the unprecedented level of luxury offered at Barnett's One57.

But Barnett had found a way to profit from that deal, too.

In 2005, he had approached the owners of a garage that had a lease in the basement of Vornado's building, and paid them an inflated price to buy a 49 percent stake in that lease. He also bought a small development parcel on 58th Street ("nothing but a little sliver of land," as one source put it) that was in the middle of Vornado's development site.

Barnett then played a war of attrition with Roth, until the titan capitulated and agreed to pay Barnett a whopping $194 million — or about $1,400 a foot — for the parcel and an agreement to surrender the garage lease.

The developers came to terms on design adjustments for their competing towers: Vornado would shift its project slightly to the west, while Extell would move its planned luxury condo on West 57th Street — what would eventually become Central Park Tower, the city's tallest residential building — to the east. Extell would also cantilever its skyscraper 28 feet to the east over the landmarked Art Students League building, a move the Times' architecture critic Michael Kimmelman said resembled "a giant with one foot raised, poised to squash a poodle."

Just a couple doors down from Barnett's One57, his old partner Kevin Maloney had teamed up with JDS Development Group's Michael Stern on a super-skinny 1,350-foot-tall tower at 111 West 57th Street near Sixth Avenue to be called "Steinway Tower," in ode to the headquarters of Steinway & Sons that once stood there. Further east, at 252 West 57th street between Seventh and Eighth avenues, Rose Associates and the World Wide Group were planning a 712-foot tower with ultra-luxury condos starting on the 36th floor.

Will and Arthur Zeckendorf had again enlisted Stern to design a 51-story tower at 43 East 60th Street, just off Park Avenue. They hoped to replicate the success of their 15 CPW, but add an even more rarified East Side air to the project, which would be dubbed 520 Park Avenue.

The lobby would be a blend of wood, metal, and Sarrancolin marble, a material the developers claimed was once favored by French kings. Residents would enjoy 15,000 square feet of amenities, the centerpiece of which was to be an underground swimming pool room, with 1,000 pieces of marble fringed by hand-carved stone lattice work under a high, vaulted ceiling, resembling a cathedral. Each of the 33 condos would encompass at least one full floor and feature stunning views. (The lowest apartment would be on the 14th floor,[98] thanks to an ingenious ploy in which they

---

98   Piore, Adam. "How Architect Robert A.M. Stern Is Reviving Manhattan's Gilded Age." *Departures*. May 3, 2018.

placed six extra-tall mechanical levels — which don't count toward the allotted square footage — on the lower floors).

The money to realize these ostentatious creations came largely from foreign sources. Roth's 220 CPS was built with a $950 million loan from Bank of China, while Barnett's key equity partner on Central Park Tower was Shanghai Municipal Investment, the largest state-owned enterprise in Shanghai. Barnett would even tap the Israeli bond markets for funds. The Zeckendorfs had also turned to the Children's Investment Fund for nearly $500 million in loans to build 520 Park. By 2015, at least five of the seven largest luxury condo projects would turn to foreign sources to finance construction.

Much of the finished product was destined for foreign hands, too. New York builders building for New Yorkers was no longer in vogue.

XXIX

Family Feud

Mentor to Tormentor

For golden boy Kent Swig, it was a master class in resilience. Throughout his long, post-recession winter, the fallen mogul had tried to keep to a routine, appearing at 770 Lexington every day, attending meetings, signing checks, and running his brokerages.

Once he left the office, however, the harsh reality of his situation was always there waiting for him. The judgments had continued to pile up, and by 2011, he owed more than $115 million to 19 separate creditors. His bank accounts remained frozen, as did his credit cards. And he had "no income whatsoever."

"I had zero — nothing," Swig would later say. "I lived on charity and the kindness of other people."

He had arranged for his rent to be prepaid. And every week, his brother sent him $400 to pay for food and other expenses. A friend bought him a six-pack of beer every week, while his business partner David Burris got him a subway pass. Others occasionally took him out to lunch and dinner. Swig used frequent-flier miles to travel. For someone accustomed to the high life, it could have been seen as hitting bottom. But in fact, Swig would later look back on those times as deeply meaningful. It certainly was different.

One night, Swig arranged for a friend who owned a restaurant to give him a meal on the house, so he could take his 18-year-old son out for dinner. When his son, unaware of the arrangement but keenly aware of Swig's financial plight, attempted to slip Swig his credit card under the table, his broke father was overwhelmed with pride. "That he would be so sensitive that I'd be embarrassed not to be able to take him out, and that he'd give me his credit card so it made it look like I took him out for dinner?" Swig recalled. "I wouldn't trade those kinds of moments for anything."

At another point, one of his sons said to him: "'I'm looking at all this stress and all this stuff and the way you handled yourself. I'm so impressed and you're my hero in this. I don't know anybody who could have handled this gracefully, didn't crack up or jump or do anything but sit there and chip away and do all this stuff and still have all this time for me, do all this stuff, and it's the most impressive thing.' So when your son tells you that, it's like 'holy shit.'"

"My day-to-day life on the one hand changed massively," he continued. "On the other hand, things didn't change. I still went to work every day. I still had my kids. I still had my friends. But yes, I guess it changed on one level but on the other level I'm more of an optimist so I wake up every day, I'm thankful I'm in New York, the sun is shining, and you do your thing. You keep going."

Swig had vowed not to declare bankruptcy, a decision that astounded many observers. But he claimed to be determined to pay back his lenders, and refused to give up the possibility he could one day resurrect his development career.

At one point, a friend of Swig offered him a pair of Yankees tickets. When Swig arrived and realized they were second-row seats, just back from the field, he was horrified. He'd taken the subway out, he didn't even have enough money to buy a beer. But his seats placed him in the sightlines of television cameras. What would his lenders think if they happened to spot him sitting in luxury seats at the game?

Swig thought a lot about his creditors. If Swig were ever to change his situation, he knew, he would first have to change his relationship with them, many of whom still felt burned.

It would take months of cajoling, and talking, and pleading. But in the summer of 2011, some 23 months into the abyss, Swig had finally had a breakthrough. To unfreeze his accounts, he managed to get 22 different people in a room, representing all the parties he owed money to. He had been working on each of them privately, even as they fought over the scraps of his shattered empire. And now he made his pitch.

"Nobody wants to be here," Swig recalled telling them. "I certainly don't want to be here. I owe everybody money. It's not a good place to be."

"I don't think you believe I'm going to pay you back," he continued. "But I'll pay back every cent, your legal fees, everything. Just give me time. Let me run my stuff. I'll give you all the dollars I make. Let me run it."

That fall, he succeeded in finalizing an agreement. It listed 18 different creditors, with a claim on $116.6 million in debts, and Swig's interests in more than 100 different LLCs and other entities subject to garnishments, along with a complicated list of disbursements, with subsections, and subparagraphs, spelling out who would get paid, how much, and when. Further, it called for the appointment of an administrator of the agreement, with the power to liquidate any and all of Swig's assets if his creditors were not paid an agreed-upon amount by May 31, 2014.

But it finally allowed Swig access to his bank accounts, and allowed him to draw a monthly salary of $10,184.34 from Brown Harris Stevens and a percentage of any other compensation from Swig Equities.

In retrospect, Swig would come to view some of his creditors as his greatest allies — since they were the ones with the greatest stake in his recovery. Only if he bounced back would they get repaid.

At the same time, Swig was surprised to find that some of his previous allies had become his greatest antagonists.

Some friends "were waiting to see you fail and then they would stomp on you to take advantage," he later said. "So that's even more than not friends. That's vicious."

Swig declined to name names. But one of his tormentors was featured prominently in the news during that time: his former father-in-law, Harry Macklowe.

In the spring of 2012, family tensions burst back into the open, when Swig filed a lawsuit accusing Macklowe of launching a systematic campaign to force him into bankruptcy.[99] Swig filed his lawsuit in response to the Macklowes' efforts to collect on the $200,000 loan they had floated Swig to pay his legal bills three years earlier.

The New York tabloids noted that Swig's divorce had turned ugly, and highlighted Swig's claim that Macklowe was "allegedly looking to get even." By then, creditors were seeking to foreclose on the couple's 740 Park Avenue apartment and Hamptons home, and had even jeopardized the trusts of the two Swig sons, leading to separate litigation between Liz and Kent.

In his lawsuit, Swig accused Macklowe of secretly orchestrating five separate lawsuits against him, including those launched by Liz, noting that Stephen Meister, one of Macklowe's go-to attorneys for real estate matters, appeared to be involved in all five.

---

99 Gregorian, Dareh. "Cry of Ruin in Real-Estate Family Feud Pop, Just Leave Me a Loan!" *The New York Post.* May 7, 2012.

"The parties arrayed against Mr. Swig have no evident means of paying legal fees, or generating any income, other than Mr. Macklowe," the suit noted.

"The one and only goal of the...litigations is Mr. Swig's financial ruin," Swig's lawyer, Tom Mullaney, said in court papers. "Mr. Macklowe's campaign of scorched-earth litigation warfare and character assassination — all public — has no other explanation."

Noting the provision in the 2009 loan agreement in which the Macklowes had promised not to support actions that would drive Swig into bankruptcy, Swig's attorneys argued that the demand for the $200,000 repayment was invalid.

"The Macklowes have treated Mr. Swig [with] unadulterated spite," Swig's suit said, adding they've engaged in a "vendetta" to "derail Mr. Swig's return to financial health following his highly publicized recent business misfortunes."

To add to Swig's biblical problems was the flood at 740 Park.

On March 1, a washing machine sprung a leak in the unit above the estranged couple's apartment in the ultra-exclusive co-op, swamping their $32.5 million digs with water, and leading to a $270,000 insurance check to pay for the damage. The fate of this check would be the next public flash point. In February 2013, the combatants were back in the news, when Swig filed court papers, accusing Macklowe of forging his signature on the check and cashing it. Macklowe denied the allegations, and Macklowe's attorney took to the tabloids to shoot back at Swig.

"It is unfortunate that in the context of a divorce proceeding Mr. Swig has chosen to resort to desperate tactics of baseless and libelous claims against the parents of his ex-wife," Meister told the New York Daily News.[100]

---

100   Gregorian, Dareh. "Titans' Cash Clash Realty Big, Son-in-Law Feud Suit: Checks Forged to Cover 270G." *The New York Daily News*. May 15, 2013.

That July, a judge ruled in favor of Harry and Linda Macklowe, agreeing that Swig did indeed owe them $260,591.12 — the principal plus interest. And on September 16, the judgment was recorded as satisfied.

XXX

Exit Stage Left

From Technocrat to Progressive

O n January 1, 2014, Michael Bloomberg, New York's richest man, completed his three terms in office, a period in which he had presided over the city's shift to a mecca for the monied, enriching hundreds of developers in the process.

His administration's impact was transformative. New York City added 40,000 new buildings during his time in office, and growth exploded in Downtown, the West Side from Chelsea to Lincoln Square, Central Harlem, Long Island City, Flushing, Williamsburg, Bushwick, and the South Bronx. His planning czar, Amanda Burden, rezoned a staggering 37 percent of the city, according to the Times, allowing for the construction of luxury housing and retail in areas once defined by industrial blight. And developers cheered him on every step of the way, profiting handsomely from the rezonings, the drop in crime rates, and the influx of wealth that happened on his watch.

The previous year, the new graduate school for techies had opened on Roosevelt Island to its first seven students — a number that would soon reach the thousands — establishing the city as a breeding ground for new tech talent.

"We have beaten the odds and the obstructionists over and over again," the mayor declared in his final State of the City address in March 2013. (He opted to deliver his swan song at the Barclays Center, part of the controversial megadevelopment known as Atlantic Yards, which was later renamed Pacific Park after a flurry of negative press about how the project was a giveaway to its developer, Forest City Ratner, and made the neighborhood less affordable.)

And, yet, the voters' choice to succeed Bloomberg seemed a direct repudiation of this legacy.

As the next mayor they had chosen Bill de Blasio, whose critiques of the real estate industry had only intensified in the four years since, as the city's Public Advocate, he had introduced the "Worst Landlord Watchlist." De Blasio had railed against the haven for the wealthy that New York had become, and vowed that the city's relationship with developers was due for a "fundamental reset."

"It used to be in New York you worried about getting mugged," de Blasio told political magazine National Journal. "But today's mugging is economic. Can you afford your rent?"

His campaign rallying cry was that New York had become a 'tale of two cities," a marvelous place for the haves, but one where the have-nots were getting further squeezed.

"[Bloomberg] governed during the greatest economic crisis since the Great Depression and he never addressed it," de Blasio said. "We will decidedly write a new chapter."

Casting an eye towards Billionaires' Row, de Blasio had proclaimed early in his campaign that, "the last thing NYC needs is another tall glass tower."

It was a message that resonated, and showed just how much resentment had been building during the Bloomberg years. Many, it was now evident, felt left behind. When the results were counted, De Blasio didn't just win — he won a landslide victory in precincts across the city, crushing his opponent Joseph Lhota, the former chairman of the MTA and Giuliani deputy mayor, by a margin of 49 percentage points — the most lopsided margin of victory since Ed Koch's 68-point win over the Liberal Party's Carol Bellamy in 1985.

De Blasio's win, the Times declared, was "a forceful rejection of the hard-nosed, business-minded style of governance that reigned at City Hall for the past two decades and a sharp leftward turn for the nation's largest metropolis."

In his victory speech, de Blasio made clear his intention to seize what he saw as an unmistakable mandate.

"My fellow New Yorkers, today, you spoke out loudly and clearly for a new direction for our city," he declared during a jubilant party in his home base of Park Slope, Brooklyn. "Make no mistake: The people of this city have chosen a progressive path, and tonight we set forth on it, together."

The backlash against the Bloomberg years was perhaps most eloquently captured in the posts of Jeremiah Ross, who in his popular blog, "Vanishing New York," obsessively chronicled the closing of beloved New York spots, the ruination of grittiness by arriving yuppies.

"Reports of New York's death are not greatly exaggerated," wrote Ross in his 2017 book named after his blog. "How did such a catastrophe befall the greatest city on earth? It didn't happen all at once. After decades of scheming on the part of urban elites — the real estate magnates, the financiers, planners, and politicians — who worked tirelessly to take the city from those they considered 'undesirables,' Mayor Ed Koch really got the ball rolling in the 1980s, Rudy Giuliani brought the muscle in the

1990s...[and] Mayor Bloomberg dealt the death blow, a stunning coup de grâce. Gentrification morphed into hyper-gentrification."

Bloomberg left behind the city in a state of record prosperity, some commentators noted, with a $2 billion budget surplus, but also with the highest number of homeless residents recorded since the Great Depression. And the city's middle-class had continued to shrink — falling to 16 percent of the population from 25 percent. Nearly a third of families paid over half their income in rent, according to the Center for Housing Policy and National Housing Conference. And nearly half of residents, according to some estimates, lived either below the poverty line or just above it.

Developers may have feared Bloomberg, and may have been frustrated that he was immune to the charms of their political donations. But he was widely respected, seen as the type of technocrat needed to take the city to greater heights in the new global economy. His encouragement of big development and his relatively hands-off approach to the kind of luxury product being churned out by builders emboldened them.

His successor promised to take the opposite approach. Big real estate, even though he readily accepted its money, became one of de Blasio's most frequent targets from the bully pulpit.

In his first State of the City address at Baruch College in February 2015, de Blasio warned that the city had gotten perilously close to becoming "a gated community."

"How did we get here?" he asked. "For decades, we let the developers write their own rules. That meant a bias toward luxury housing. This administration is taking a totally and fundamentally different approach."

Over his reign, the backlash against high-end development would grow, as would de Blasio's willingness to seize on it as a political issue.

"If I had my druthers, the city government would determine every single plot of land, how development would proceed," he told New

York Magazine in September 2017. "And there would be very stringent requirements around income levels and rents. That's a world I'd love to see." In response, one developer told the press that de Blasio "didn't stop at Bernie Sanders; he went straight to Chairman Mao."

Despite de Blasio's fiery rhetoric, the real estate industry still had plenty of prominent allies in Albany to protect some of its most important priorities. But de Blasio's election was a harbinger of things to come. The backlash was just beginning. (Later, Democratic Socialist politicians came to power and pushed through reforms that sought to challenge the idea that building housing could be a for-profit endeavor.)

De Blasio wasted little time diving into the thorniest of local real estate issues.

In October 2015, his administration announced it had reached a deal with the Blackstone Group aimed at finally bringing the saga of Stuy Town–Peter Cooper Village to an end. The investment giant would acquire the 11,232-unit complex from the property's special servicer for about $5.3 billion — $100 million less than Tishman Speyer had agreed to shell out in its ill-fated top-of-the-market deal some nine years earlier.

As part of the deal, Blackstone promised that 4,500 of the apartments would remain affordable for the following two decades, reserved for middle-income families. A family of three earning just under $130,000 would pay $3,200 a month for a two-bedroom, compared to market-rate rents of around $4,200. An additional 500 apartments would be set aside for families making even less.

In exchange, the city agreed to provide Blackstone with a $144 million loan to help make the purchase, while also waiving $77 million in mortgage recording taxes. (That loan, as *The Real Deal* learned, turned out to be a giveaway to Blackstone, as the city provided the loan at zero interest and agreed to forgive the principal over a 20-year term.)

Meanwhile, Rob Speyer, who had been at the center of the previous controversy around the complex, had recovered quite nicely. As the industry began to emerge from the downturn a few years earlier, the would-be Hudson Yards developer had made it clear that he was not eager to reenter the domestic residential business.

"We put Stuyvesant Town firmly behind us," he'd told Bloomberg. "We've moved forward. Our activity in the United States in the last couple of years has been focused on office."

He declined to say he would steer clear of residential acquisitions for good, but noted that "the last nine deals we've done in the last 18 months in America have all been office. The next nine deals will likely be mostly office." By opting to stay out of it, Speyer would avoid the third rail of the city's housing politics, which were making a sharp leftward turn.

A few months later, the seven present and former chairs of the Real Estate Board of New York arrived at the trade organization's Lexington Avenue headquarters and joined REBNY President Steven Spinola in the Harry Helmsley Boardroom. Over deli sandwiches and chocolate-chip cookies brought by developer Larry Silverstein, the conclave discussed who should serve as the titular head of REBNY. Present were Ross, Brookfield Office Properties co-chairman John Zuccotti, Glenwood Management CEO Leonard Litwin, Tishman Speyer co-CEO Jerry Speyer, Jack Resnick & Sons CEO Burton Resnick, CBRE Tri-State CEO Mary Ann Tighe and Silverstein. This was an era when the lobbying group still held serious sway over local and state races, when developer money had not yet become toxic for those aspiring to office.

The panel settled on Rob Speyer, tapping him to be the group's youngest-ever chairman. Speyer, who had joined his father as co-CEO of Tishman Speyer in 2008, was by then running the company's global operations. He had also quietly emerged as a powerful behind-the-scenes player in New York politics. In 2011, Speyer had founded a nonprofit called the Committee to Save New York that raised and spent $12.1 million to buy TV and radio ads in support of Governor Andrew Cuomo's agenda. He had also taken a position as chair of the Mayor's Fund to Advance New York City, a nonprofit that raised private money for some of Mayor Bloomberg's highest-priority projects. And he had established himself as a reliable financial backer of political candidates at every level.

All of which made him the obvious choice for chairman, a role that would require him to lobby elected leaders who oversee everything from zoning to tax policies.

"Due to the outsized role of the Committee to Save New York during Governor Cuomo's tenure, it's difficult to argue that any other non-elected official has dominated the state's political discourse as much as Mr. Speyer," groused Bill Mahoney, research coordinator for the New York Public Interest Research Group, a nonpartisan nonprofit that had been carefully tracking Speyer's efforts.

The links were so blatant that the previous January, sign-waving protestors had converged outside REBNY's annual gala to denounce the tax reductions and pension reform policies that the Committee to Save New York has been advocating.

REBNY was gearing up for the change in the city's political guard that would take place at the end of Bloomberg's third term.

"No one can say who will be the next mayor and what their direction will be. But we wanted someone who had strong ties to [city] elected officials, but also strong ties to Albany," outgoing chairwoman Tighe said at the time. "And we need someone who is up-to-date on the issues currently facing the board. Rob has been involved for a long time."

Tishman Speyer continued to shore up political capital. It would eventually donate over $60,000 to Cuomo's re-election campaign. And in 2014, when Cuomo sought to strike a deal with New York Republicans to ensure his reelection, Speyer reportedly hosted a meeting between the governor and several high-profile members of the party, including the now-disgraced former Republican Senate majority leader Dean Skelos.

In the wake of the Stuy Town debacle, Speyer hired Michelle Adams — the influential executive director of the Association for a Better New York, who also served as an aide to the group's chairman, Bill Rudin — to oversee Tishman Speyer's public and government affairs and help rehabilitate the firm's reputation.

"You learn from your mistakes and we certainly learned from that one," Speyer would later tell *The Real Deal*. "The biggest lesson was about our use of leverage. [Virtually] every investment we've had since 2010 has been 50 percent equity and 50 percent debt."

XXXI

West Side Story

Hudson Yards Takes Shape

Throughout 2015 and 2016, the evidence of Related's progress at Hudson Yards was on display.

To successfully build a new neighborhood, Ross would need to address the same challenge that had allowed his company to "activate" Columbus Circle and transform it from a dead hole in the donut into a vibrant and teeming public space.

A major component of this transformation fell into place on a sunny Sunday morning in September 2015, when Mayor Bill de Blasio presided over a ribbon-cutting ceremony at a gleaming new subway station at 34th Street and 11th Avenue — the opening of the first new train station in 25 years, part of the $2.4 billion 1.5-mile link connecting the Far West Side to the rest of the city.

"This extension connects this extraordinary development happening here — a whole new city being created within our city — connects it with thousands of jobs in neighborhoods like Flushing and in central Queens, bringing people from those neighborhoods to the jobs here," de Blasio said, declaring the day "monumental."

"Just like in the 20th century, when the 7 train created neighborhoods like Long Island City, Sunnyside, and Jackson Heights, this extension instantly creates an accessible new neighborhood right here in Manhattan," the authority's chairman, Thomas F. Prendergast, said.

Meanwhile, Ross had revealed the name of the artist he would rely upon to complete a second major piece of the plan back in 2013, selecting British designer Thomas Heatherwick to produce what he hoped would provide a year-round tourist draw to the area akin to a 365-day-a-year Rockefeller Center Christmas Tree.

On the site of the plaza, Ross announced he would erect a massive copper-colored lattice of 154 staircases, 2,000 individual steps, and 80 landings that resembles a shiny upside-down 16-story beehive. The structure was dubbed "The Vessel," (although, Ross, according to Fisher, sometimes has a different name for it: He calls it "my baby"; critics have called it "The Shawarma").

"I fell in love instantly," Ross would tell the New Yorker's Ian Parker. "My guys around here thought I was out of my goddamn mind. It was too big, too this, too that. 'How are we going to build it?' 'What's it going to cost?' I said, 'I don't care.' The cost, I figured, would be seventy-five million." (According to Parker the cost, with landscaping included, topped $250 million.)

But to implement what would perhaps be the most challenging remaining part of the plan, Ross had turned to the same collaborator and partner who had done so well by him at Time Warner Center: Ken Himmel would be in charge of the retail.

Restaurants would again be a crucial part of the mix. Himmel knew he also wanted something big on top to draw people into the shopping center, just as he had relied on Jazz at Lincoln Center at Time Warner Center.

Himmel had thought that the right kind of department store might do the trick. When he was a young man building Copley Place back in Boston, he'd looked at sales volumes in Back Bay and found steady demand at Saks and Lord & Taylor, a few blocks from his proposed site. He had determined that not only was the market underserved, but there was very little opportunity for anyone else to build to the scale that would take up the slack because there were so few building sites. Himmel, however, had a site, and used this information to his advantage, knowing no one would later be able to dilute his market share.

A similar dynamic was at work on the West Side of Manhattan, he believed.

"You can actually put a profile together of exactly how people are performing, and you can develop a whole matrix of where there is enough demand, where you think if you deliver in the following categories, you should be able to do well, if there's enough demand for people to have good sales performance," Himmel said. "It's very scientific when you're in the business and you have access to everyone, all the good brokers and all the retailers."

The pitch he'd prepared for retailers was convincing: The West Side ranked as one of the top seven markets in America, in terms of density, income, buying power, and visitors, he noted. A new shopping center there would draw traffic from Times Square, Chelsea, the Meatpacking District, and the Upper West Side, including leisure and business travelers.

To the east was Herald Square, Macy's, and Penn Station. Closer by, the expanded Jacob K. Javits Center and the northern terminus of the High Line promised to deliver a steady flow of people. North and south on 10th

Avenue, a number of other residential buildings already existed. But the 2005 rezoning of the Hudson Yards District had also opened the way for several other notable projects.

Most significantly to the east, Brookfield had acquired the parcels, running from along Ninth and Tenth avenues between 31st and 33rd streets, in several transactions. The eight-acre site, a little more than a third of the size of Related's Hudson Yards, had been largely dormant since the 2008 crash, but the company was watching Related closely and was poised to get going on construction in early 2014.

There, Brookfield would construct a six-building mixed-use development of their own to be called Manhattan West, adding more than five million more square feet of office buildings, luxury apartments, some retail and restaurants and two acres of open space.

Neiman Marcus, Himmel knew, had been eyeing Manhattan for years. The same company that owned Neiman, however, owned Bergdorf Goodman and would not want to put a store anywhere near their flagship on Fifth Avenue. But Himmel recognized Hudson Yards was far enough away and would target an entirely different market. Himmel turned to Howard Elkus and asked him to come up with a plan that would dazzle Neiman CEO Karen Katz and her board. Together, the pair flew down to Dallas to deliver a presentation.

Not only would this be Neiman's first time in New York, Himmel told them, but they would have the opportunity to "do something very unique."

"You're going to be the top of the project," he said. "You get the penthouse levels."

Himmel then laid out his vision for the retail component of Hudson Yards, with Neiman at the center. While most shopping centers are horizontal, placing department stores from one end to the other, Himmel planned to turn Neiman vertical. Neiman would be located on levels four, five, and six, and he would surround them with eateries that would draw people to it.

"Our restaurant story here is unprecedented, in any project I've ever heard of in the world, including Asia — the sheer number of people coming to these incredible restaurants," Himmel told them.

When Katz and her board signed on — the deal became official in September 2014 — it provided an important seal of approval and opened the way for a number of other deals.

"In order to establish the credibility of leasing at Hudson Yards, it had to start with Neiman, before anything else," Himmel said. "The entire retail project has to be built around that. I mean, you can't just suddenly fill the top of the building."

From there, Chanel, Louis Vuitton, and 15 other luxury brands that already had relationships with Neiman took space. On levels three and four, Himmel added H&M and Zara. The sheer volumes these stores did attracted other complementary retailers such as Sephora, Lululemon, and Aritzia. On the plaza level, there would be Rolex and Patek Philippe.

It was shaping out to be a powerful roster.

The following May, the first tower in Hudson Yards opened — the 52-story 10 Hudson Yards — with tenants that included Coach and L'Oréal.

But even as Himmel and Ross sought to replicate the success they had achieved at Time Warner Center, that earlier grand-slam project was about to get some unwanted scrutiny.

XXXII

Ill-Gotten Gains

The Money Laundering Question

I n February 2015, the New York Times splashed an explosive story across the front of its Sunday edition that would reverberate through the real estate industry for years to come.

Penned by investigative reporters Louise Story and Stephanie Saul, the story, the first in a series called "Towers of Secrecy," pulled back the curtain on New York's high-end real estate market and revealed that the explosive luxury-condo market had been fed in part by an influx of shady foreign criminals, who had used the shiny apartments as a way to launder money.

Story and Saul had chosen to bring the problem to life by focusing on one specific development: Time Warner Center.

Steve Ross's prized development, Story would later explain, "was a turning point in New York real estate" not only from a geographical standpoint — shifting the center of gravity to the West Side — but also in the way it was sold. It was heavily marketed abroad in a way that "few had done as aggressively," she said. And the share of units purchased by shell companies there, the reporters found, had risen from about one-third in 2003 when the project was launched to more than 80 percent in 2014.

Though many of the buyers at Time Warner Center represented a broad spectrum of U.S. wealth, from CEOs to celebrities to doctors and Wall Street traders, the report also found a growing proportion of wealthy foreigners — at least 16 of whom had been the subject of government inquiries around the world, either personally or as heads of companies. The cases ranged from housing and environmental violations to financial fraud.

"Four owners have been arrested, and another four have been the subject of fines or penalties for illegal activities," the article noted.

The owners, which included government officials or close associates from Russia, Colombia, Malaysia, China, Kazakhstan, and Mexico, "were able to make these multimillion-dollar purchases with few questions asked because of United States laws that foster the movement of largely untraceable money through shell companies," the reporters wrote.

In case anybody might miss the fact that much of this wealth had been produced through illicit activities and, in some cases, the possible looting of national treasuries, the profiles of some of the tenants made the connection clear.

One unit, which sold for just under $16 million, was connected to a Russian oligarch named Vitaly Malkin, who had been forced to resign from Russia's upper legislative house after an anti-corruption activist revealed he had failed to disclose property he owned in Canada, and noted that he had been involved in a 1996 deal to restructure the government of Angola's $5 billion debt to Russia in an "arrangement that has become a symbol of official plundering in Africa among anti-corruption advocates." (Malkin, the article noted, received $48.8 million as part of the deal.)

Another unit was connected to a Colombian former provincial governor

named Pablo Ardila, who had previously admitted his parents set up a
shell company to buy the $4 million unit, and was subsequently jailed on
charges of enriching himself illegally.

Of course, Time Warner Center was hardly unique. The problem of
money laundering had been an open secret for decades. Story had become
interested in the issue in early 2013, while reporting a series of articles for
the Times' business desk in the wake of the financial crisis. After moving
over to the paper's investigative team, she began thinking about a longer
project on the subject when she came across a report by Global Financial
Integrity, an obscure Washington, D.C.–based think tank that tracked the
flow of illicit money out of developing countries.

The report showed a huge uptick in the lucre leaving these countries.
Story wondered where all that money was going, and decided to find out.
She expected her reporting would lead her to offshore havens such as the
British Virgin Islands and Panama. She began by calling law firms known
for their expertise in tracking down the funds looted by corrupt foreign
officials, and chatting up lawyers known as "asset-recovery specialists."
She figured they could help her navigate through the byzantine shell
corporations and offshore banking systems often used to launder funds.
When she asked them to tell her where they thought all that money was
going, however, she was surprised by their answer.

"Yes, it goes through offshore centers," she recalled them saying. "But
it ends up right here in New York or in London. It ends up where people
want to live and spend it."

Because real estate wasn't governed by the same due-diligence rules
that had been imposed on the banking industry in the late 1990s and early
2000s, and because ownership could be masked in public records, it had
become an increasingly attractive destination for those looking to park
large sums of money with few questions asked, she learned.

Story began mining databases for the names of prominent international politicians along with their relatives and business associates and cross-referencing those names against the names of those associated with the largest real estate transactions recorded in the U.S. over the past decade. These initial efforts failed to yield many hits, and when she realized why, she grew even more intrigued. Virtually all the deeds had been recorded under the names of shell companies, or "LLCs." And Story learned that the use of LLCs for luxury real estate deals had skyrocketed over the decade.

By 2014, of the U.S. residential purchases valued at more than $5 million, nearly half were through shell companies.

At the suggestion of anti-money-laundering experts, Story, by now joined by Saul, began analyzing huge datasets to see where luxury buyers were flocking to. This led the reporters straight to some of the most high-profile developments in Manhattan, many of which were clustered around Central Park, including the Plaza, Bloomberg Tower, Barnett's One57, and Trump International.

To them, Time Warner Center seemed the ideal case study because, with 10 years of history, there was more of a chance that the anonymous buyers behind the shell companies would inadvertently have left a paper trail.

The story highlighted the real estate industry's laissez-faire approach to understanding the origin of a buyer's money, particularly when it came to condo units.

"They have to have the money," Sotheby's Elizabeth Sample, the ace Manhattan broker with several deals at the building, was quoted as saying. "Other than that, that's it. That's all we need."

Their findings came as no surprise to Elise Bean, former chief counsel for the Senate Permanent Subcommittee on Investigations. Real estate's role in enabling money laundering had been on Bean's radar since the eve of the new millennium.

"Realtors back in the 1970s, from the very beginning, were identified as people who dealt with a lot of money, sometimes in cash, and so they were considered a group that had to have anti-money laundering obligations," Bean said. "So, from the very beginning, realtors had been identified. But the industry has managed to avoid it."

In those initial hearings in the early 2000s, however, Bean and her colleagues focused on another link in the chain: The role of private bankers and wealth managers — the very individuals Sotheby's Nikki Field and her colleagues had cultivated as an entrée to a new pool of overseas buyers (Field and her fellow brokers would later insist that money laundering was the last thing on their minds when they approached bankers and offered them investment opportunities).

Overall, Bean's panel found that as much as half of the estimated $1 trillion in criminal proceeds laundered worldwide each year went through American financial institutions, much of it through private banks where "a corporate culture of secrecy and lax controls" were guiding principles.[101] The committee highlighted figures ranging from Raul Salinas, the eldest brother of former Mexican president Carlos Salinas de Gortari, to Gabon's president Omar Bongo and Asif Ali Zardari, the widower of former Pakistani Prime Minister Benazir Bhutto.

The hearings helped shape sweeping anti-money laundering legislation that was pushed through in the wake of 9/11 as Title III of the USA Patriot Act. The new laws vastly expanded the list of industries required to conduct some level of due diligence on buyers of jewelry, hedge funds, and real estate. It stipulated that those involved in selling such assets would be required to analyze risk, know their clients and take steps to avoid handling dirty money.

But the real estate industry launched a furious lobbying campaign, playing down the risks.

---

101   Berkeley, Bill. "A Glimpse into a Recess of International Finance." *The New York Times*. November 12, 2002.

"Everybody was covered [by the regulations]," Bean recalled. "But then the regulators said, 'Oh my God, we have to cover so many people, we can't do them all at once!'"

Promising to return to other categories later, the Treasury Department set out first to increase efforts to monitor the flow of money through banks, securities firms, insurance companies, and money-service businesses. Realtors were temporarily exempted, along with investment advisors, and those selling yachts and aircraft.

"It was a temporary exemption," Bean said in 2018. "Here it is 17 years later and they never removed the exemption."

Back at the Times, Story and Saul methodically peeled back the layers obscuring the ownership behind the more than 200 shell companies that owned or had owned condos at the Time Warner complex. When the paper trail led them overseas, they tapped the newspaper's vast network of bureaus for assistance — tasking Times correspondent Carlotta Gall to knock on doors in Tunisia, reaching out to reporter Joe Cochrane in Indonesia and Alejandra Xanic von Bertrab in Mexico, they would later write.

"It was almost like taking apart the layers of a Russian doll through various jurisdictions including looking at lawsuits, looking at various ways of searching, reverse searching phone numbers, looking at import records, looking at IP registrations, talking to people," Story said. "I was talking on the phone to people all over the world — we reported on people from over 20 countries and in each place, once we would figure out who was behind the unit, we didn't just stop there. We then reported out who they were, how they made their money, what do people who know them know about their background and that was as time-consuming as it was to even break the shell companies."

They narrowed down the people they intended to mention publicly and reached out for comment. Once, Story was followed out of the Times building and told to "back off" and leave one of the subjects alone. Letters were sent to the editors, and when she went abroad to report on the story, she was followed by individuals who snapped her picture.

"Normally when you're reporting on something and call somebody for a comment you just get a comment or they might send you a written comment," Saul said. "In this case, it was a lot of big law firms, writing really, really long letters to us going over points case by case by case. And in some cases the letters were like 20 pages long."

In subsequent articles, Story and Saul broke out profiles that delved deeper into the background of some of the more intriguing buyers. Then in early February, they splashed a photograph of a figure unmistakable to regulars at the city's hottest nightclubs, and certainly to some of the city's biggest developers.

The photo was of Jho Low, a wealthy Malaysian investor. The chubby, baby-faced 31-year-old was close to the family of Malaysian Prime Minister Najib Razak, did deals with Middle Eastern sheiks, and was an "advisor" to Malaysia's sovereign wealth fund, which he had helped to establish. He was said to have backed Martin Scorsese's recent hit, "The Wolf of Wall Street," starring Leonardo DiCaprio and produced by Razak's stepson, Riza Aziz. But it was Low's nightclub exploits that had made him irresistible tabloid fodder. The enthusiasm with which Low spent money even caught the attention of heiress Paris Hilton, to whom he once handed a Cartier watch and $250,000 in gambling chips as a birthday present. In 2010, in St. Tropez, Low's younger brother, Zhen Low, squared off against New York real estate scion Winston Fisher in a battle to see who could order more champagne. (Zhen won, spending $2.6 million, according to Page Six.)

Low had toured a 76th-floor penthouse at Time Warner Center that had once been home to Jay-Z and Beyoncé, and a few months later had used a shell company to buy it for $30.6 million. Low had also partnered with Steve Witkoff and Howard Lorber, CEO of Vector Group and chair of brokerage firm Douglas Elliman, to purchase the 46-story 605-room

Helmsley Park Lane Hotel at the foot of the park on Central Park South on Billionaires' Row.

The location offered park views fit for a billionaire — indeed, Hemsley and his wife Leona had once lived atop it in a three-story triplex. Low had agreed to pony up 85 percent of what would eventually be a $654 million play for the property. Once bidding started, he offered to put up a $100 million nonrefundable deposit,[102] twice the customary amount — prompting the owners to choose Witkoff's group over competitors with a slightly higher offer. At the last minute, Low reduced his stake to 55 percent and sold a 30 percent stake to Mubadala, the Abu Dhabi sovereign wealth fund.

It was Low's close ties to the family of Malaysia's prime minister that made the buy noteworthy for Story and Saul. In 2010, the reporters noted, Low had also used a shell company to purchase a $23.9 million apartment in the Park Laurel condominium Downtown. Then, three years later, he had sold it to another shell company owned by Riza Aziz. Around the same time, Low paid $17.5 million for a Beverly Hills mansion and also flipped it to a shell company connected to Aziz.

The Jho Low story was already the subject of a simmering scandal in Malaysia. It would soon explode into a major incident ensnaring not just the Malaysian leader but a wide range of other figures. Low had played an important role in bringing Middle Eastern investors into deals with the Malaysian government, and had helped to set up a Malaysian sovereign wealth fund, called 1Malaysia Development Berhad, which was overseen by Razak. Rumors had begin to circulate that money from 1MDB might be funding the extravagant spending of Razak's wife, who was known to wear ostentatious diamond jewelry and had a collection of Hermès Birkin

---

102   Bagli, Charles V. "Malaysian Money. Opulent Ideas. But Now, for Park Lane, a Forced Sale." *The New York Times*. May 23, 2017.

bags said to be on par with Imelda Marcos's infamous shoe collection.

Where had the money come from to buy the Time Warner penthouse? Story and Saul couldn't answer the question. At the time of the buy, Low told people he represented a group of investors, but he now claimed the unit was owned by his family trust, they wrote.

"One thing is clear: As with nearly two-thirds of the apartments at Time Warner Center, a dark-glass symbol of New York's luxury condominium boom, the people behind Penthouse 76B cannot be found in any public real estate records. The trail ends with Jho Low."

Just a couple of weeks later, Clare Rewcastle Brown,[103] a British investigative journalist with ties to Malaysia, published an article headlined "Heist of the Century." In it, she referenced a series of leaked documents that appeared to show that Low had siphoned hundreds of millions of dollars from 1MDB. Soon after, Malaysian law enforcement agencies jumped into action, and what would come to be known as one of the largest government corruption scandals in world history, later chronicled extensively in the book "Billion Dollar Whale," began to unfold.

Industry figures who teamed up with Low say they were caught unawares.

"I thought he was a totally legitimate guy when I met him," Witkoff said, noting that his company had followed government "know your customer" anti-money laundering regulations. "I mean, that's how he read. He was partners with Goldman Sachs, with Blackstone, he was partners with sovereign wealth funds, we ran background checks, we're a very thorough operation."

Witkoff, however, came to realize that something was wrong when it came time to refinance the original loan on the Park Lane property. He

---

103   Hope, Bradley, et. al. *Billion Dollar Whale*. Hachette. September 18, 2018.

had lined up a deal with JPMorgan, but when the firm tasked its Southeast Asia desk with confirming Low's family wealth as part of a reputational assessment, a fortune purportedly worth $800 million, they could find no indication his father and grandfather existed as he had described them. Eventually, the bankers would share a shocking assessment with Witkoff: They believed Low had photoshopped photographs of his father and grandfather in military gear, making them appear to have played a prominent role in the history of the country.

When Witkoff and his team confronted Low, he brushed it off.

"JPMorgan has a vendetta against us because we do all our business with Goldman Sachs," Witkoff recalled Low telling him. "So we're going to have to find a loan somewhere else because they'll never approve me."

"Right then and there, I knew he was a liar," Witkoff said. "He is a snake in the grass. He's the worst guy, the most manipulative human being I ever dealt with."

In January 2016, prompted in part by the Times' series, the Treasury's Financial Crime Enforcement Network (FinCEN) finally took action to "pierce" the veil of secrecy allowed by LLCs. It instituted what it called a "Geographic Targeting Order," focusing on anonymous, all-cash transactions of more than $3 million in Manhattan and over $1 million in Miami. The new rule required title insurance firms to identify the true owners of shell companies seeking to purchase residential real estate with cash.

It was a timely change, as other high-profile money-laundering cases continued to come to light, including that of Nigerian energy magnate Kolawole "Kola" Aluko, who purchased a full-floor, 6,250-square-foot penthouse at Gary Barnett's One57 for $51.9 million in 2014, with money the U.S. Justice Department would later claim in a lawsuit was looted from his home country.

By then, the market for the city's top-end apartments had already started to slip, with resale prices for the top 20 percent falling every month after hitting a peak in February 2015.[104] Some attributed the drop to a saturation of overpriced product. And some warned the new rules would only further dent the market.

"It's almost like the requirement for people to go through security checks at the airport," real estate attorney Terrence Oved said at the time. "Someone who's carrying contraband is going to feel more nervous, but it will have a negative effect on the regular person who'd rather not get padded down. It may cause developers, sellers, and brokers to think again in terms of where their ultimate consumer is coming from."

In an analysis done by FinCEN a few months later, the agency revealed that more than 30 percent of the newly identified true owners had previously been named in "suspicious-activity reports," filed voluntarily by banks or other financial service providers to flag transactions that might be related to money laundering or illicit activities.

And indeed, one report done a few years later by the Federal Reserve of New York found that since the targeting program was introduced, the number of companies using all-cash to buy homes plummeted. The program has since expanded to more than a dozen counties across the country, including in parts of California, Texas, and later, Hawaii.

Despite the decline, few actually believed the problem had gone away: One of the report's authors later speculated that many corrupt foreign buyers had simply opted to use straw buyers, or put property used to launder funds in the names of family members. Indeed, while the use of shell companies for all-cash real estate purchases declined by 66 percent, the number of individually named foreign buyers jumped 50 percent, the author said.

As details of Jho Low's chicanery leaked out, meanwhile, it would

---

104   Carmiel, Oshrat, et. al. Transparency Sought for Cash Buyers. *Bloomberg News.* January 17, 2016.

continue to provide a gritty cautionary tale.

By the spring of 2016, the Park Lane project had been "all but scuttled," according to some accounts, with Wells Fargo refusing to release the funds needed to purchase the property. In July 2016, ownership of the property was effectively frozen for Low and his partners, when U.S. Attorney General Loretta Lynch announced that the government intended to seize more than $1 billion in Low's assets — assets Lynch alleged were purchased with money looted from 1MDB.

What followed, Witkoff recalled, was "three years of hell." Witkoff had to sit tight and deal with bad press until June 2019, when the ownership group, now with Mubadala in control of Low's former stake, refinanced the property with a $615 million loan from Deutsche Bank and JPMorgan. Witkoff was finally free of Low.

The 1MDB scandal would have legs. Goldman Sachs bankers would eventually be ensnared. The Justice Department documents also named two figures who had become prominent players in New York real estate in the wake of the financial crisis: Khadem al-Qubaisi, the former head of Abu Dhabi sovereign wealth fund IPIC, and Mohamed Al Husseiny, his former deputy who ran IPIC subsidiary Aabar. It was Aabar that had provided the massive infusion of cash that had funded Gary Barnett's pioneering construction of One57 during the downturn. Both had been mysteriously removed from their posts by the government months earlier. Barnett was never implicated of any wrongdoing.

Jho Low snuck into China, where he's reportedly been living as a fugitive ever since. It's a claim China denies.

The New Kings of New York

XXXIII
Three Amigos in a Room
Shelly Silver Goes Down

T he fallout from the Low scandal and the spotlight it brought to the foreign money infiltrating the market provided further fodder for activists and politicians looking to reform the city's housing market.

In spring 2016, the average price of a Manhattan apartment hit a record $2 million, an increase of 18 percent compared with the first quarter of 2015, according to a Douglas Elliman report authored by Jonathan Miller. The surge was caused by super-luxury apartments — at least half of which were sold to foreign buyers, mostly from China, Europe, and Brazil for use as "safety deposit boxes" to protect their fortunes, Miller noted. The Guardian newspaper noted that with Manhattan's price per square foot hitting a record high of $1,713, "a standard six-foot-by-eight-foot prison cell would cost $82,000."

Of the more than 2,800 apartment sales between January and March,

46 percent were paid for in cash, the Guardian reported. It came as the U.S. Treasury launched a crackdown on cash sales to unidentified owners, "which the government said corrupt foreign officials and international criminal masterminds have used to disguise their ownership and wash 'dirty money.'"

"We are seeking to understand the risk that corrupt foreign officials, or transnational criminals, may be using premium U.S. real estate to secretly invest millions," Jennifer Shasky Calvery, director of FinCEN, told the newspaper.

Meanwhile, the weakening of New York's political old guard through scandal was bringing about further change and ushering in a new era of progressive-minded lawmakers.

In late January 2015, federal authorities unveiled a sweeping series of corruption charges against Sheldon Silver, 70, the Democratic speaker of the New York State Assembly, and one of the most powerful politicians in the state. Money laundering, it seemed, wasn't the only flavor of crime to beset the industry.

In an explosive indictment, Preet Bharara, the U.S. Attorney for the Southern District of New York, accused Silver, a Democrat from the Lower East Side of Manhattan, of collecting about $4 million in bribes and kickbacks, which he disguised through a personal injury law firm he was affiliated with. Among his "clients" was Glenwood Management, one of the biggest developers and owners of luxury rentals in the city. Glenwood had paid Silver $700,000, unreported on Silver's annual financial disclosure statements, at a time when Silver's chamber was considering legislation of crucial importance to the real estate industry in general — and Glenwood in particular.

Silver had directed Glenwood to the law officers of Jay Arthur Goldberg, who ran a two-person law firm in Lower Manhattan and had previously worked for Silver in Albany. Then the politician collected a "referral fee" for his efforts.

Glenwood had a lot at stake. About a third of its buildings received tax breaks and special financing under the state's 421a program, which awarded developers who set aside 20 percent of their units for low- and moderate-income tenants. At least nine of the company's Manhattan apartment buildings had received 421-a tax breaks worth more than $700 million.

"As we are reminded today, those who make the laws don't have the right to break the laws," FBI agent Richard Frankel said at the news conference announcing the indictment.

More politicians would be ensnared. And in the months that followed, it would emerge that both Steve Witkoff and Rob Speyer had been pressured by the state's political leaders to ante up. (Neither Glenwood, Witkoff, or Speyer were ever charged with any wrongdoing.)

The taint of the indictment threatened to spread even to players who weren't directly involved. The first indictment came seven months after New York Governor Andrew Cuomo had shut down an anti-corruption panel he'd appointed three years earlier, just as it had begun to probe the sources of outside income procured by the state's legislative leaders.

Though Cuomo wasn't implicated, the timing was embarrassing. Just the day before Silver's arrest, Cuomo had delivered his annual "State of the State" address and had mentioned he had brought along Silver and the Republican Senate Majority Leader Joseph Bruno on a series of international trade missions. During the speech, Cuomo had displayed a doctored image depicting the three men on horseback in the Mexican desert wearing black sombreros and matching Mariachi band costumes. It was a reference to a previous corruption scandal — in 2009, former Senators Carl Kruger, Pedro Espada, and Ruben Diaz had formed an alliance after Democrats had won control of the Senate chamber for the first time in four decades. The gleeful new leaders had purchased Mexican hats, declared themselves the three amigos and, in the months that followed, allied with the Republican caucus, and orchestrated a coup that for a time paralyzed the state government. Two of the three amigos, Kruger and Espada, were subsequently charged with corruption and sent to federal prison.

"These three Amigos are different," Cuomo had quipped, standing in front of his doctored "three Amigos" picture. Not that different, it seemed.

Five months later, in May 2015, the FBI arrested Cuomo's second "amigo," the Republican Senate majority leader Dean Skelos, on charges of extortion, fraud, and bribe solicitation. In the complaint, prosecutors accused Skelos, 67, of pressuring Glenwood to direct more than $200,000 in "commissions" to his son Adam Skelos through a company they owned a piece of called AbTech. In addition to the payments to AbTech, which sold filters designed to remove pollutants from stormwater, Skelos also directed Glenwood to make another $20,000 payment to his son through a title insurance company, which was disguised as a commission.

In addition to Glenwood, Tishman Speyer's Rob Speyer also made a cameo: According to prosecutors, Adam Skelos emailed a supervisor at the title company where he worked in January 2011, bragging that he planned to have lunch with the president of a major commercial development company, "and he wants to start giving me his work." The company, according to press reports, was the owner of the Chrysler Building, which is controlled by Tishman Speyer.

On February 10, 2011, both the Senate majority leader and his son did have lunch with Speyer at Rockefeller Center. And a month later, Tishman Speyer emailed Adam Skelos "asking him to produce a title report for a $250 million mortgage of the Chrysler Building complex," according to the complaint, which did not say how much Mr. Skelos was paid. In a statement to the Times, a spokesman for Tishman Speyer said, "we have been contacted by the U.S. attorney's office with regard to its investigation and are happy to continue to answer any questions they may have."

But most of all, the scandal cast a spotlight on Glenwood's mild-mannered 101-year-old founder Leonard Litwin. Litwin had begun his career with his father's Depression-era plant nursery on Long Island and built a New York City residential real estate empire with nearly 9,000 apartments, most catering to the well-heeled. He held the title of "Lifetime Honorary Chairman" of the Real Estate Board of New York, and his company had made no secret of their desire to influence the trajectory of legislation affecting the real estate industry. By some estimates, over the previous decade Glenwood had contributed more than $12 million in legal campaign contributions to state assembly and Senate candidates and party committees, according to an analysis by Common Cause New York, which included donations from related companies and individuals. In 2014, the company had shelled out $900,000 to hire eight different lobbying firms to lobby state officials.

Glenwood's "business model depends in substantial part on favorable tax abatements and rent regulations that must be periodically renewed" in Albany, according to the criminal complaint.

In a story about the new indictments, the Times would note that while the complaint did not indicate what Glenwood's top lobbyist Charles Dorego thought he would get in return for steering work to the Silver-affiliated law firm, "a battle in the State Legislature in 2011 over renewing the 421-a tax program as well as rent regulations that govern one million apartments in New York City provide some clues."

Housing and tenant activists wanted major changes to both programs. In one instance, in April 2011, after Glenwood contributed $25,000 to the Senate Republican Campaign Committee, the firm's representatives met with Skelos to discuss real estate regulations and legislation affecting Glenwood, according to the indictment. In the end, lawmakers agreed to renew the 421-a program, and made modest changes to the rent-regulation laws.

In December 2015, both Silver and Skelos were convicted of all the counts leveled against them and both were expelled from the State Legislature, where each had held office for more than three decades. The cases dragged on for years in appeals, eventually requiring a second trial. But both would eventually serve prison time.

The real estate industry emerged from the scandal seemingly unscathed — no major player was charged and in the indictments and press Glenwood, Wtikoff, and Speyer were cast as secondary characters, victimized and pressured by rapacious politicians.

But the repercussions were coming. In the months that followed, the fall of the two leaders, and some of their lieutenants, coupled with the rise of Donald Trump, would help feed a populist tide that would fundamentally change the dynamics in Albany — and threaten some of the very same programs the industry had worked so hard for so long to defend.

XXXIV

Piper Paid

Swig Steps into the Sunlight

O n a glorious day in June 2016, Kent Swig kneeled on the floor of his office at 770 Lexington Avenue, the sun streaming in through glass windows, the air redolent with the promise of a long summer. Chewing sunflower seeds, humming to himself, Swig placed folder after folder stuffed with legal documents into large cardboard bankers boxes, and sealed them up.

Swig had finally managed to pay off all his creditors and lawyers. His divorce was done and dusted.

Condo sales at the Sheffield were going strong, and soon there would be a dividend that surprised almost everybody else but partially vindicated Swig: $54 million in profits. It was just a fraction of the amount of money Fortress would make on their investment. (Though the firm declined to reveal the size of their windfall, Swig would later claim it was among the most profitable bets they have ever made.)

Newly debt-free, with time on his hands, Swig was getting ready to turn back to the future.

"I took thousands and thousands of pages of documents that I didn't need anymore and put them in storage, and cleaned out my office, cleaned out my desk and only focused on new opportunities and the current business," he would later recall. "Scanned them all and chucked them. It was cathartic."

He would now turn his attention to Helmsley Spear, growing the commercial brokerage he had acquired just before the crash, and one that he hoped would generate income in both good times and bad. He went on a hiring spree, increasing the brokers from 5 to 21 — a number that would top 35 by 2021.

"We've got 83 Maiden Lane, a 250,000-square-foot building downtown — we lease-manage that," he would later say. "We're closing, you know, several deals. Well, we're closing a deal a week, plus or minus. So, I mean, we're active."

He also devoted time to his construction company, Falcon Pacific. In the months that followed, the company won a job to build an eight-story building, ground up, in Queens, a residential tower on the Upper East Side, and a number of other smaller projects. There was no need to try for the grand slam.

When buried in debt, he would later reflect, "you have to be very calm and very methodical and very patient and keep chipping away little by little, every piece." The same applied to building his new businesses. Swig would even, ever so gingerly, go back into buying mode, purchasing a building in Tribeca, which he planned to gut renovate and turn residential — though he took efforts, he said, to disguise his identity as the buyer in order to keep it out of the press.

It was a far cry from the size and scope of Swig's Sheffield days, though he could still dabble. In collaboration with Brookfield Properties, the Swig family trust had recently purchased the HBO building in its prime

Midtown location across from Bryant Park, next to the Grace Building, which they already owned. With HBO moving over to Hudson Yards, the partners had reached a deal to lease the entire 386,000-square-foot 15-story building to Bank of America, and planned a gut renovation. The bank was taking another 120,000 square feet in the neighboring Grace Building. Though Swig wasn't involved in the day-to-day running of the deal, he sat on his family's investment committee, allowing a perch from which he could apply his hard-earned wisdom.

Early on during his crisis, he had learned a mantra: Respond, don't react. And through it all, he had cultivated patience.

A couple years later, Swig sat in a conference room in his office on the 44th floor of a Lexington Avenue skyscraper and reflected back on the experience. The lines on his face, along with a new, golden beard, lent him a wizened, slightly rabbinical air. It was a picturesque tableau, the East River and a cityscape of buildings silhouetted against a cloudless blue sky. A master-of-the-universe kind of view.

Though the lessons and the memories would stay with him, he was happy to put the past behind him and embrace new challenges.

"We're in a market that's very unique," Swig said. "I think it's one of the great opportunities for people to buy. This is a wonderful time to be an agent in the marketplace and for our clients to be buying and selling. Well-priced things are moving very quickly."

One thing Swig had no immediate plans to do was dive into the super-high-end market that had emerged in the post-crash world.

"I don't need to wait seven years to sell my product," he said. "No offense. Look, we make a great living at that with Brown Harris Stevens [as a brokerage]. We dominate that in everything, but as a developer, as a developer, to go out and build a product that takes...if I put 68 units at 432 Park and it takes me seven years to sell, that time thing will eat up your returns. I don't want to play in that end of the spectrum."

Reflecting back on his travails, Swig maintained he had won the respect of many of his former creditors. And when he has needed loans or refinancings in the years since, he has been pleased by lenders' reactions.

"When I now paid off all this, I went to go do other deals, I had a bank tell me that I would be their greatest client ever because under any economic circumstances that exist, and you went through the worst, we know what kind of person you are, and that's the kind of banking relationship we want," he said.

Swig added: "I don't want to go through anything like that ever again, so don't get me wrong, but it's turned out to be a career-building enhancement as opposed to a detriment, because the bank saw under the worst circumstances, which I went through, both the physical, you know, surgery and a matrimonial nightmare and a financial meltdown of the U.S. global environment."

Swig was not the only prominent real estate figure putting things in boxes in the spring of 2016. His former father-in-law, Harry Macklowe, also apparently was doing some packing.

In late May, Page Six revealed that Macklowe had informed Linda, his wife of 57 years, that he was leaving her for another woman, setting off a salacious public spectacle that would make Swig's own battles with his former in-laws look tame.

Macklowe, it would soon emerge, had been secretly housing a mistress for two years in a luxury apartment complex he owned at 737 Park Avenue, just a couple blocks away from the Plaza penthouse he shared with Linda. Macklowe had met his blonde 60-year-old French paramour, a businesswoman named Patricia Landeau, years earlier at a museum event.

"Harry told his wife last week he was divorcing her — completely out of the blue — then moved straight in with his girlfriend," one source told Page Six. "This is a total shock to everybody because he's been married to Linda a long time. Harry is almost 80, he's been married for [almost] 60 years, and suddenly he has a girlfriend. And he's been running around town and the Hamptons with her."

The story would become tabloid fodder for months to come. At stake was a fortune estimated at $2 billion, which included a $1 billion family art collection that had reportedly been put in Linda's name around the time of the 2008 market crash to shield the assets from creditors.

In a later filing, Macklowe would also reportedly turn against his son Billy, filing court documents the following fall, accusing Billy of breach of fiduciary duty, misuse of company funds, and "usurping control" over the domain names HMacklowe.com and Macklowe.com (Billy, 48, denied the claims). Some speculated that both these episodes were the legacy of the 2008 Equity Office debacle, in which Macklowe had been forced to sell the GM Building.

"This is a vindictive move by Harry because Billy has sided with his mother in the divorce. Harry is not just divorcing Linda; he's divorcing Billy," one source told Page Six.

Yet the drama did not seem to slow Macklowe down at work. That September, a penthouse at 432 Park Avenue sold for nearly $88 million. Macklowe also announced plans to convert an Art Deco office building at One Wall Street, formally BNY Mellon headquarters, into 566 condos.

In an interview with the New York Times that appeared in January 2017, Macklowe cracked jokes, dodged questions about his messy divorce, and reflected back on his colorful career.

While "the upper end of the market is justifiably slow," he told a reporter, "we're very confident that our pricing structure is correct and we'll sell." But he acknowledged the top of the market had weakened, and added, "We wouldn't start a 432 Park today." (It wasn't just the high-end that was about to get hammered, however. In Albany, a far more consequential change was under consideration. And it would hit the industry where it truly hurt.)

Macklowe contended he had never actually stumbled "not even in 2008 when he was forced to relinquish seven properties to lenders and to sell four others, including his crown jewel, the General Motors building." Exhibiting the same unabashed confidence exuded by another brash New York developer who just took office in Washington, Macklowe reasoned, "I've never had a bad deal," he said. "I've only had good deals that, because of timing, haven't worked out."

Two months after the Times interview, *The Real Deal* revealed that Macklowe's backer on the One Wall Street project was Hamad bin Jassim bin Jabar Al Thani, the former Prime Minister of Qatar and one of the Middle East's most prominent billionaires. "If you've got that kind of equity behind you," one developer active in the market remarked to *The Real Deal*, "you can't be in trouble."

XXXV

The Everything Store Checks Out

Amazon Dumps NYC

I n September 2017, Amazon announced it planned to open a second company headquarters in an as-yet-unnamed location — and called on cities throughout North America to submit proposals for the project. The winner could expect more than $5 billion in construction investment, as many as 50,000 new high-paying jobs, and "tens of billions of dollars in additional investment in the surrounding community," the company said.

In many ways, what the e-commerce behemoth, one of the world's five most valuable companies, was offering was the ultimate big-city prize — the kind of prize Dan Doctoroff, Michael Bloomberg, and their like-minded allies in the business community had begun working towards the moment they began pushing to rezone all that fallow former manufacturing space across the city in the early aughts. Doctoroff had championed a "virtuous cycle," one in which a rising tax base, falling crime, and high-paying jobs created opportunity for everyone. Bloomberg and his deputy Robert K. Steel had made the connection to a thriving tech sector explicit. And though de Blasio had risen to power playing up the downsides of the city's transformation — with his "Tale of Two Cities" — he had continued to support the city's emergence as a tech hub.

The previous month, de Blasio had joined Bloomberg and Gov. Andrew Cuomo at the official opening of the Cornell Tech campus on Roosevelt Island, which by then the city could brag had already graduated students who had spawned more than 50 startups and raised $60 million from investors. More than 500 had been hired by Google, Bloomberg, Microsoft, and other tech companies, the New York Times would later note.

What's more, the institution's dean and vice provost Daniel Huttenlocher was on Amazon's board of directors.

And in the days following Amazon's announcement about the search, de Blasio hailed an unrelated decision by the company to open a new office in Manhattan in 2018 and create more than 2,000 new jobs, touting the company's arrival as a boom for New York City workers.

"New York City has the most talented workforce and the most diverse economy in the country, and the world's most innovative companies want to be here," de Blasio said at the time.

In a triumphant article headlined "New York Matures as a Hub for Technology," the Times reflected back to 2003, noting that back then, efforts by a Google computer scientist to set up an engineering outpost in Manhattan were met with skepticism "that he could even find 15 'Google-worthy' software developers in the city."

"The attitude was that pretty much all the good software engineers were in Silicon Valley," the engineer, Craig Nevill-Manning, recalled. "It seems crazy in retrospect."

By the time the Amazon headquarters was in play, Google employed about 7,000 people in New York, Salesforce with 1,000, Facebook had 2,000, and IBM had chosen to headquarter its Watson artificial intelligence and cloud computing divisions in the city, the article noted. All told from 2010 to 2017 alone, according to government statistics, tech sector employment grew by 53,000 in the city, or 65 percent, to an estimated 134,700. And the average salary of $147,300 in 2016, the most recent estimate available, was far higher than the citywide average of $89,100 for all private employers.

But some had begun to question the growth-at-all-costs approach to urban planning. It wasn't just New Yorkers perplexed by the ugly towers for foreign billionaires ringing Central Park. Even Richard Florida — whose book "The Rise of the Creative Class" had provided the most compelling case for big tech and put a modern spin on Lew Rudin's "virtuous cycle" — was becoming a critic.

Florida had been appointed to the board of directors for Toronto Global, the entity behind that city's Amazon bid, which, along with New York, would make the cut and become one of the 20 finalists. Florida complained that the process by which most cities were handling the package of incentives was shrouded in secrecy.

"I think the lack of transparency of this whole process is galling," he told the Times. "This has to be all out in the public. This is taxpayer money."

Florida then remarked on the irony of mayors like de Blasio and Rahm Emanuel of Chicago, who claimed to be focused on housing and affordability, courting Amazon with tax incentives.

"They are about ending inequality and creating more inclusive cities," Florida said. "Now they're in a game competing with one another to throw money at one of the most powerful companies in the world run by one of the world's richest men."

Eventually, Florida warned, whoever won the bid would have to reveal how much money Amazon was promised. When that happened, he warned presciently, "there is going to be hell to pay." At the time, it was easy to dismiss Florida's warning — after all, hadn't the city worked hard to compete for the Olympics, rezone a huge chunk of the five boroughs, develop Hudson Yards, and create a tech hub on Roosevelt Island? Few, it seemed, had made such a fuss when the Bloomberg administration went about its plans — or at least, the ones who made a fuss didn't have the clout to spoil the party.

In early November 2018, news broke that Amazon executives had met separately with both de Blasio and Cuomo, and that the state had offered potentially hundreds of millions of dollars in subsidies.

"I am doing everything I can," Cuomo told reporters when asked about his courtship of the firm. "I'll change my name to Amazon Cuomo if that's what it takes," he quipped. "Because it would be a great economic boost."

On November 5, the day before New Yorkers headed to the polls for midterm elections, the New York Times delivered the news that thrilled business leaders across the city: Amazon was finalizing the details. New York City would split the prize with Arlington, Virginia. Long Island City would be home to a sprawling new headquarters, housing 25,000 skilled high-paid workers. The news became official a week later.

At a press conference soon after, Cuomo and de Blasio, who had spent years taking potshots at each other, appeared together jubilantly and spent the day basking in the glow of their victory. Just nine days after Bloomberg had first taken office back in 2002, he had chosen Long Island City as the setting for a press conference, appearing just below the rumbling tracks of the Queens Plaza elevated train station with his police commissioner, promising to build on the Giuliani years, wipe away the gritty New York, and usher in a new modern era, open for business. Now, in an area once dominated by shuttered industrial warehouses, business was coming. A business of the most modern kind.

"We've never seen 25,000 new jobs at once," Cuomo crowed. "We've never come close. And that's the contractual minimum on the table with the potential to go to 40,000. This is big, big news."

"This is a giant step on our path to building an economy in New York City that leaves no one behind," de Blasio added. "We are thrilled."

With the announcement, the package the city and state had used to lure the company finally became public. The cost was steep: With promises of just over $1.5 billion in incentives — including $1.2 billion in tax credits over the following 10 years, $180 million in infrastructure upgrades, job training programs, and a helipad — the incentives package was roughly twice the size of that offered by Virginia. (In addition, by some estimates, the company was eligible for as much as $900 million in existing city tax credits over the next 12 years.)

Nor was that the only compromise. After the company had expressed concerns about the city's planning process, and the ability of the City Council to veto projects, de Blasio and Cuomo had agreed to a process that would let the state control the approval process, by allowing it to perform a "friendly condemnation" of the city-controlled land.

It was a maneuver that had helped clinch the deal in the final stretch. But it would feed a backlash that would soon grow far more vehement than anyone could have anticipated.

As it happened, the Amazon deal was not the only big news in the state that day.

Energized and outraged by the policies of hated native son President Donald Trump — who had improbably seized victory the previous year and become the nation's first developer-in-chief — liberal-leaning New Yorkers had turned out in droves to vote in the midterm election on November 6, the day after news had first broken that the city was a likely winner. As the company and city and state political leaders had rushed to finalize plans for a triumphant announcement of the deal, a political earthquake was occurring.

For the majority of the previous 100 years, real estate–friendly Republicans had a lock on the state Senate. (Though Democrats had briefly won control of the Republican-controlled state Senate in 2009 and 2010, wayward Democrats had formed an alliance with Republicans and effectively ceded back the power.) In the election of 2018, Republicans dropped Senate seats in Long Island, Brooklyn, the Hudson Valley, and elsewhere. And Democrats swept to the majority.

The new revolution promised to upset the delicate balance of power that Cuomo had used so effectively over the previous years to govern as a centrist. It also presaged serious consequences for the industry — and signaled that the backlash many had long feared was finally beginning to manifest.

To protect precious rent laws and lucrative tax incentives, the real estate industry had come to rely on a group of Democrats known as the Independent Democratic Caucus, a small core of loyalists they had showered with donations, and counted on to consistently vote with Republicans to support industry priorities. Some observers had long noted that the arrangement benefited Cuomo — allowing him to appear moderate, since he could rely on the IDC to advance legislation and deflect the heat for measures that might offend the party base, but helping to bottle up legislation that might offend his financial backers on Wall Street and in real estate.

But in the primaries, progressives had backed a slate of six candidates to take out the IDC. All six declined to take money from real estate developers — and all six won.

The decline of the IDC was just one potential trouble spot.

One of the architects of the Democratic takeover was Senator Michael Gianaris, a powerful Queens Democrat who ran the Democratic Senate

Campaign Committee, a fundraising group, and a frequent Cuomo thorn. Over the years, Gianaris had accepted more than $250,000 from real estate interests. This time, he announced that neither he nor the party's Senate committee would accept any money from the industry.

Ominously for the Amazon deal, Gianaris's district included Long Island City, and he had openly worried about the impact Amazon would have on the local infrastructure.

Not to mention concerns about the cost of living. During the Bloomberg years, the mayor and his administration had touted Long Island City as the site of thousands of units of new middle-class housing — they had offered it up as a consolation prize of sorts to affordable-housing advocates disappointed at the city's decision not to intervene in the calamitous Stuy Town auction. Looking back, to many it seemed a bitter irony — to meet Stuy Town's steep price tag, the Speyers had anticipated the deregulation of hundreds of rent-controlled apartments in that complex, which could then be rented to the growing population of upwardly mobile young professionals flooding into the city for banking and tech jobs.

Now, just a few short years later, the new mayor and the governor were proposing to transform the new middle-class housing area into a tech hub that would attract exactly this same kind of tenants, driving up rents for the old-timers, and ensuring that the gentrification that had overtaken Manhattan would engulf Long Island City.

In the days following the election, Gianaris had appeared on CNN and made clear he had not been involved in or consulted on the deal, and said that the area was "already being overdeveloped."

"My understanding is the public subsidies that are being discussed are massive in scale," Gianaris said. "Why we would need to give scarce public dollars to one of the richest companies on Earth is beyond me."

"Offering massive corporate welfare from scarce public resources to one of the wealthiest corporations in the world at a time of great need in our state is just wrong," he said in a joint statement with Council member Jimmy Van Bramer, whose district included Long Island City. "We were not elected to serve as Amazon drones. The burden should not be on the 99 percent to prove we are worthy of the 1 percent's presence in our communities, but rather on Amazon to prove it would be a responsible corporate neighbor."

"We're going to tell Amazon to take that welcome mat, roll it back, put it back in the package, and send it back to Seattle," he vowed.

The election also marked the arrival of Alexandria Ocasio-Cortez, a 29-year-old socialist elected to represent New York's 14th Congressional district in Queens and the Bronx. And when the terms of the deal became public a week after the election, though Ocasio-Cortez's district did not include the Amazon site, she quickly made clear where she stood.

"Amazon is a billion-dollar company," she tweeted. "The idea that it will receive hundreds of millions of dollars in tax breaks at a time when our subway is crumbling and our communities need MORE investment, not less, is extremely concerning to residents here. Displacement is not community development. Investing in luxury condos is not the same thing as investing in people and families. Shuffling working class people out of a community does not improve their quality of life."

Nor were newly emboldened Democrats the only ones who found fault with the deal. In the days following the official announcement that New York had won the prize, both the Times and the Post published editorials attacking the terms of the deal.

The blowback was so fierce that Cuomo felt compelled to pen an op-ed defending what he called a "historic transformative moment for the entire New York City region."

"I have done enough development work during my career to know there is no large development project that is accomplished without controversy, especially in a city like New York and especially in this polarized, hyperpolitical time," he wrote. "While I appreciate the ideological and political points of view, we must still govern and analyze based on facts. In fact, given the current political turmoil, it is more important than ever."

The controversy continued to grow.

In the weeks after taking control, the newly empowered Democratic Senate Majority tapped Gianaris to serve as Deputy Majority Leader — then chose him to represent them as one of three voting members of the Public Authorities Control Board, a board Cuomo had previously stated would have the oversight on the Queens development plan. It was the same board that had previously derailed Bloomberg's ambitious plans to build a West Side stadium 14 years earlier.

The City Council, it was by then clear, was likely to file a lawsuit aimed at killing the deal, taking aim at the end-run de Blasio and Cuomo had engineered around the local zoning process.

On Valentine's Day 2019, Amazon dumped the city.

"For Amazon, the commitment to build a new headquarters requires positive, collaborative relationships with state and local elected officials who will be supportive over the long-term," the company said on its website. "While polls show that 70 percent of New Yorkers support our plans and investment, a number of state and local politicians have made it clear that they oppose our presence and will not work with us to build the type of relationships that are required to go forward with the project we and many others envisioned in Long Island City."

It was a devastating blow to the local real estate scene. Lightstone Group's David Lichtenstein summed up the industry's sentiment, telling *The Real Deal* that Amazon's about-face on its New York megacomplex was the "worst day for NYC since 9-11."

"Except this time," he said, "the terrorists were elected."

XXXVI

Big Bird Comes Home to Roost

The Hudson Yards Backlash

"**A**lright, have you got the rope, everybody has the rope? Alright, on the count of three, you're going to pull it, ready? One, two, three!"

Sporting a blue-and-red tie, Big Bird guided Steve Ross, CNN's Anderson Cooper, Jeff Blau, and others through the process, which released a wave of confetti into the sky. It was March 15, 2019, and Hudson Yards, the $25 billion 26-acre city-within-a-city on the Far West Side of Manhattan, was officially open.

The previous night, Related had thrown a star-studded invite-only party for New York's glitterati that showcased the project's retail space. Liza Minnelli had belted out her classics in the Neiman Marcus store, Lin-Manuel Miranda posed on the red carpet with chef José Andrés, and Ross held court with the likes of Tom Brady and Gisele Bündchen at what was sure to become the city's latest power-lunch hotspot, the high-end Greek restaurant Estiatorio Milos.

Many industry players had showed up to pay tribute and to see in the flesh what they had all been hearing about for nearly a decade.

"Hats off to them for being able to actually open, and in a challenging retail environment," HFZ Capital's Ziel Feldman said. "Everything looks beautiful."

"This is like SimCity on steroids, but real," said developer Sharif El Gamal of Soho Properties. New-development consultant Anna Zarro likened the Vessel to "real estate's answer to J.Lo's ring."

By the end of the year, in many ways, Ross's big bet — the biggest any developer in the country could have hoped to make — looked to be paying off.

Nearly six million square feet of office space across the three new skyscrapers had been fully leased to the likes of L'Oréal, Coach, Wells Fargo, and Facebook. "When considering the next phase of our growth in the city, it was important that our newest office space was situated in the heart of a vibrant community that offered access to arts, culture, media, and commerce," a Facebook representative said in a statement announcing the 1.5 million-square-foot deal.

The seven-story retail mall was nearly fully spoken for, with top-tier tenants, and two of the luxury condo towers were ready for occupancy. Meanwhile, the Vessel had arguably replaced the High Line as Instagram's favorite New York totem, with throngs visiting on a daily basis.

Related had already cashed in big time. By bringing in equity partners such as Mitsui Fudosan and doing office condo deals with the likes of Wells Fargo and Time Warner, the company had managed to bank major profits and insulate themselves. The project had cemented the company's status as the alpha developer, the one firm to rule them all. From a real estate player's perspective, Hudson Yards was an unmitigated triumph for

Ross, who had seen his net worth more than double over the past six years to $7.6 billion.

And yet, if Ross expected the undertaking would be universally celebrated, he was wrong.

In the weeks prior to and after the opening, Hudson Yards received a barrage of unflattering press, depicting the project as woefully out of touch, lacking coherence, and operating in a wealthy bubble rather than embracing the city at large.

In addition to brutal reviews in both New York Magazine and the New York Times, the New York Observer noted that "neighborhood" wasn't the right word for Ross's development.

Hudson Yards is "a mall, augmented with luxury housing units and a sci-fi-inflected arts center known as the Shed. (The homegrown simplicity of all these names seems engineered to offset the development's own focus on the 1 percent)."

The negative reaction helped explain why both Governor Andrew Cuomo and Mayor Bill de Blasio, still reeling from the scotched Amazon deal, skipped the ceremony.

Standing inside the entrance to his new mall after the ceremony, Ross greeted well-wishers, including NBA Commissioner Adam Silver. When a reporter approached and asked him what he thought about all the negative press, he shrugged it off.

The billions of dollars in tax breaks Hudson Yards received were "a way to grow a whole new part of New York," he argued. And he noted he had built some affordable housing in the development as part of the deal.

"Look, today we have a lot of politicians, who are extreme left," Ross grumbled. "They killed the Amazon deal, it's like the popular thing for them to do right now. That's not where the mainstream is. So you know it just shows irresponsibility."

Ken Himmel, the Related vet who put the retail and restaurant component of the project together, offered a different explanation for the criticism.

"I think it's because no one is taking the time to understand what this is," he said. "There's something here for everybody."

In the months that followed, the backlash would only grow. Soon Hudson Yards would inspire its own line of sex toys, including a butt plug shaped like Thomas Heatherwick's Vessel and a dildo shaped like Kohn Pendersen Fox's 10 Hudson Yards.

"The city and developers have been jerking each other off for decades, so naturally we wanted to join in the fun," Wolfgang & Hite, the studio behind the toys, said to design magazine Dezeen. "Masturbation is a great metaphor for the latest wave of development in New York City."

XXXVII
The Rent Riot
Tenants Strike Back

T hroughout the morning on June 4, 2019, buses deposited demonstrators of all ages and races outside the State Capitol in Albany. Inside the building, the crowd of chanting, clapping activists in matching red T-shirts emblazoned with the words "Housing Justice for All" continued to grow, clogging the ornate, high-ceilinged hallways. They were there to show their support for a slate of legislation known as "universal rent control," which tenants-rights advocates were billing as a once-in-a-generation opportunity.

Some had been there for the Stuyvesant Town protests. Many remembered the Sheffield.

"All nine bills!" They chanted. "All nine bills!"

As nervous legislative aides slunk by and state troopers stood watch in their wide-brimmed hats, demonstrators leaned against doorways and sprawled out on marble landings. Others climbed the Capitol's central staircase, stood on the balconies overlooking the gallery, with its stone arches and ornate chandeliers, and tossed down fake $100 bills printed with the faces of Governor Cuomo and real estate industry figures. Outside the legislative chambers of the Assembly and Senate, activists refused to allow staffers and lobbyists onto the floor. One contingent hammered on the glass doors to Cuomo's office.

Scuffles broke out. Over by the Senate chambers, a group of men reached over the shoulders of a group of activists who were blocking the entrance, and attempted to yank the doors open, as the activists shouted and strained to keep them shut. Two people struck the Assembly sergeant-at-arms. They were hauled away in handcuffs. Senior citizens shouted and waved signs. By the end of the day, 61 people were arrested and charged with disorderly conduct, among them Jumaane Williams, the New York City public advocate and a former tenant organizer.

The demonstration was the culmination of months of organizing and lobbying by tenant activists. On June 15, a little more than a week away, the state law regulating one million rent-stabilized apartments, was set to expire. The legislature was expected to act. And for the first time in ages, tenant activists had reason to believe they might finally get what they were seeking.

In the 2018 elections, Democrats had gained a 40-23 majority in the state Senate, and a 106-43-1 majority in the Assembly, to go along with Democratic control of the governor's mansion. It was only the third time the Democratic party controlled the full legislature in more than half a century. And the victory had put the surging cost of living in the state's most populous city onto the front of the agenda.

Over the course of the previous 14 years, since those halcyon days when Kent Swig had first fallen in love with the Sheffield and Tishman Speyer had so disastrously won the bidding war for Stuy Town, more than one million apartments renting for $900 or less in New York City had been converted to market-rate housing.

"One million low-rent units gone, disappeared, never existed," the City's Comptroller Scott Stringer had declared at a Manhattan press conference unveiling a new report detailing those numbers the previous fall. "Today we are sounding an alarm and together with this coalition we are taking the fight for housing justice all the way up to Albany. Because of the changing winds, this is a fight we can win."

Now, a little more than six months after Democrats had won their statewide seats — four months after the stunning withdrawal of Amazon — here was the chance, finally, to do something about it.

"This is something that is so huge, which is why you're seeing so many people here and so militant," Jeanie Dubnau, an 80-year-old member of Washington Heights' Riverside Edgecombe Neighborhood Association, told a reporter from the New York Times.

The sweeping rent-regulation reform dramatically limited how landlords could increase rents on stabilized apartments and opened the door for rent stabilization to spread outside of New York City. The bill abolished "vacancy decontrol," a provision that allowed landlords to lift apartments out of regulation and charge market rates when their rents pass a certain threshold (a rule that had led to the deregulation of more than 155,000 units since it was enacted in the 1990s). It repealed the "vacancy bonus," which gave landlords the right to raise rents by up to 20 percent whenever a tenant moved out of a rent-stabilized apartment. And it placed limits on the ability of landlords to raise rents to help pay for building renovations. Also, for the first time, these laws were made permanent, meaning they wouldn't sunset after four years.

All of those provisions took aim at tactics that had been exploited, most famously at Stuy Town, to displace old tenants and make way for newcomers willing to pay market-rate rents.

But the bill didn't just add protections for rent control. It opened the door for its expansion.

To the horror of some in the industry, the bill included a provision to allow municipalities in counties outside the city — that have a vacancy rate of less than 5 percent — to opt into rent stabilization.

Finally, the bill closed loopholes that had allowed the industry to use LLCs to pour vast amounts of money into the campaign coffers of state legislators — one of their primary means of influence.

Real estate trade groups called the proposed legislation an "existential threat" to building owners, warning in an ad blitz that the changes would put small landlords out of business because they wouldn't be able to raise rents to cover their costs. But the truth was, the industry had totally misread the political zeitgeist.

Ominously, industry advocates warned, if the bill passed it would force many, out of necessity, to let their buildings fall into disrepair. The Rent Stabilization Association, representing 25,000 landlords, released an independent study arguing that in 2018 alone, landlords of rent-stabilized properties reinvested $13.3 billion in building and individual apartment upgrades, improvements, maintenance, and operations. They also cited another study showing the spending had an overall $22.4 billion impact on the city's economy from 2003 to 2018.

"If lawmakers eliminate rent increases generated by major capital improvements and individual-apartment improvements in rent-stabilized buildings, it would result in the loss of hundreds of thousands of jobs and billions of dollars in business and tax revenue," Joseph Strasburg, president of the Rent Stabilization Association, told the Daily News.

But, for the industry, the outlook was looking bleak.

As it became clear that the bill was likely to pass, New York's real estate industry had turned its attention to lobbying Governor Cuomo. A group of top developers who had long helped finance his campaigns, including Douglas Durst, Richard LeFrak, and Bill Rudin, called him directly to ask for help.

But it was too late. Used to winning all the battles, some suggested, New York City developers had ignored the Democratic-led Assembly for too long, and failed to cultivate a sufficient firewall of support in the newly Democratic-controlled Senate, overestimating their ability to bottle up the legislation. Having worked closely with Cuomo, they had thought they could rely on him, underestimating the force of the political backlash the industry was facing.

"They thought the governor would step in and negotiate a compromise," Strasburg would later explain to one reporter.

Cuomo had just survived an unlikely primary challenge during his 2018 reelection campaign from actress Cynthia Nixon, who had played up the governor's ties to the industry and attacked him for not doing enough to support tenants. To veto the bill, most agreed, would be political suicide. And in the days leading up to its passage, Cuomo promised to bless whatever the legislature sent him.

In late June, Cuomo signed the bill.

Michael McKee, a longtime tenant advocate, hailed the legislation. Speaking with reporters for a local newspaper serving Stuy Town residents, he invoked the battles of the early aughts where speculators like Kent Swig and Tishman Speyer bought up buildings in the hopes of unlocking hidden value.

"These last 25 years, with the weakening of the rent laws, it allows speculative landlords to move in," said McKee. "That's over now. There's no vacancy decontrol. No longevity bonus. Major capital improvements will be based on need, not speculation, not a business model that relies on displacing people. They don't have the mechanisms."

Real estate groups and landlords called the changes "devastating" and predicted they would result in the decline of the city's housing stock and the flight of investors to other areas of the state and outside New York.

"The construction of future affordable units will slow, if not end altogether, and the housing vacancy rate will worsen and nothing will have been done to make it easier for those who struggle to pay their rent," Real Estate Board of New York President John Banks said. "There was a path to responsible reform that could have protected tenants as well as owners, jobs, and revenue, but Albany chose not to take it."

Two weeks later, Banks stepped down from his post at REBNY, and ceded control of the top industry lobbying group to his number two, Jim Whalen. On Banks's watch, the industry had suffered a hiding. It was time for new blood.

It was a stunning reversal for New York City developers, who had gone from saviors of the burning city to political foils. Politics had come full circle.

XXXVIII

Killing the Golden Goose?

Defining the Future of New York

Back when he was a student at Columbia in the 1970s, Paul Whalen used to marvel at the timeless masterpieces fashioned in previous eras. Around him at the time, the city's streets were littered with garbage, the Bronx was burning, and the city was teetering on the edge of bankruptcy. But any time Whalen wanted, he could catch the No. 1 train from 116th Street, head downtown to Tribeca, and walk over to 233 Broadway, just by City Hall Park, the address of the Woolworth Building.

Whalen would stroll through the ornate lobby, with its sculptures and mosaics, then step outside to take in the regal 30-story limestone base, topped with its iconic 30-story limestone-and-terracotta tower. He would think back to 1913, and he would shake his head.

"Who would ever want to build a tall, skinny office building like that?" he would wonder. "How could they ever have afforded it?"

In 2018, standing over a table at Robert A.M. Stern Architects, the firm where he is a partner, Whalen motioned to the renderings and drawings piled on his desk, and the mockups of some of his current and recent projects, among them 15 Central Park West, 520 Park Avenue, and 220 Central Park South — buildings every bit as opulent as the one he used to marvel at in the 1970s.

"For a long time in New York, you'd look at buildings like the Woolworth and you just couldn't understand it," he said.

"We're at a time now," he reflected, "where there is that kind of money around. The entire world economy is roaring. So there are extraordinary buildings being built that people haven't seen before."

"But," he added forebodingly, "the good times don't last forever. They end, and these will be markers of this time in New York. The last time that happened in the '20s and '30s, we had to wait more than 60 years for it to happen again."

On January 23, 2019, hedge-fund magnate Ken Griffin closed on a quadplex penthouse at Vornado's 220 Central Park South for $238 million, smashing the record for the city's most expensive home by more than a factor of two.

Among the brokers who peddle such rarefied product, the mood was ecstatic.

"It exemplifies belief in New York from a long-term perspective," said Compass's Michael Graves at the time of the Griffin deal. "It's a nod to value in New York's luxury market." His colleague, Leonard Steinberg, added that "all in New York should be celebrating this close because the volume of revenue it delivers for New York City is spectacular."

Griffin, estimated to be worth nearly $23 billion — about 100 times what he paid for his unit — had been on an ultra-luxury real estate buying spree, picking up a $122 million mansion overlooking St. James's Park in London as well as Miami's most expensive condo, at $59 million. He had, in fact, inked the contract for the 23,000-square-foot-pad at 220 CPS back in 2015, when the luxury market was afire and developers were scrambling to satisfy demand for palaces in the sky. Still, the closing of the transaction snagged global headlines, and set off a spirited debate about the very character of New York, at a time of worsening income inequality and a growing sense of frustration with the economic system that allowed it. And it resurrected talk in Albany of a pied-à-terre tax on second homes.

"The plutocrats continue brazenly flaunting the excesses that have enraged much of humanity," Anand Giridharadas, author of "Winners Take All," a book about how the superrich worsen income inequality, told the Times. "They're displaying very little awareness of the moment that we are in."

Developers and brokers had long warned that such a tax would decimate the luxury market; almost every industry figure, when asked about this, offered up the "killing the goose that laid the golden egg" analogy. Many of the biggest buyers of this boom, including Griffin, Bezos, and Dyson, do not count Manhattan as their primary abode.

Meanwhile, the pricey closings at 220 CPS kept coming, and Vornado declared that it would become the most profitable condo project of all time.

"There is two-odd billion dollars coming out...with no debt requirements," said Michael Franco, Vornado's chief investment officer, during a company earnings call in July 2019. "That all comes into our treasury."

Observers also noticed a uniquely New York phenomenon in play: big-ticket buyers were moving from older mansions in the sky to newer, even glitzier ones.

In its day, 15 Central Park West had been the alpha dog of condos, attracting buyers such as music legend Sting and hedge-fund bigwig Daniel Och. Now, those very same buyers were jumping to 220 CPS: Sting paid $65.7 million for a penthouse at 220 CPS and sold his 15 CPW abode for $15 million; Och's 15 CPW pad was asking $57.5 million, while he closed on his 220 CPS pad for $95 million in December.

"There's nothing better than a rich mercurial billionaire with an appetite for real estate," broker Donna Olshan told the Journal. "It's a broker's dream."

Others who had built into the heady market of 2015 and 2016 reaped their rewards when the deals started closing a couple years later after inking their contracts to buy. The Zeckendorfs's 520 Park Avenue, for example, saw buyers such as billionaire vacuum-cleaner mogul James Dyson, who paid $73.8 million for a 60th-floor penthouse. Frank Fertitta, co-founder of the Ultimate Fighting Championship, paid $67.9 million for a duplex penthouse. At 212 Fifth Avenue, developed by Madison Equities, Building and Land Technology, and Thor Equities, Amazon boss Jeff Bezos set a record for the priciest condo under 42nd Street, paying $80 million for three adjacent units that he planned to combine.

And yet, as the decade drew to a close, it was clear that the go-go days of the residential boom were also coming to an end. According to a year-end report from Olshan Realty, which analyzes contract signings above $4 million, there were 935 of them representing a total value of $7.65 billion in 2019. That was the lowest-dollar volume since 2012.

"It's a fragile market by any measure," said Olshan, the report's author. "And it seems obvious that a sustained uptick in sales cannot be realized until the market resets its prices."

Given this new reality, there were some big question marks sitting on the skyline.

Gary Barnett's Central Park Tower was one. The supertall, which topped out in September 2019 at 1,550 feet, had projected a total sellout of $4 billion, making the 233-unit project's offering plan the most expensive in the city's history. Extell had priced nearly 10 percent of the units at a staggering $60 million and up.

At the topping out, Barnett acknowledged that those prices may have been a tad aspirational.

"We have to be flexible when we're selling really large units," he said, noting that his units were priced 15 percent to 20 percent below those at 220 CPS. "It's a more challenging market for sales."

Other players were changing tack, too. Anbang, the Chinese insurer that had paid nearly $2 billion for the Waldorf Astoria in 2015, had intended to convert it into an ultra-luxury condo project, betting that its iconic pedigree — Frank Sinatra paid $1 million a year to maintain a suite there — would bring in the wealthiest of buyers.

But the Chinese government put an end to the party in late 2016, when it instituted capital controls meant to curb the very kinds of excessive spending in which Anbang got involved. In May 2018, its former chairman Wu Xiaohui was sentenced to 18 years in prison after being convicted by a Chinese court of orchestrating a $12 billion fraud.

Under new leadership, Anbang sold a number of those trophy acquisitions, often stomaching losses. It decided to hold on to the Waldorf, but changed tack: Instead of shooting for the stratosphere across the board, it decided to include both ultra-luxury units and pads for more modest millionaires.

In 2018, overall sales in Manhattan saw their largest decline since the financial crisis, according to a report by Douglas Elliman. By the end of 2018, there were a total of 8,000 new condos on the market, according to Jonathan Miller, who authored Elliman's reports. In 2019, as the Fed used all its tricks to keep the economy from falling into a recession, and interest rates hit new lows, sales had started to rise again. Sellers, notes Miller, had finally capitulated to the weaker conditions and agreed to lower their prices.

Then COVID hit. And the consequences were cataclysmic. The good times, it seemed, had finally drawn to an end.

Whether it would take another six decades to see the kind of development that gave us Billionaires' Row and Hudson Yards remained an open question. But looking around the city in the fall of 2020, members of the real estate industry found plenty of reason for pessimism.

In October 2020, residential sales were down more than 50 percent from previous years; the hotel occupancy rate was hovering at a miserable 39 percent, down from 95 percent the previous year. By some estimates, nearly one third of the city's 240,000 small businesses were unlikely ever to reopen. And Manhattan rental vacancies reached 5 percent in August, the highest level in 14 years, according to Miller Samuel data. As a result, rental prices were falling, and many were predicting an eviction tsunami.

Neiman Marcus, the anchor tenant for Steve Ross's Hudson Yards, and the venue for Liza Minnelli's opening-night performance, declared bankruptcy. Related had agreed to an arrangement that involved Neiman paying a portion of sales in exchange for rent, but that had not been enough — the retailer closed the store after being open for just 16 months.

But perhaps most alarming of all was what the pandemic did to the office market. Only 10 percent of workers had returned to Manhattan offices as of late October, according to a survey from Partnership for New York City. No one knew for sure when — and if — they would come back.

The real estate industry seemed to be getting remarkably little sympathy from the politicians in Albany. To some, the situation had bleak parallels to the dark days of the 1970s.

"There's been a tremendous amount of anti-wealth, anti-landlord, anti-development sentiment in the political zeitgeist in Albany since the midterms," Miller said. "And COVID has brought on this real hunger to make up for budget shortfalls. There's a tremendous amount of uncertainty in front of us. The massive disruption that was brought to retail and office in the city is unprecedented."

Even assuming the city recovered some of its former economic bustle, would it go back to the heady pro-development days of the first two decades?

Even Richard Florida had begun to rethink the wisdom of his much-vaunted theories. What surprised him was not that cities like New York have managed to transform themselves into playgrounds for the "creative class" — and that this had in fact attracted more wealth. It was exactly what Florida predicted. But what's shocked him and other experts is the pace and ferocity with which this metamorphosis has occurred.

"If you look back to when I wrote 'Rise of the Creative Class,' no one would have imagined this — no one," Florida now says. "Not a single mayor, not a single urban pundit, not a single urban economist. And it's happened in a flash."

"I think the urban economists got it wrong," he concedes. "It's not that you just have to build more housing and increase density. What we have found is that just doing that, developers build more rich-people housing. Cause that's where their profit margins are because land is expensive in places like the West Side of Manhattan. So you have to make provisions to build affordable housing just to round this out."

But more taxation isn't the answer, Barnett believes.

"There are plenty of big buyers who want to own something in Manhattan," Barnett told *The Real Deal* as the decade drew to a close. "If you drive those buyers away, you can forget about the values in the residential market."

JDS's Michael Stern noted another impediment: Land for towers adjacent to Central Park is all spoken for. Billionaires' Row is all built up.

"We just lived through an era," Stern told *The Real Deal*. "Make no mistake — these [new luxury projects] aren't happening anytime soon. It was a small window."

Epilogue
Macklowe and the Wedding Present

E ven as critics were bashing Hudson Yards, and progressives were celebrating the Amazon defeat, pedestrians walking by 432 Park Avenue were treated to the kind of wedding present only a New York developer could conjure up.

Two photographs, measuring 24 feet wide and 42 feet high — just three feet shorter than the Hollywood sign — were plastered across the skyscraper. They depicted Harry Macklowe, the picture of newfound love and contentment, gazing adoringly at his new wife, Patricia Landeau.

"Since I wasn't getting married during the summer in the Hamptons," Macklowe told the Times, "I wasn't able to hire an airplane with a banner to go up and down the shoreline. I thought, 'I own a building. Why don't I just hang a banner from my own building?'"

Macklowe deemed the stunt a "proclamation of love." But it could also have been seen as the ultimate fuck-you to his ex-wife of nearly 60 years,

Linda Macklowe, whom he had just finalized a divorce with after a bitter 14-week trial. In the end, the judge had ordered the couple's fortune split down the middle: An art collection by then estimated to be worth $700 million was ordered sold; Macklowe got to keep control of the commercial properties but had to pay Linda half of what they were worth; he got to keep the yacht; she got to keep the jewelry; they split $62 million in cash.

At one point in the trial, Macklowe had preposterously pegged his personal net worth at negative $400 million, largely as a result of deferred capital gains from the $2.8 billion sale of the GM Building in 2008. John Teitler, Linda's lead lawyer, dismissed the gambit as a "case study in divorce accounting 101."

"Mr. Macklowe himself knows these types of [capital] gains are never actually realized by real estate developers," Teitler said.

Macklowe's courtroom battles with Linda and nonstop global romancing with Landeau — the Post memorably dubbed him a "lusty long-in-the-tooth Lothario" — had not dimmed his drive to keep building, however. His ability to stitch together daredevil, skyline-shaping deals while fighting whatever stood in his way remained undimmed, a pugilistic, money-chasing spirit reminiscent of New York itself.

He had been assembling a parcel on East 51st and 52nd streets near St. Patrick's Cathedral where he was planning another supertall tower, his office counterpart to 432 Park.

Dubbed Tower Fifth, the skyscraper could be as big as a million square feet. It is slated to rise nearly 1,500 feet high. In October 2019, Macklowe received a nearly $200 million refinancing for properties that included that assemblage, bringing his dream of a new skyscraper one step closer to reality.

The lender? Fortress Investment Group.

Acknowledgments

The idea for this book came from the minds of Amir Korangy and Stuart Elliott, who summoned me, quite mysteriously, to their offices a few years ago and offered me what would turn out to be the mother of all story assignments. I'm grateful to them for entrusting me to pull it off. Though, of course, I had a lot of help. I'm indebted to Amir, Stuart, and Hiten Samtani for their patience, sage guidance, and brilliant editing, and for mobilizing the rest of their team. Thank you Paul Dilakian, Sydney Winnick, Andy Lefkowitz, Suzanne Williams, Victoria Tuturice, and all the others who helped make this book happen.

I extend my sincere thanks to Alan Segan, an early believer in this project, who shared his considerable wisdom and convinced many a reluctant mogul to sit down with me and share their stories. Gordon Runte at Fortress was equally kind with his time and helped plead my case with his normally tight-lipped colleagues at the financial powerhouse. Joanna Rose, formerly of Related, was a big help in facilitating my first interviews with Steve Ross, Ken Himmel, and others.

This book would not have come to life without the industry figures who gave me an insider's view into the most opaque of businesses. Thanks to Kent Swig, Steve Ross, Gary Barnett, Michael Stern, Arthur and Will Lie Zeckendorf, Dan Doctoroff, Joe Rose, Steve Witkoff, Jonathan Miller, Bill Mack, Darcy Stacom, Ismael Leyva, Robert A.M. Stern, Steve Stuart, Pete Briger, Chris Linkas, Dean Dakolias, Yair Levy, Kevin O'Shea, Dov Hertz, Nikki Field, Ziel Feldman, the late Alex Garvin, and the countless other players who shared their experiences and insights with me. I'm also grateful to Charlie Bagli, Vicky Ward, Michael Gross, Louise Story, Stephanie Saul, Steven Gaines, Michael Lewis, Lynne Sagalyn, and Steve Cuozzo, whose books, articles, and perspective helped fill in some of the missing pieces. And I have tremendous gratitude for the reporting staff, past and present, of *The Real Deal*, whose dogged and colorful coverage is indispensable for anyone interested in how New York is shaped.

Joe Ulam (the best Manhattan real estate broker I know), Roger Lipman, Eric Hedman, and Pete Doyle also provided sage counsel on the inner workings of the industry.

Finally, I'd like to thank my two kids, Marcus and Natalia; my father, Michael Piore; and my sister, Ana. My mother, Nancy Kline Piore, a wonderful writer and editor, often served as my first reader while I was working on this book, and I am grateful for her insight. And, of course, my brilliant wife, Dr. Sara Diaz, who has been a constant source of support and wise counsel.